D0411624

LIVERPOOL INSTITUTE
OF HIGHER EDUCATION

LIBRARY

WOOLTON ROAD,
LIVERPOOL, L16 8ND

Human Geography

Edited by Michael Dear and Derek Gregory

Published

Michael Dear and Jennifer Wolch, *Landscapes of Despair*★
John Eyles and David M. Smith (eds), *Qualitative Methods in Human Geography*★
Kevin Morgan and Andrew Sayer, *Microcircuits of Capital*★
Allan Pred, *Place, Practice and Structure*★
Susan J. Smith, *The Politics of 'Race' and Residence*

Forthcoming

Stephen Daniels, *Landscape, Image, Text*
Derek Gregory, *An Introduction to Human Geography*
Nigel Thrift, *Social Theory and Human Geography*

★ *for copyright reasons this edition is not available in the USA*

The Politics of 'Race' and Residence

Citizenship, Segregation and White Supremacy in Britain

SUSAN J. SMITH

Polity Press

Copyright © Susan J. Smith 1989

First published in 1989 by Polity Press
in association with Basil Blackwell.

Editorial Office:
Polity Press, Dales Brewery, Gwydir Street,
Cambridge CB1 2LJ, UK

Basil Blackwell Ltd
108 Cowley Road, Oxford OX4 1JF, UK

Basil Blackwell Inc.
432 Park Avenue South, Suite 1503,
New York, NY 10016, USA

All rights reserved. Except for the quotation
of short passages for the purposes of criticism
and review, no part of this publication may be
reproduced, stored in a retrieval system, or
transmitted, in any form or by any means,
electronic, mechanical, photocopying, recording or
otherwise, without the prior permission of the
publisher.

Except in the United States of America, this book
is sold subject to the condition that it shall
not, by way of trade or otherwise, be lent,
resold, hired out, or otherwise circulated without
the publisher's prior consent in any form of
binding or cover other than that in which it is
published and without a similar condition
including this condition being imposed on the
subsequent purchaser.

British Library Cataloguing in Publication Data
Smith, Susan J.
  The politics of 'race' and residence: citizenship,
  segregation and white supremacy in Britain.
  1. Great Britain. Housing. Racial discrimination
  I. Title
  363.5'1
  ISBN 0-7456-0358-0
  ISBN 0-7456-0359-9 Pbk

Library of Congress Cataloging in Publication Data
Smith, Susan, 1956–
  The politics of 'race' and residence: citizenship, segregation
  and white supremacy in Britain / Susan J. Smith.
    p. cm.
  Bibliography: p.
  Includes index.
    ISBN 0-7456-0358-0 (U.S) – ISBN 0-7456-0359-9 (U.S.: pbk.)
    1. Discrimination in housing—Great Britain. I. Title.
  HD7288.76.G7S64 1989
  363.5'1–dc19   88-36873
                                                CIP

Typeset in 10 on 12 pt Plantin
by Hope Services, Abingdon
Printed in Great Britain by
T. J. Press Ltd, Padstow

Contents

    Relations' of Housing Consumption   80

    Private renting and the 'independent' sector   81
    Owner occupation: choosing an asset or forced to buy?   87
    Council housing: uneven rations of a scarce resource   92
      Access and eligibility   93
      Allocation and transfer   96
    Dispersal versus equality   99

5   Political Interpretations of 'Racial Segregation'   105

    The politics of race   106
    The colonial legacy at the end of an empire   109
      Conceptions of race: the Commonwealth ideal   109
      Segregation: a passing phase in immigration history   112
      The policy response: laissez-faire   114
    Constructing 'Little England': the racialization of residential
      space   115
      Conceptions of race: an indigenous racism   115
      Segregation: from incipient ghetto to insurgent state   118
      Avoiding the ghetto: remove or disperse?   122
    The euphemization of race and a new segregationism   126
      *Race rephrased: economic individualism and the ascent of
        culture* ✓   127
      Segregation: the view from the market   129
      *The conservative problem: segregation as a symptom of urban
        malaise*   131
      The authoritarian solution: containing the crisis   134
    Conclusion   142

6   'Common Sense' Racism and the Limits to
    Resistance   146

    'Common sense' racism   147
    Racism and resistance in the struggle for space   151
      Racism at the ballot box   151
      Attack and defence   158
      Ritual and rebellion   163
    Conclusion   167

Preface and Acknowledgements

In some parts of the world, public life is soaked in the symbolism of 'racial segregation'. The stigma of apartheid, the odium of Jim Crow and the volatile North American ghetto spring quickly to mind whenever the legacy of slavery or the politicization of colour are discussed. In Britain, however, analysts have usually been more concerned about the economics of labour migration, the politics of immigration legislation and the sociology of 'race relations' than about the geography of settlement. Since this is not a generalization which applies to British politicians, who have frequently been preoccupied with the residential clustering of 'racial' minorities, it is puzzling that research on this theme in Britain has been restricted to a handful of geographers and a sprinkling of housing analysts. Moreover, the politics of race have rarely impinged on this scholarship. Instead, segregation has been studied primarily as a spatial pattern, sometimes as a product shaped by markets or institutions, and occasionally as a medium through which ordinary people structure their social lives.

I was first alerted to the much broader implications of 'racial segregation' through the writings of two historians – John Cell and George Fredrickson. Their critiques of segregation in South Africa and the American South suggest not only that the distinctions between *de jure* and *de facto* 'racial' separatism are finer than might be expected, but also that racial (racist) exclusivity may be less a legacy of the past and more a strategy for the future in advanced industrial economies.

This book is, for the most part, an essay in geography rather than history, a work of synthesis rather than originality, and based on the experience of a nation with no history of domestic slavery or enforced segregation. Nevertheless, I am persuaded that the practice of segregation and the ideology of segregationism are not passing corollaries of immigration history but rather a force to be reckoned with in Britain today.

What follows is, therefore, an attempt to use recent trends in the politics of race to explore the theme of 'racial segregation' which lies at the heart of traditional social geography. It is an attempt to show that where people live does matter, and that what politicians think about where people live has important implications for legislation. My subject is not that of cultural preference or residential choice, but rather the force of what is commonly termed 'racism' – that set of ideas and practices which sustains the notion that races are real and which constructs and reproduces systematic inequalities between the groups so defined.

The text must, because of this, be unbalanced. It is about power and conflict not accommodation or altruism; it monitors the setting up rather than the tearing down of social barriers; it condemns legislative blunders before celebrating political achievement; and it underplays the rich social heterogeneity of the black population. In short, the book refers to the exercise of racism not the experience of culture, and to this end it focuses primarily on white authority rather than black resistance.

Because of this emphasis, the book also contains another kind of imbalance. It focuses on racism more than on patriarchy, exposing the difficulties faced by black people to a greater extent than those experienced by women in the same society. These oppressions are linked, of course, and my final chapter suggests a framework – rooted in access to the rights of citizenship – through which their origins and interdependencies may be explored. The text as a whole, however, is limited by a preoccupation in housing research with the experience of households, rather than with relationships between the individual men, women and children who form them; and it is bound by length to an argument which, for the moment, is unable fully to accommodate the position and struggles of black women. Neither of these themes is inherently less important than those that *are* addressed and, together, they form the core of another work.

An emphasis on 'race' rather than culture does not mean that I am uninterested in the lifestyles, aspirations and achievements of the many different Asian, Afro-Caribbean and British black populations, that I am unimpressed by cultural variety or that I am opposed to the pursuit of good 'community relations'. It means rather that I regard the obvious threat to these niceties of social life as an important prior consideration – especially for a white academic.

The problem in adopting this perspective is that it can too easily help perpetuate the myth that black people *must* be poor, oppressed and disadvantaged (and therefore that to be a 'black' human being is somehow intrinsically different from being 'white'). This is not a view I support, and I acknowledge that even where inequalities are deeply entrenched there is some scope for black people to advance individually and collectively within the opportunity structure of British society. Equally, though, I am convinced that there is overwhelming evidence that black people in Britain are treated – within as well as outside the law – *as if* being black is (and should be) intrinsically different from (and inferior to) being white. In exposing such evidence, this book is primarily a critique of the practices and ideas which make it more difficult for the typical black citizen than for his or her white counterpart to be economically active, socially mobile and eligible to receive a fair share of resources and life chances.

While acknowledging that these practices and ideas are deeply entrenched and widely pervasive, I shall nevertheless argue that the processes involved are not so hidden and inaccessible that they are beyond human control. Ultimately, it is not the tenacity of racial inequality that I wish to emphasize, but rather its susceptibility to change. Part of the power of modern racism is the seeming inevitability with which, in incident after incident, time after time, it is uncovered. This book is an attempt to show that such inequality is not inevitable – that it has to *be made*, that it can be resisted and that it could be undermined.

I have been fortunate as an author to work in the lively intellectual atmosphere created by colleagues at the ESRC's Centre for Housing Research. I am indebted to David Clapham, Phil Cooke, Duncan Maclennan, Peter Kemp, Bob Miles, John Mercer, Ceri Peach, Deborah Phillips and John Western for comment and criticism on various parts of the text. I also owe considerable thanks to the organizers and participants of several conferences and seminars where aspects of this work were debated (these include Phil Cooke, Peter Jackson, David Ley, Alisdair Rogers and Steve Vertovec). Glasgow's Housing Diploma students have continually reminded me of what it means to write a book about *Britain*. Racism in Wales is poorly documented, and while the Scottish case remains under-appreciated I hope I have at least indicated some of the country's distinctive features. Finally, Mike Summerfield provided valuable assistance of a practical as well as an intellectual nature; while Derek Gregory, the series editor, displayed characteristic enthusiasm, encouragement and patience.

Susan J. Smith

List of Abbreviations Used in the Text

AMA	Association of Metropolitan Authorities
CAC	Conservative Party Annual Conference
CRE	Commission for Racial Equality
FBHO	Federation of Black Housing Organizations
HC	House of Commons Debates (Hansard)
LFS	Labour Force Survey
NCWP	New Commonwealth and Pakistan
NFHA	National Federation of Housing Associations
NF	National Front
OPCS	Office of Population Censuses and Surveys
PEP	Political and Economic Planning
PSI	Policy Studies Institute

List of Tables and Figures

Tables

Figures

L. I. H. E.
THE BECK LIBRARY
WOOLTON RD., LIVERPOOL, L16 8ND

1 Preamble: on 'Race', Residence and Segregation

'Racial segregation', the theme of this book, has interested social scientists and policy makers for more than half a century. The subject has inspired extremes of opinion and behaviour, eliciting approval as well as condemnation, and inciting passions which range from active encouragement to resigned acceptance or violent resistance. The notion is soaked in symbolism, basking in images which link a 'benevolent' colonial segregationism with the terrors of apartheid, the spectre of Jim Crow, the threat of the North American ghetto and the demise of the British inner city. The rhetoric of 'separate but equal' vies with 'oppression and inequality', confirming that whatever reality it represents 'racial segregation' is not a neutral term.

In common usage, the meaning of 'race' is ideologically biased, and the concept of segregation implies that social differentiation is systematically organized and actively sustained. Because these definitional issues are so important – politically and morally, as well as theoretically – this introductory essay is devoted to them. Some appreciation of the salience of 'race' and the relevance of segregation is required if subsequent chapters are to consider adequately what form 'racial segregation' takes, how it is sustained and why it has persisted for more than forty years in Britain.

I begin, therefore, by exploring the idea of race, arguing that it is fundamentally a social construct which is important both at the level of ideology and in the world of lived experience. I then examine the concept of segregation, which, notwithstanding its conventional appeal as a spatial index of social process, can also be regarded as part of the imagery and practice of racial exclusivism. Having clarified these terms of reference, I provide a short introduction to the remainder of the book. This indicates how each chapter accounts for the incidence, character and consequences of 'racial segregation' in Britain.

The salience of 'race'

The erroneous belief that human races exist as distinct biological types, identified by physical traits and reflected in cultural diversity, has longstanding, widespread and disturbingly enduring appeal. In Britain, fragments of racial consciousness may have emerged as early as the fifteenth century, marking an awareness which intensified during the overseas explorations of the Elizabethan Renaissance. Later, in the nineteenth century, notions of racial differentiation, linked with concepts of white superiority, were used to legitimize the exploitation of black labour in the colonies.

For Miles (1982a) the colonial era is most directly implicated in the construction of race as a relevant category for the organization of political and social life. In Britain, moreover, the effects of commercial colonialism and political imperialism were reinforced by domestic factors. The development of a rigid Victorian class structure, for instance, established skin pigmentation as an index of social inferiority when black people became associated with servile and labouring tasks. Equally, a growing popular patriotism (arguably encouraged to blunt working class consciousness) prompted solidarity among white Britons against black 'outsiders'. These themes are discussed in more detail by Barker (1978), Biddis (1979), Lorimer (1979) and MacKenzie (1984).

Fuelled by the popularity of social Darwinism, spurious racial typologies, based on a grading of skin colour from pale to dark, soon became infused with pseudo-scientific meaning. 'Racial' traits were linked with environmental setting, racial conflict was regarded as inherent in humanity's struggle for survival, and racial difference became linked with beliefs about the intellectual, moral and cultural superiority of white Europeans (a process discussed by Banton 1977; Stepan 1982).

Notwithstanding the force of this historical legacy, scientific developments in the twentieth century have proved that human populations are not naturally divisible into what are popularly conceived of as racial categories. Races, science reliably informs us, are simply social constructions. There are no phenotypic (physically observable) or genetic differences within the human population that correspond with, or cause, cultural differentiation. Unfortunately, such enlightenment has not dislodged the myth of race from daily life, nor has it undermined a quest for the natural origins of racial differentiation (which has found renewed impetus in sociobiology's preoccupation with the genetic determinants of human behaviour – despite the fact that this area of scholarship treats *Homo sapiens* as a single species).

Thinly disguised racism still nibbles at the crumbs of respectable science in ways which retain the language of race in academic, political and public discourse. But informed commentators can no longer be excused for sustaining this myth, either explicitly or tacitly. The most important question to address before proceeding, therefore, is whether, despite its popular reality and notwithstanding the authenticity of black people's experiences of racist (colour) discrimination, there can be any reason for retaining the notion of race as an *analytical* category in modern social science.

There can, of course, be no justification for continuing uncritically to use race as an explanatory construct. Neither appearance nor lineage – nor any of the phenotypic or genetic variables that appearance or lineage are popularly assumed to represent – can, of themselves, shape identity or behaviour. It is the social significance attached to physical traits that has a bearing on action and attitude. Where this is not acknowledged, and where the implications are not followed through, the routine incorporation of race into the language of academic discourse can only add spurious legitimacy to a reservoir of erroneous beliefs about the natural origins of social difference.

On the other hand, because of the demonstrably inequitable consequences of actions sustained by individuals, institutions and societies operating *as if* races are real, the salience of race as a *social construct* (culturally, politically and economically constituted) cannot be ignored. In analysing this, however, interest should centre not on what race explains about society, but rather on the questions of how, why and with what effect social significance is attached to the racial attributes that are constructed in particular political and socio-economic contexts.

Most authors agree that the processes involved here are negotiable, contestable, diverse and changeable, and that the significance of race can only be grasped in relation to particular historical, cultural, political and economic contexts. This does not mean that 'racial' boundaries are arbitrary: in so far as they distinguish the powerful from the powerless, and the dominated from the oppressed, they cannot be. It does mean that the constitution and reproduction of races (sometimes referred to as a process of racialization) is an empirical (measurable and experiential) as well as a theoretically deducible question, the answer to which must change as societies, politics and economies develop. Thus, while some of the generalizations made in this book are widely applicable (relating to the legacy of colonialism, the experience of migrant labour and so on), much of what I have to say refers specifically to the circumstances of modern (post-war) Britain. Elsewhere in Europe, North America and Australasia the processes of racialization may be quite different.

Having redefined the analytical task as that of accounting for the constitution of races, I will now go on to show that this occurs both at the level of meaning and at the level of experience. Racial differentiation is both an ideological construct and a more tangible product of the organizations, markets and institutions which drive the relations of production, distribution and consumption. I shall consider these elements in turn.

Ideological underpinnings: racism, nationalism and segregationism

To say that race is an ideological construct is to recognize that it is rooted in the production, contestation and transformation of social meanings. In detail, however, the nature of ideology generally, and of racial ideology in particular, is the source of considerable debate. This is unlikely to be resolved in the short term, but my own position is as follows.

I regard ideology as a fundamentally political, prescriptive and purposive (though not necessarily coherent or logically consistent) medium through which the popular legitimacy of iniquitous social and economic arrangements is secured. Ideology is political because it arises from the circumstances of collective decision making. It reflects the necessity, particularly in democratic societies, for those in power to gain popular support – or at least grudging acceptance – for strategies adopted (ostensibly) in pursuit of the common good. Ideology therefore refers to 'the modes in which exploitative domination is legitimised' (Giddens 1981: 68).

Additionally, ideology may be regarded as the medium by which competing sets of interest seek to 'gather, assemble, husband, defer and control the *discharge* of political energies' (Gouldner 1976: 26). Ideology is therefore prescriptive, providing the means by which 'one group of people persuades another to accept a certain vision of how things are and *ought* to be' (Reeves 1983: 39, my emphasis). It is also purposive because it tends to be 'put to use in the service of particular social groups, who use it to justify the world as they would like it to be, at the expense of possibilities proposed by other groups' (Reeves 1983: 40). This does not mean that the ideas deployed are easily imposed or readily accepted. Ideology is, above all, the locus of a struggle for power in which the ideas and beliefs of both the powerful and the powerless are contested, transformed, appropriated and reused. Because of the interplay of ideology with material circumstances, i.e. because there is a link between the power accrued through markets and institutions and the power that groups have to disseminate particular kinds of knowledge and ideas, some ideological formulae are particularly enduring.

Racial ideologies are among the most pervasive systems of belief in the Western world. The commonest of these is racism, which Barker (1981: 4) claims 'sees as biological or pseudo-biological, groupings that are the result of social and historical processes'. Miles (1982a: 78) defines racism as an ideology which 'ascribes negatively evaluated characteristics in a deterministic manner (which may or may not be justified) to a group which is additionally identified as being in some way biologically (phenotypically or genotypically) distinct.' Racism, as ideology, provides a reservoir of imagery and justifications for those who believe, or wish others to believe, that variations in appearance have some biologically rooted social or behavioural significance and may be used as a basis on which to include or exclude individuals when apportioning rewards, opportunities and life chances. This kind of reasoning, incoherent and unfounded as it may be, has had, and retains, a powerful influence on public and political life. It has been the main source of legitimation for the policies and practices whose consequences (whether expected or unanticipated) have differentially dispensed material resources and political rights according to 'physical' criteria. It is not, however, helpful to regard racism as the only manifestation of racial ideology in the modern world.

Here, following Fredrickson (1981), I shall restrict the term 'racism' to the doctrine of biological inequality, in order to recognize the historical specificity as well as the continuing importance of that system of beliefs. I shall also identify other forms of racial ideology which are undoubtedly racist in the common usage of the word but which, for analytical purposes, should be distinguished from racism as sources of legitimacy for the social reality of race. If race is regarded as a social construction based on perceptions of some combination of pigmentation, physique, descent, historical or geographical origin, dress, language and cultural norms (see Reeves 1983: 7), then racism is just one body of ideas informing the practices which draw on these perceptions to create and sustain racial categories. Reeves (1983) points out that when reference is made to race as a 'natural' source of social differentiation, discussion frequently alludes not only to biologically inherent traits, but also to culturally determined or divinely ordained sources of human variability. 'Nature, nurture and providence' may be used simultaneously or interchangeably, but they seek legitimacy for racial differentiation from very different pools of ideas (natural science, philosophy and theology, respectively).

Racism may, then, be seen as one of several racial ideologies which collectively consist of a broad set of beliefs that first 'accounts for events in the social world by making extensive use of racial descriptions and explanations, and assigning major causal significance to racial categories' and then uses these racial evaluations and prescriptions to guide attitudes and behaviour (Reeves 1983: 31). At a given time and place the specific doctrines used, singly or in combination, to justify these beliefs and actions may differ; while racism may be the most obvious, there are others – including nationalism and segregationism – which may be as pervasive.

Miles (1987) argues that English nationalism (although always a complex and contentious construction) has played an important role in the process of racial categorization. Popular patriotism feeds on the notion that national identities are natural and inevitable, and while biological allusions are part of this, the sense of racial awareness involved reaches beyond crude racism to find a rationale in birthplace and history rather than in gene pools or environments. Ideas about the intrinsic properties of human nature in different parts of the world can help shape national identity without drawing on the doctrine of biological inequality. As a racial ideology in its own right, nationalism can be presented as a celebration of difference rather than as an assertion of superiority and this, · as Barker (1981) has shown, can secure new found (though morally indefensible) respectability for racial exclusivity. (I am not suggesting here that nationalism *must* take the form of racial ideology; I would simply point out that it can, and frequently does, take on this role.)

In the same vein, much of this book is concerned with a third racial ideology – segregationism. This may be regarded as a system of beliefs which seeks justification for racial exclusivity *within* national boundaries. While it overlaps and interacts with racism and nationalism, it is not reducible to either of these doctrines. Segregationist ideology is discussed at greater length in the second part of this introduction. Prager (1982, 1987) gives a good illustration of its currency when discussing the symbolic exclusion of black people from full participation in American society. He shows that just as slavery was bolstered by beliefs about the essential inhumanity of blacks, so 'the conception of the cultural distinctiveness of blacks today serves to explain and thereby tolerate a largely divided American society' (Prager 1982: 103). This reaffirmation of the salience of race has as much to do with contemporary ways of life as with the legacy of colonial exploitation: racism may persist, but other racial ideologies – including segregationism – now help to sustain and reproduce racial differentiation.

By defining racism as one among several overlapping and interacting racial ideologies (the number of which is not fixed), I am not arguing that there is some inexorable sequence of racial ideologies such that racism has been, or might soon be, made redundant. I am certainly not suggesting that racism is any less powerful now than it has been in the past. Racial ideologies may, and do, coexist; indeed, their common end may be furthered by the appearance of competition (e.g. between racism and ostensibly more 'respectable' racial ideologies), which marginalizes any serious challenge to their collective legitimacy.

Ideological struggle is an important arena of social conflict in its own right which can sustain the salience of race – and the structures of racial inequality – relatively independently of events in the material world. Nevertheless, it is important to appreciate that races are not defined solely in the world of ideas. Racial differentiation is also a practice, constituted through a network of economic, social and political relations. If the impetus for racial categorization can be said to originate anywhere, these more tangible conditions of existence, which I consider below, are where it must be lodged.

Material origins: economy, welfare and politics

In the crudest sense, racial ideology may be seen as a system of beliefs which legitimizes not only the identification of racial attributes but also their alignment with dimensions of inequality. (In analysing modern Britain, I shall be particularly concerned with attributes related to skin pigmentation, although the racialization of Jewish and Irish migrants in other times and places illustrates that other (equally arbitrary) principles of identification can be important.) It is therefore only by probing the mechanisms of resource production, distribution and consumption that explanations for the salience of race can finally be established. My argument here is that, ultimately, the significance (indeed existence) of racial ideology rests on its origins in, impact on and 'utility' for the conditions of existence and experience. This focuses attention squarely on the worlds of economic management, political practice and public policy.

It is usual to define the practices which sustain racial inequality as 'racist'. However, it follows from what is written above that if racism as ideology is one of several interlocking racial ideologies, then racist practices may be just one element in a web of action reproducing racial categories and sustaining the inequalities that divide them. Following Cell (1982) and Fredrickson (1981), I shall link this wider set of practices with the project of 'white supremacy' – a set of social relations encapsulating 'the attitudes, ideologies, and policies associated with the rise of blatant forms of white or European dominance over "non white" populations' (Fredrickson 1981: xi). Racism, then, may be conceptualized as just one realization of that broader category of social relations which works towards 'the restriction of meaningful citizenship rights to a privileged group characterised by its light pigmentation' (Fredrickson 1981: xi). The way in which this is achieved varies between nations and over time, and in the process racist actions coexist and overlap with other practices organized to sustain racial difference and inequality (including the practice of segregation, which is considered below). Taking this reasoning a step further, it could be argued that white supremacy is itself a subset of 'racialized relations'. This notion differs radically from the concept of 'race relations' which is more familiar to social and political science.[1] It has the advantage of challenging the intrinsic reality of racial differentiation while creating some much-needed theoretical space to analyse racial categorization as a product of power *struggle* rather than as something imposed by white society and passively accepted by black people.

Those who agree that the impetus for racial differentiation originates in the practice and experience of everyday life are often divided in their views about the precise mechanisms involved. The flavour of this debate can be appreciated from three sets of arguments. Each identifies a route by which 'meaningful citizenship rights' (economic, social and political, respectively) are made less available to black people than to their white counterparts. Later in the book I will show how the rights they refer to are manipulated through the practice of segregation to construct patterns of inequality. Here, however, I will sketch the theses separately, drawing on the work of Robert Miles, John Rex and Paul Gilroy.

Miles (1982a) explores a first element of the link between racial ideology and practice in his discussion of the racialization of migrant labour from the New Commonwealth in post-war Britain. He regards the increasing political significance of race during this period as the ideological corollary of a process of class fragmentation. Races in this sense may be conceptualized as class fractions, constituted through but not reducible to the labour process. Miles argues that migrant labour occupies a structurally distinct position in British society: economically, such migrants are part of the working class (in that the rationale for immigration was the sale of labour) but ideologically they are marginalized (by a reservoir of racist imagery that is carried over from a colonial past and gains new impetus among the uncertainties of industrial restructuring). The ideological process of racialization has, Miles argues, 'served to reinforce and maintain the economic stratification of wage labour' (p. 171). According to Castles (1984: 98) this is part of a more general process wherein 'capital uses racial, national and sexual categorisation to differentiate between groups of workers, splitting the labour force, and permitting super-exploitation of certain sections'. From this perspective, the process of racial differentiation is functional for capitalism even though, by adding a new dimension to class struggle, it also changes the form of capitalism.

The achievement of Miles's analytical framework is that it replaces biology with economics in accounting for the material origins of 'races', and it displaces the niceties of culture with bitter ideological struggle as the source of legitimation for racial inequality. Additionally, his work suggests a mechanism – racism or, more broadly, racial ideology – that is able not only to reproduce patterns of domination and subordination in the labour market, but to extend such inequalities beyond the workplace. In particular he and Annie Phizacklea (Miles and Phizacklea 1981; Phizacklea and Miles 1980) draw attention to the significance of racist imagery for a white working class that is struggling to make sense of, and resist, the process of urban decline in late capitalist Britain.

Miles's scheme is most appropriate for explaining the racialization of migrant workers in the post-war years and, especially, during the 1960s. It does not directly account for the position of the large proportion of Britain's black population who were refugees, or for the 40 per cent of black people who are not migrants at all. The basic thesis can be elaborated, of course, to account for the continuing vulnerability of black labour, as illustrated by Doherty (1973); Miles (1982a) himself examines the possible role of black youth as a new 'reserve army' of surplus labour. This may even be taken a step further, since, in a political climate favouring the ascendency of the market in all spheres of life, it would seem appropriate to seek explanations for the constitution of race not only in the varying capacity of the working classes to sell their labour, but also in the public's differential access to property rights more generally.

A second link between racial ideology and the material world may be established by moving beyond the economics of labour migration and wealth accumulation. If the unequal dispensation of economic rights contributes to (or seeks legitimacy in) the process of racial differentiation, then the same might be true of unequal access to a range of other citizenship rights in a given national setting. This possibility is built into Rex and Tomlinson's (1979) conceptualization of the black population as an underclass. The notion is most fully developed by Rex (1986a), who uses it to refer to black people as a population not only marginalized by the labour process and disadvantaged in the market place, but also excluded from full incorporation into the welfare state. He argues that in societies where collective responsibility for welfare is institutionalized in the state, the working classes can be defined or identified in terms of their eligibility for a range of basic rights. These rights include the freedom to engage in collective bargaining, security in the event of unemployment, a minimum standard of health, access to education, the right to decent housing and so on. It is not, Rex implies, helpful to regard those effectively (or legally) excluded from these universal rights as members of the working class.

Moreover, he argues that black people in Britain 'have not enjoyed the benefits of the working class in the Welfare State', either because of discrimination by those who dispense the benefits, or because working class organizations have not been prepared to allow black people the kind of protection offered to other workers (Rex 1986a: 122). Because black people are not on an even footing with whites, whatever their socio-economic status, they might best be viewed, for analytical purposes, as an underclass: 'a quasi-group with a distinct class position and status weaker and lower than that of the [white] working class' (Rex 1986a: 74).

It is doubtful whether either Rex or Miles would consider their approaches to be compatible. From Miles's perspective the whole of social policy would be portrayed as a requirement for maintaining the social relations of production, whereas in Rex's thesis social policy would inspire and sustain forms of social stratification that are lodged outside the labour process. Nevertheless, irrespective of whether black people constitute a fraction of the working class or a stratum apart from it (and currently this is effectively a question of philosophical belief or political commitment) Rex's thesis is helpful in suggesting that differential access to welfare rights contributes to the reproduction of racial differentiation within the bottom end of the class structure. Groups which might be united in their exclusion from economic rights could be divided over their eligibility for welfare.

A framework which locates the material basis of racial categorization in differential access to economic rights, and which finds impetus for the reproduction of race in terms of social rights more generally, would be incomplete without also considering the significance of political and legal rights in this same process. The politics of race is, however, a relatively neglected topic in Britain. Much of the 'race relations' literature has been reluctant to explore political theory, while political science has often failed to embrace the significance of racism. The importance of political conflict and legislative history is, of course, acknowledged in the work already summarized, but there is little explicit analysis of the political constitution of 'race' in its own right.

One important exception is the work of Gilroy (1987), which re-conceptualizes race as a political category – the endpoint of a political process of 'race formation'. Gilroy defines this as 'the manner in which "races" become organised in politics' (p. 38), at both an individual and an institutional level. This suggests that racial differentiation is not only a product of white exclusivity but also a locus for black resistance, much as suggested by researchers at Birmingham's Centre for Contemporary Cultural Studies (1982). Race is, for Gilroy, a significant analytical category because its manifestation 'refers investigation to the power that collective entities acquire by means of their roots in tradition' (p. 247). This scheme does not present 'race formation' as an alternative to class formation, but rather as a process able to 'relate the release of political forces which define themselves and organise around notions of "race" to the meaning and extent of class relationships' (p. 38). By drawing a distinction between class as a phenomenon of the material world and 'race' as a social construction, Gilroy narrowly avoids conflating these categories, and succeeds in drawing attention to the role of political conflict in establishing the forms that the social construction of race can take.

To summarize, the material origins of racial differentiation may be attributed to entrenched inequalities in the apportionment of a range of economic, social and political rights associated in Britain with permanent residence and citizenship. Racial ideology, though important in its own right, may be viewed primarily as a vehicle legitimizing these inequalities. Viewed from this perspective, 'race' *must* be regarded as a valid analytical category; not as an explanatory concept, but as a powerful social myth, with far-reaching human consequences, which itself requires explaining. However, before moving on to examine the relevance of segregation to this broader explanatory task, a diversion on terminology is required.

Language and meanings

Even from a critical perspective that is fully aware that racial differentiation is not 'natural' in a biological (or indeed theological) sense, it is easy to slip into dialogue which unthinkingly sustains popular racial categories without exposing and challenging the assumptions they encapsulate. It is therefore important to clarify the terms of reference – the languages of race – that are used in this book.[2]

At least two broad vocabularies are commonly used to articulate debate about race in Britain. The first draws attention to the broad differences in opportunities and achievement experienced by 'black' and 'white' members of society. Regarding this as a fundamental cleavage, Ramdin (1987) uses the term 'black' to refer to all non-white people of Afro-Caribbean or south Asian origin or descent. The reasoning here is, first, that black people have in common the experience of a recent history of migration into a predominantly white post-colonial society; secondly, that despite their wide variety of national origins, these migrants and their descendants have undergone a strikingly similar process of racialization; and finally, that they all are subject to forms of 'racial' – colour – discrimination embedded in British markets and institutions, and in the organization of social life. Modood (1988) takes a similar line, but prefers to recognize 'black' and 'Asian' separately as racialized categories and as principles of resistance, reserving the former only for those who perceive themselves as Afro-Caribbean.

Robinson (1982, 1986) on the other hand, having exposed the variable circumstances, experiences and achievements of the different Asian groups in British cities, urges that monolithic descriptive terms such as 'blacks', 'Asians', and 'West Indians' should be abandoned. Instead, analysts should focus on the subtle cultural, religious, linguistic and national divisions subsumed by the broader, less sensitive categories that are in more common use.

I agree with Robinson that it is critically important to recognize that all (black and white) immigrants and their descendants in Britain have unique personalities and attributes, and form a variety of groupings based on perceptions of common histories, interests and shared cultural values. At an analytical level, however, questions relating to culture and community are not the same as questions referring to racial categorization. Cultural variety is certainly a theoretically legitimate and morally important area of analysis, and it is an aspect of study that requires a high degree of sensitivity to internal differentiation within the population as a whole, black and white, immigrant or not. Racial ideology and inequality – forms of white supremacy – are also a pressing (and, for the most part, different) object of enquiry. Here analytical concern centres on the social cleavage forged between representatives of a colonial periphery and defenders of an imperialist core.

The second of these themes is more central than the former as a point of departure for this book. I shall therefore use the term 'black' to refer to people of both South Asian and Afro-Caribbean appearance who, whether born in Britain or overseas, can trace their extended family histories to the New Commonwealth and Pakistan. Where it seems appropriate to make distinctions within this group, I use the labels Afro-Caribbean and Asian (unless qualified, therefore, these terms do not refer to birthplace). Likewise, I use the term 'white' to refer to people of Caucasian appearance whose extended family histories are linked with Europe, North America and parts of Australasia. When speaking specifically about *immigrants*, I refer to groups in terms of their area of origin (East Europeans, Northern Irish, Caribbeans, Indians, East Africans, etc.).

My analysis is not, however, intended to be insensitive to culture. Culture is in many ways central to the argument I wish to make, although I restrict my investigation of this largely to the belief systems of white legislators. Throughout the text, I use the term 'culture' to refer to systems of shared meaning based on perceptions of common identity and experience (whether past or present). Culture is not equivalent, or reducible, to ideology, although it may play an important role in expressing or contesting particular ideological forms. Culture is not necessarily political, purposive or prescriptive. It need not coalesce around the manipulation of power, even though it can be regarded as an expression of, or response to, the material conditions of existence (and therefore as a signifying system mediating between individuals and the social and economic structures in which they must operate). There is, in my view, no necessary correspondence between birthplace and culture (although national heritage, language and religion may all be part of culture), or between 'race' and culture (although shared experiences in a process of racial categorization may begin to infuse terms such as 'black,' 'African' and 'Asian' with new meanings for their incumbents). Referring to this latter combination, Birmingham University's Centre for Contemporary Cultural Studies offers a helpful definition of race as a cultural response or resistance to structured subordination. This is not (as critics have suggested) a reification of race, but an account of how a position in the social and class structure is experienced, lived and shared by some individuals and groups.

My view of culture therefore rejects the idealist position, rooted in the anthropological writings of Alfred Kroeber and Robert Lowie, and in the geography of Carl Sauer, which defines culture as the pre-given 'informing spirit' of a way of life. Culture, in the sense I refer to it, is dynamic and changeable, expressing present circumstances as much as a shared past. It is not a rigid formula transported between continents, but a system of meanings, norms and expressions, moulding and adjusting to new challenges and changed circumstances.

This materialist and interactionist definition of culture allows me to dispense analytically with the notion of 'ethnicity'. Again, I would not deny the popular currency of this term nor question its usefulness as a concept introduced to overcome the rigidities of an idealist conception of culture. However, in the British context, it seems to me that ethnicity has become euphemism for race: when it is not referring to culture, it is a way of signalling that black people are the object of concern. As such, its effect is to sustain the meanings associated with race while appearing not to subscribe to this much cruder concept. Ethnicity is, as Miles (1982a) has shown, too readily employed as an uncritical reference to the social and behavioural significance of phenotypical characteristics. Sivanandan (1983) argues compellingly that the notion of ethnicity has masked the problem of racism and weakened the struggle against it, diluting the political voice of black people by fragmenting it into diverse communities of interest. Although there *are* times when ethnicity is used to refer to religious, linguistic or national, rather than to racialized groups, this meaning, for the non-idealist, is adequately incorporated within the term culture.

Therefore, for political and theoretical reasons the language of ethnicity is excluded from this text.

The relevance of segregation

Drawing on these arguments concerning the idea, meaning and language of race, I can now examine a related issue concerning how the practices and beliefs underpinning particular forms of residential segregation help to account for the persistence of racial inequalities in access to economic, welfare and political rights. Segregation in its broadest sense refers to the organization of all social life. It has to do with the conditions of interaction or avoidance, the construction of group identity and the structuring of social, economic and political activity. This book is concerned primarily with *residential* segregation, which human geography has conventionally regarded as an index or expression of a much wider set of social relations than those embedded in the production and consumption of housing. In assessing this wider relevance of residential segregation to the analysis of race, there are two areas of social science which are particularly helpful.

The first is the empirical tradition of social geography or 'spatial sociology', which has a longstanding interest in the measurement of specifically *racial* segregation. This work is rooted in a 'contact' hypothesis' borrowed from Robert Park and the Chicago School of Sociology and Human Ecology. It is assumed that there is a relationship between social and physical distance such that levels of segregation provide a measure of the frequency or quality of social intermixing. The practical aim is to explore the possibility that 'one's behaviour and attitudes towards members of a disliked social category will become more positive after direct interpersonal interaction with them' (Miller and Brewer 1984: 2). This kind of question has focused analysts' attention firmly on issues concerning the intensity and the patterning of segregation. The majority of published work has therefore provided empirical answers to essentially empirical debates about the configuration of residential differentiation; a large portion of the literature is bound up with the task of developing, contesting and refining a range of measuring tools.[3]

Obviously such work is invaluable if we are to have any grasp of the empirical facts about segregation or make any impact on policy debate (see Clarke 1982). However, preoccupation with the empirical project has too often meant that the task of specifying or isolating the 'racial' dimension of segregation is regarded as an end in itself. Race becomes the explanation for segregation rather than a facet of segregation *to be* explained. There is a temptation to regard segregation as something which, in Kantrowitz's

(1981) words, 'just is', and the import and significance of which is tied to its measurable intensity.[4] There is a reluctance to consider that segregation has *meaning*, in social, political and economic terms, quite irrespective of the degree of spatial separation it entails. Consequently, more attention has been paid to the absolute magnitude or degree of segregation than to its social significance within specific (national) political economies.

This empirical tradition has at least been prepared to recognize the salience of race, even though it can be criticized for treating the category as unproblematic. A second tradition, of interest because it makes a more sophisticated theoretical statement on the social significance of residential differentiation, is conspicuously silent on the topic of racial categorization. With only a few exceptions – including the work of Sarre (1986) and Shah (1979) – interpretations of segregation drawing on recent advances in social theory are more concerned with 'class' (variously defined) than with other axes of social differentiation. Whether viewing urban structure as a reflection of the class structure (Johnston 1980) or as a factor in class formation or fragmentation (Harris 1984; Harvey 1975), the tendency among urban theorists has been to regard race as marginal to the relations of production and consumption which structure residential space (largely ignoring the extent to which ideas about race are embedded in or constituted through these relations). There is, in short, a theoretical gap in the literature between political theories directly concerned with race but reluctant to explore the significance of residential segregation as a basis for racial ideology, and innovative theories of residential segregation which fail to recognize the salience of race.

This second tradition does suggest that if our focus in studying race is to explore the constitution and reproduction of this resilient category of social, economic and political life, then residential segregation, properly conceptualized, is one of the most obvious points of departure. If viewed from Harvey's (1985b: 123–4) perspective as 'an integral mediating influence in the processes whereby class relationships and social differentiations are produced and sustained', segregation must be recognized as one of the most neglected facets of the reproduction of social relations (including those implicated in the constitution of race).

Although empirical social geography and recent urban theory both shed light on the links between 'race' and residence, neither as yet offers an adequate conceptualization of racial segregation in its entirety. This is because while both express an interest in the role of segregation in the apportionment of material resources (and therefore in the reproduction of inequality), neither fully grasps its symbolic significance or historic specificity (thus ignoring its import as racial ideology). Some attention has, however, been focused on these themes by historians, whose point of departure has been the two classic examples of *de jure* segregation: apartheid in South Africa and the Jim Crow laws of the old American South. Such examples seem far removed in space, time and circumstances from late twentieth-century Britain. However, from the work of John Cell (1982), George Fredrickson (1981) and Paul Rich (1984/5, 1986a, b) in particular, some pointers of relevance to contemporary Britain emerge.

First, in its *de jure* form racial segregation was, and is, sustained for ideological as well as (and sometimes in opposition to) material (especially economic) reasons. Race, then, cannot only be seen as a form of stratification required for the economy, and racial segregation cannot simply be regarded as an instrument of social structuring. These more tangible concerns may be overlaid (and superseded) by an ideology of segregation*ism* which disculpates a range of iniquitous social and political practices (including, but reaching beyond, those referring to the production and use of residential space).

Secondly, history challenges the comfortable assumption that segregationist beliefs and practices have been confined to two anachronistic national instances. Rich (1984/5) draws attention to the export of this doctrine from the American South, and traces its import not only to South Africa, but also to the UK. In the early 1900s, British politicians were more than ready to be persuaded of the merits of segregation, and segregationist ideologies shaped the development of policies of Colonial Trusteeship and indirect rule. Frenkel and Western (1988) show how residential segregation between 'natives' and colonial officers was advocated in the tropics, apparently to protect the latter from malaria. On the other hand, philanthropists viewed segregation – specifically, the proposal to set aside portions of the colonies for native use – as a benevolent means of securing black people's political advance. Others, influenced by the doctrines of Anglo-Saxon superiority that were popular in North America, favoured segregation as a means of precluding 'miscegenation', and supported their demands for territorial separation on a global scale with Darwinian notions of environmental 'fitness'. Only towards the end of the 1940s did segregationism fall from favour, and by then an informal 'colour bar' had begun to operate in Britain itself, affecting employment, service provision, lodgings, social events and interpersonal relationships (see Fryer 1984).

Finally, a historical perspective shows that segregationism is not the dying cry of a crumbling Empire, but a relatively new concept in political and public life. Neither the term nor the practice became popular before the early twentieth century, and once introduced, the idea gained momentum for more than fifty years. The doctrine of racial separatism is not, then, buried as deeply as politicians might like to imagine in the history of industrial capitalism. The USA did not repeal the last of the Jim

Crow laws until 1967,[5] and *de facto* segregationism is even now a politically volatile issue in both North America and Western Europe. Despite the South African 'anomaly' legally enforced segregation *might* soon be a diminishing legacy of a colonial past. But history testifies to the possibility that just as the content and practice of racism has changed, so too is segregationism a flexible and adaptable doctrine. Indeed, both Cell (1982) and Fredrickson (1981) suggest that segregationism might be more sophisticated than crude racism as an instrument of white supremacy; certainly, in its *de facto* form it might prove infinitely more resilient.

Segregationism is resilient because it captures much more than mere physical separation and it expresses much more than the differential distribution of material rewards. It encapsulates, rather, 'an interlocking system of economic institutions, social practices and customs, political power, law, and ideology' (Cell 1982: 14). It may, of course, be argued that the attitudes, ideologies and policies associated with racial segregation in modern Britain differ dramatically from those now, or ever, associated with South Africa or the American South. It was, after all, events in both those countries that prompted Britain to abandon its policies of 'benevolent' segregationism in the colonies and to make dispersal and integration the touchstone of immigration and race relations legislation. Modern Britain has no history of domestic slavery, has never operated a policy of *de jure* segregation and, during the main period of migration and settlement, was developing a welfare state designed to redistribute wealth according to need among the socially disadvantaged and economically deprived. Nevertheless, 'racial' segregation has been a consistent theme of this country's urban geography for more than forty years. No laws explicitly sustain it, and it may simply be a passing phase in the adjustment of markets and institutions to the needs and demands of a recently established black population. On the other hand, residential differentiation in Britain may be an expression of entrenched racial inequalities that are politically and socially, as well as economically, inspired. It is this possibility that I want to explore.

'Racial' segregation in Britain

I begin chapter 2 with a description of the development of residential segregation in post-war Britain. The discussion is confined to this modern period primarily for pragmatic reasons, as well as to achieve conceptual clarity. More than one volume would be required to encompass the long history of black settlement in Britain (catalogued by Fryer 1984), and only a much fatter book could delve with satisfaction into the archives of the late nineteenth and early twentieth centuries (fortunately the work of Paul Rich is beginning to provide a firm basis for our understanding of segregation in this earlier period). The past forty years do, nevertheless, cover the main period of immigration to Britain from the Caribbean, South Asia and East Africa, and these four decades offer some unique insights into the relationships between political ideology, racial differentiation and the changing labour requirements of a restructuring economy.

Chapter 2 draws together a range of evidence from the post-war period to specify the 'racial' dimension of residential segregation at both a regional and an intra-urban scale. Neither the size nor the concentration of the black population in Britain has allowed 'ghettoization' to develop on a scale or intensity comparable to that in the USA. Segregation of this racialized minority is, nevertheless, marked and enduring, and it can no longer be regarded as a passing legacy of immigration history. The challenge is to explain the persistence of segregation now that primary migration has all but ceased and 40 per cent of the black population was born in Britain.

This tour of the empirical 'facts' also illustrates that segregation is not a neutral expression of cultural preference. It is, rather, the fulcrum of racial inequality – in the labour market, in the housing system and, consequently, in access to a wide range of opportunities and life chances. This inequality stems primarily from the systematic denial of some key economic rights (associated with employment opportunities and property ownership) to migrant labourers and their dependents and descendants. Increasingly, however, such inequality is sustained by the operation of the housing system and by the restructuring of welfare rights that has accompanied the economic and ideological changes of the late twentieth century. Chapters 3 and 4 examine in more detail the policies that underpin this observation.

Chapter 3 is concerned with the extent to which centrally dispensed decisions have affected black people's access to residential space. Successive rounds of housing policy, developed in response to economic contingency and shaped by an ideological struggle over the appropriate role of the public sector, have imposed unmistakable, if seemingly unanticipated, constraints on black people's locational choice. These policies have rarely been formulated with explicit reference to race or racism, and it has never been considered appropriate to build a concept of racial disadvantage into mainstream housing legislation. Rather, it is assumed that the 'racial' dimension of inequality will be dealt with by urban policies designed to alleviate *general* deprivation, and by race relations legislation designed to eradicate racial discrimination. A review of these two sets of initiatives shows that while much *has* been achieved, such reasoning is fundamentally flawed. As a consequence, central governments have inadvertently devised policies which simply sustain segregation in its present, inequitable, form.

Over the course of forty years, formal responsibility for managing race-related issues (in the fields of housing, urban and anti-discrimination policy) has been gradually devolved to the local authorities.Chapter 4 examines a variety of processes impinging on patterns of housing consumption at a local level, where local governments exert an influence on black people's quality of life both through their management of public housing and through their wider responsibilities under the 1976 Race Relations Act. A wide range of research is interrogated to expose the initial complacency of the local authorities in catering to the needs of black people and the subsequent impotency of local governments as their financial and democratic autonomy has been undermined by the political centre.

Chapters 3 and 4 together expose the policy mechanisms which help to explain *how* the patterns of segregation described in chapter 2 are sustained. They show, in effect, that overlaid on black people's economic marginality is a progressive denial of certain rights to welfare – rights which scholars of social policy have usually regarded as a means of offsetting the impact of economic inequality in a capitalist system. This does not, however, explain *why* it is possible, in a supposedly enlightened liberal democracy, for residential space to be allocated or withheld, chosen or avoided, according to racially discriminatory criteria. This is the issue addressed in chapters 5 and 6, which identify a tendency towards segregationism in political and popular thought that lends tacit (if spurious) legitimacy to the principle of racial separatism.

To persist (i.e. to be reproduced) social inequality requires both a material base and a degree of normative support. To explore the latter, it is necessary to conceptualize racial segregation as a cultural symbol as well as an institutional practice. It must be analysed not only as a facet of residential differentiation, but also as a politically constructed problem and as a socially constructed way of life. Taking these in turn, chapters 5 and 6 examine the meaning of segregation in political and public opinion, showing that both the culture of high politics and the 'common sense' world of popular culture contain elements of racial exclusionism which license rather than challenge existing forms of racial inequality. In a sense these chapters are concerned with the contribution of racial ideology generally, and of segregationism in particular, to the legitimacy of the policies and practices outlined in chapters 3 and 4. Conceptions of race and beliefs about segregation do not *cause* racial inequality, but they do explain why a broadly egalitarian society tolerates such arrangements.

Chapter 5 might be regarded as the core of the book, since it is concerned with those centrally dispensed policies which most decisively affect black people's opportunities and life chances in British society. The discussion shows that such policies have an unstated as well as a stated rationale. Once this is appreciated, the unanticipated outcomes of government actions are much easier to understand. Developing an argument introduced elsewhere (Smith 1988), I explain how the politics of race have tacitly informed and explicitly rationalized a wide range of policy decisions. (A chronology of the main political and policy events drawn together here is given as an appendix.) While it is largely the *orientation* rather than the origins of policy that are accounted for in this way, the beliefs underpinning the fine tuning of the legislative agenda are shown to have an important bearing on black people's quality of life.

Chapter 5 shows that, throughout the post-war period, the imagery of racial segregation, and the pitfalls of building race into mainstream legislation, were uppermost in legislators' minds. The spectre of ghettoization and the stigma of the 'colour bar' were to be avoided at all costs. Attempts to balance the demands of this stated agenda with those of a more complex unstated agenda (concerning the future of Empire and Commonwealth) helped determine the character of segregation as a problem defined (and responded to) by politicians. As a consequence, political constructions of racial segregation have always been less effective in identifying the roots of inequality than in creating a model of racial disadvantage that can be tackled without offending the sensibilities of a predominantly white electorate. In this sense the politics of racial segregation have subscribed to the ideological assertion that races are real (rather than socially constructed), spawned policies which sustain rather than ameliorate the racist dimension of social inequality and, most recently, given *de facto* racial separatism greater force in British life than ever before.

The culture of 'high' politics is not, however, the only source of normative support for the reproduction of racial segregation. The 'common sense' of a general public also plays a vital role in sustaining the social reality of race and in legitimizing racial inequality. Chapter 6 examines the confrontation between white racism and black resistance in the struggle for urban space, exploring a range of attitudinal and behavioural norms which either sustain or fail to challenge racial exclusivism on a neighbourhood scale. A review of voting behaviour, street politics and popular protest unearths little resistance among the general public to the notion that relative segregation rather than relative integration is the British urban norm.

Having exposed a disjunction between the theory and reality of representative democracy as a vehicle for building black people's interests into public decision-making, chapters 5 and 6 both indicate that the racial inequalities expressed in segregation testify not only to a differential distribution of economic and social rights, but also, and fundamentally, to an uneven distribution of effective political rights.

The story of racial segregation in Britain is, on the evidence of chapters 2 to 6, a tale of the progressive *de facto* (and, indeed, *de jure*) curtailment of the rights of black Britons as established by the British Nationality Act of 1948. Chapter 7 draws from this a re-theorization of racial segregation based on differential access to the rights of citizenship. I suggest that segregation in Britain is an expression of unequal access to all these rights, but that political inequality lies at its core. My conclusions therefore speculate on the prospects for change, distinguishing those political strategies and policy frameworks which could promote reform from those which promise 'more of the same'. As a whole, the book is offered as an attempt to expand our understanding of the *meaning* of racial segregation in a modern liberal democracy, where, in the apportionment of residential space, the niceties of cultural preference are overlaid with the stark realities of a struggle for privilege and power.

Notes

1 The more conventional notion of 'race relations' refers to 'a general body of knowledge which tries to bring together in a common framework studies of group relations in different countries and in different periods of history' (Banton 1977: 2). In contrast, racialized relations are transactions which seize on arbitrary attributes to define groups for political, social and economic purposes.
2 As part of this strategy, I refer to 'race' and 'racial segregation' in inverted commas whenever it seems necessary to emphasize that the idea of race is problematic and originates in the social world. Racial inequality therefore refers to the imbalance of power dividing racialized minorities; racial equality is an ideal which, on attainment, dissolves into the principle of anti-racism.
3 At least two 'index wars' have been waged to determine which mathematical formulation best summarizes observed residential patterns (see reviews by Duncan and Duncan 1955; James and Taeuber 1985a; Taeuber and Taeuber 1965; exchanges involving Reiner 1972; Winship 1977, 1978; Falk et al. 1978; and a comment by Peach 1981). The limitations of common indices have been exposed (see Morgan 1980, 1982; Morgan and Norbury 1981; Sims 1981; Woods 1976) and new measures have been developed in their wake (see Farley 1984; Lieberson 1981; Lieberson and Carter 1982; Robinson 1980a).
4 This is well illustrated in work which, by applying techniques of direct or indirect standardization to common indices of segregation and residential

dissimilarity, attempts to isolate the contribution of race, or racial discrimination, to segregation by *filtering out* the contribution of class, housing tenure, language, education and so on. Such approaches make a theoretical error by trying to take away the very factors through which race is constituted; and they make an empirical error by inferring the extent of racial discrimination without exposing the policy mechanisms and institutional practices that are responsible for it.

5 The end of the Jim Crow era in the American South came with the Civil Rights Acts of 1964 and 1965 (which, respectively, demanded equal access to public facilities and protected black people's voting rights), and with the Supreme Court rulings banning segregation in public schools in 1954 (*Brown* v *Board of Education of Topeka*) and declaring state laws preventing inter-racial marriage unconstitutional in 1967 (*Loving* v *Virginia*).

2 'Race' as a Dimension of Residential Segregation

They congregate where the employment prospects are good and, almost inevitably, where the housing shortage is most acute.

Patricia Hornsby-Smith, 3 April 1958

Nothing meaningful may be said about the significance of segregation without first establishing what form it takes. To an extent, therefore, this chapter may be regarded as a ground-clearing exercise, drawing together information on the composition and distribution of Britain's black population nationally, regionally and at an intra-urban scale. This includes a detailed summary of measures of 'racial' segregation and of observable dissimilarities in the residential locations of 'black' and 'white' Britain. Those not interested in the minutiae of this analysis, and who do not need to be persuaded that such patterns are entrenched and enduring, may use the opening sections simply for reference and rejoin the text at page 36. There, I go on to argue that the intensity of segregation is ultimately less important than its place at the intersection between labour markets and the housing system. It is at this point that residential segregation is directly implicated in the structuring of racial inequality.

Britain's black population

Inferences from the 1981 census suggest that 2.2 million people with personal or family histories in the New Commonwealth or Pakistan live in Britain (see Ballard 1983; OPCS and Registrar General of Scotland 1983).[1] The census also shows that, in 1981, *immigrants* originating in the NCWP numbered just over 1.5 million (they account, therefore, for about 45 per cent of that part of Britain's population which was born outside the UK, and this represents a steady increase from 13.9 per cent in 1951, 24.5 per cent in 1961 and 38.6 per cent in 1979). Among people of New Commonwealth origin or descent now resident in Britain, as many as 20 per cent may be white; the enumerated black population therefore constitutes around 3.6 per cent of the total – a figure broadly confirmed by the Labour Force Surveys (LFS) for 1983–5, in which 3.3 per cent of respondents identified themselves as West Indian, Indian, Pakistani or Bangladeshi in origin.[2] Table 1 shows the composition of the black

Table 1   Britain's black population in the 1980s

National origin	Family background 1981[a] (%)[c]	UK-born 1981 (%)[d]	Self-ascribed 'ethnicity' 1983–5[b] (%)[c]
Caribbean/West Indies	24.7 (1.0)	50.1	22.5 (1.0)
India	30.5 (1.3)	38.8	32.4 (1.4)
Pakistan	13.4 (0.6)	40.0	16.1 (0.7)
Bangladesh	2.9 (0.1)	26.2	3.9 (0.2)
East Africa[e]	8.2 (0.3)	26.8	n.a.
Other[f]	20.2 (0.9)	39.6	25.1 (10.9)
Total	100.0 (4.2)	40.6	100.0 (4.3)
Number	2 207 245	895 592	2 349 000

[a] Census data: country of origin based on birthplace of head of household of all persons resident in private households with head of household born in the New Commonwealth or Pakistan (NCWP).
[b] Based on LFS figures averaged over three years.
[c] Proportion of total non-white population formed by each national group. Figures in parentheses refer to proportion each group forms of the total population of Great Britain.
[d] Proportions of those in column 1 who were born within the UK.
[e] 'East African' is not a category used in the ethnic question of the LFS. However, special tabulations show that among those born in East Africa (0.5 per cent of the population in 1983), the majority (76 per cent) perceived themselves as Indian, while most of the remainder claimed to be white. East Africans, therefore, form 13 per cent of the Asian population and 21 per cent of Indians in Britain (see Saggar 1985/6).
[f] Including Mediterranean and Far East in LFS, and Southern Africa, Western Africa, South East Asia, Mediterranean and several other islands and territories in the census.
Sources: OPCS and Registrar General of Scotland 1983; Central Statistical Office 1987

population based on the geographical classification of the 1981 census and the measure of cultural identification elicited by the LFS.[3]

South Asians now comprise over half the non-white population, a numerical dominance which is relatively recent, although there is documentary evidence of the significance of Asian communities in Britian for at least 120 years. The largest national sub-group is the Indians, about 20 per cent of whom were born in, or migrated via, East Africa, to which many had first been drawn as indentured labour. The majority (four-fifths) of the remainder originated in the East Punjab (primarily in the Jullundur Doab) with smaller groups from the Gujerat. Over two-fifths of the Indians are Sikhs, and a little under a third (rising to almost two-thirds of East Africans) are Hindus; just one in six are Muslim (Brown 1984). The population of Pakistani origin is less than half the size of the Indian group, although again the majority originate from the Punjab (primarily the Mirpur and Rawalpindi districts). They, like the much smaller Bangladeshi population (whose links are primarily with rural Sylhet), are predominantly (96 per cent) Muslim.

Simmons (1981) sketches some key characteristics of the Asian communities in Britain, although the most incisive account of their migration and settlement is given by Robinson (1986). Although a fairly steady flow of South Asian immigration was sustained throughout the 1950s, it was not until the 1960s that the numbers involved matched or exceeded migration from the Caribbean. (A substantial proportion of the increase, especially between 1965 and 1968, was accounted for by refugees from Kenya.) By 1971, well over three-quarters of the Indian and Pakistani population in Britain consisted of people who had settled in the past ten years. These were joined in the early 1970s by more refugees from East Africa (primarily Ugandans), who contributed significantly to the 10 per cent increase in the size of the Asian population that occurred between 1971 and 1981. (Between 1971 and 1983, net immigration from India, Pakistan, Sri Lanka and Bangladesh averaged 18 200 per year, mostly consisting of dependents since primary immigration from these areas had been brought virtually to an end.)

People of Afro-Caribbean origin or descent form about a quarter of the black population in Britain. Of those born in the West Indies, the majority (56 per cent) are Jamaican; Barbados (8.5 per cent), Guyana (7.3 per cent) and Trinidad and Tobago (5.5 per cent) each account for a much smaller proportion of the West Indian total. The migration history and present characteristics of the Afro-Caribbean communities are succinctly outlined by Peach (1968, 1986a). He shows how the major period of immigration occurred during the 1950s, peaking in 1961 and giving way to net emigration by the early 1970s. Comparisons between the 1971 and 1981

L. I. H. E.

THE BECK LIBRARY

WOOLTON RD., LIVERPOOL, L16 8ND

censuses, insofar as they are possible, show that not only has the Caribbean-born population decreased in size, but there has also been a slight decrease in the numbers of black people of Caribbean descent.[4] However, my over-riding concern in this book does not relate to the absolute or relative size of the black population, but rather to the questions of where and in what conditions black people live, and why.

Black and white Britain: regional trends

Although studies of residential differentiation rarely dwell on regional patterns, table 2 indicates that this broad area scale is an important starting point when considering the 'racial' dimension of segregation. Almost 30 per cent of the black population (and over two-fifths of those who identify themselves as Bangladeshi or Afro-Caribbean) would have to move to attain the same degree of regional dispersal as the white population.

Table 2 Indices of dissimilarity[a] for selected populations[b] in England, by region, 1983–5

	All non-white (1)	White (2)	West Indian (3)	Indian (4)	Pakistani (5)	Bangladeshi (6)
1	–	29.8				
2		–	42.5	35.9	31.3	44.5
3			–	19.4	45.5	7.5
4				–	33.9	21.3
5					–	44.7

[a] The index of dissimilarity (ID) is defined in note 6 to this chapter.
[b] Self-identification by respondents to the LFS.
Source: Central Statistical Office 1987

   Table 3 indicates that black people are statistically over-represented in the South-East (where the concentration of Afro-Caribbeans, Bangladeshis and East African Asians is particularly marked), and the West Midlands (where there is a notable clustering of the population of Indian and Pakistani origin), and that they are well-represented (mainly as a consequence of Pakistani settlement) in the North-West and Yorkshire/ Humberside, as well as in the East Midlands (where the Indian and East African Asian populations are more dominant). Only between 3.2 and 3.5

per cent of black people (as compared with over 14 per cent of white people) live in Scotland or Wales, and they are similarly under-represented in the North and the South-West. There is, then, both an overall regional concentration of the black population and considerable inter-regional variability among the sub-communities concerned. The most marked distinction in this latter respect occurs between Afro-Caribbeans and Pakistanis who cluster, respectively, in Southern and Northern regions. Figure 1 gives a more detailed picture of the nature of this variability.

These patterns of under- and over-representation were established in the earliest phases of Afro-Caribbean and Asian migrations and show few signs of change. Peach (1986a) shows that the present distribution of the Caribbean population (focused on the South-East and West Midlands) was more or less set by 1961. It reflects the role of West Indian migrants as a replacement labour force that was attracted not to regions of high unemployment, nor indeed to the most prosperous locales, but rather to areas where demand for labour was high in occupations unable (because of employment opportunities elsewhere) to retain a white labour force.

Robinson (1986) uses a similar argument to account for the sustained prominence of the South-East and West Midlands as destinations for South Asian migrants. However, reflecting a change in the distribution of employment opportunities, which occurred at a time when West Indian migration was declining and Asians were beginning to enter the British labour market, this study also shows a rapid growth (from 1961 to 1971) of the Lancashire textile towns and East Midlands as Asian centres. Subsequently, the North-West has also strengthened its position as a centre of Asian (especially Pakistani) settlement.

Broadly, therefore, the pattern identified in Jones's (1978) elegant analysis of the 1971 census can be seen as an elaboration of a trend well established by 1961 and set to continue during the 1980s. For the most part, black people remain statistically over-represented in Greater London (which accommodates three times more black people, in proportionate terms, than whites), the West Midlands and the largest textile towns of Lancashire and Yorkshire. They are less prominent in the coalfield regions and the spatially peripheral heavy industrial regions of Scotland and the North. Moreover, given that the growth rate of the black population is relatively low in sparsely settled zones, it seems likely that the regional polarization of 'black' and 'white' Britain will continue (see Peach 1982).

Not only are black people much more likely than whites to live in the metropolitan regions of England, but within these regions, they are also more likely to be found in the metropolitan counties. Table 4 shows that just over three-quarters of white people but almost 90 per cent of the black

Table 3 Population distribution in Great Britain 1981–5:[a] percentage of residents in private households

	Total	Black[b]	West Indian[c]	Indian	Pakistani[d]	Bangladeshi[d]	East African[e]
Scotland	9.5 (9.3)	2.1 (1.8)	0.3 (0)	2.4 (0.8)	3.4 (5.3)	1.3 (0)	1.8
Wales	5.1 (5.1)	1.1 (1.6)	0.6 (0.6)	1.0 (0.9)	1.1 (1.6)	2.1 (2.2)	0.9
North	5.7 (5.7)	1.2 (1.6)	0.2 (0)	1.3 (0.7)	2.1 (2.9)	1.6 (2.2)	0.7
Yorkshire/Humberside	9.0 (9.0)	7.0 (7.4)	4.9 (4.9)	6.3 (5.3)	20.4 (19.9)	7.0 (6.5)	2.8
North-West	11.8 (11.7)	7.6 (9.0)	4.8 (5.3)	8.1 (8.5)	15.2 (15.7)	11.4 (4.4)	5.4
East Midlands	7.0 (7.1)	6.4 (6.5)	5.2 (4.4)	9.2 (11.8)	4.0 (3.5)	3.3 (0)	12.3

West Midlands	9.5 (9.5)	14.8 (16.8)	15.5 (15.0)	20.3 (21.5)	21.0 (25.7)	14.2 (16.3)	8.0
East Anglia	3.5 (3.5)	1.3 (1.2)	1.0 (1.0)	1.1 (0.5)	1.3 (1.1)	1.1 (1.1)	1.6
South-East	31.0 (31.1)	55.6 (52.2)	64.7 (66.7)	47.3 (48.8)	30.1 (23.3)	56.5 (67.4)	64.0
South-West	8.0 (8.1)	2.9 (2.0)	2.7 (2.1)	3.0 (1.1)	1.5 (1.1)	1.4 (0)	2.4
Number (1981)	54 814 500	2 207 245	545 744	673 704	295 461	64 561	181 321
Number (1983–5)	54 118 000	2 349 000	528 000	762 000	377 000	92 000	

[a] 1981 census and (in parentheses) LFS averages for 1983–5. These two sets of figures are not directly comparable.

[b] Census data refer to those in households where the head of household was born in the New Commonwealth or Pakistan. LFS data refer to those whose self-ascribed 'ethnic' category is not 'white'.

[c] LFS grouping; census designation is 'Caribbean'.

[d] LFS figures include people born in East Africa.

[e] LFS does not distinguish East Africans (but see table 1, note e).

Sources: OPCS and Registrar General of Scotland 1983; Central Statistical Office 1987

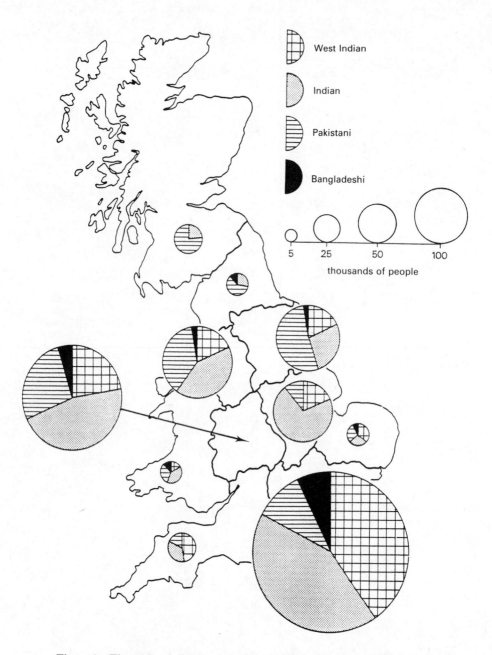

Figure 1 The regional distribution of the black populations of Britain (based on LFS estimates, averaged over 3 years, 1983–5)

Table 4 Population distribution within the metropolitan regions of England

Region	Non-NCWP	All NCWP	Caribbean	Indian	Pakistani	Bangladeshi	East African
				% of regional population			
North							
Tyne & Wear	37.0	43.3	36.3	46.9	33.6	65.9	40.1
Elsewhere	63.0	56.7	63.7	53.1	66.4	34.1	59.9
Yorkshire/Humberside							
South Yorkshire	27.1	15.9	27.2	9.5	14.8	13.8	12.0
West Yorkshire	40.9	76.7	69.9	81.4	84.0	70.2	72.2
Elsewhere	32.0	7.4	2.9	9.1	1.2	16.0	15.8
North-West							
Greater Manchester	40.1	59.3	77.6	54.5	57.1	73.5	60.9
Merseyside	24.0	8.8	9.9	6.2	1.6	6.0	5.6
Elsewhere	35.9	31.9	12.5	39.3	41.3	20.5	33.5
West Midlands							
West Midlands MC	49.1	87.4	91.2	88.2	88.5	89.9	79.7
Elsewhere	50.9	12.6	8.8	11.8	11.5	10.1	20.3
South-East							
Greater London	37.1	77.0	86.9	70.2	58.8	79.1	78.1
Elsewhere	62.9	23.0	13.1	29.8	41.2	20.9	21.9
Total in metropolitan counties	47.9	78.8	88.1	74.9	74.4	81.0	77.4
Total elsewhere in metropolitan region	52.1	21.2	11.9	25.1	25.6	19.0	22.6
% in England in metropolitan regions	77.9	89.1	91.0	86.2	92.8	94.0	83.2

Census data: based on persons resident in private households with head of household born in the NCWP (see note 1).
Source: OPCS 1983

population lived in the five metropolitan regions of England in the early 1980s and less than half the former but nearly 80 per cent of the latter lived in the major urban centres.

The dissimilarity between the intra-regional distributions of the black and white populations is greatest in Yorkshire/Humberside (where Indian and Pakistani Asians are twice as likely as whites to live in West Yorkshire), in the South-East (where 87 per cent of Afro-Caribbeans but only 37 per cent of whites live in Greater London) and in the West Midlands (where all the black populations cluster disproportionately into the Wolverhampton–Birmingham–Coventry axis). Overall, 50 per cent of black households as compared with 21 per cent of whites live in Greater London and the West Midlands and, with the exception of London and Birmingham, there are no common cities in the top five urban centres ranked according to the proportion of the black and white population they contain. Again, this is a pattern firmly set by 1971, and it has been modified only by some very minor changes among the Asians as their urban system expanded with population growth (as illustrated by Robinson 1986).

The most prominent theme, then, is one of marked and persistent inter- and intra-regional disparity between the distribution of the black and white populations. This has led Peach (1987: 42) to identify Britain's experience as 'the classic case of the black immigrant population as a replacement population'. Finding high negative correlations (of $r = -0.93$ and -0.89, respectively) between West Indian and Asian settlement and overall population increase (by county), he shows that black people consistently live within zones that are losing whites. The 'racial' basis of residential segregation thus seems likely to endure.

The pattern is not, of course, exclusively one of clustering and concentration. In the context of a net increase in the size of the black population, it is hardly surprising that the urban system they occupy has expanded (by 1981 as many as 155 cities or London boroughs contained over 2000 NCWP-born residents, representing an increase of 46 over the previous decade). Similarly, as many as 295 of the 366 English local authorities (London boroughs, metropolitan districts and district (borough) councils) in 1981 had at least 500 people living in households headed by a person born in the New Commonwealth or Pakistan; and there were only 9 districts (including seven London boroughs) whose populations were less than 80 per cent white. This intra-regional spread must, nevertheless, be set in the context of the distinctive patterns of intra-urban segregation that are exhibited by the highly urbanized black populations. As I will show, even signs of intra-regional dispersal can mask a high degree of residential concentration at a local level.

Segregation in cities

Only 3 per cent of black people (in contrast to the national average of 24 per cent) live in rural enumeration districts, and three-quarters live in a set of urban enumeration districts containing just 10 per cent of all whites (Brown 1984). This means that about half the white population lives in neighbourhoods containing no black residents and only about 1 in 16 whites lives in an enumeration district with a 'coloured immigrant' population of 5 per cent or more (although these zones accommodate 60 per cent of all black people). Although there is evidence of some residential dispersal between 1971 and 1981, the 1980s began with a higher proportion of black people living in the most segregated urban areas than did the 1970s. There was no significant growth in the intercensal decade in the proportion of black people living in electoral wards where they have historically been under-represented. Only in wards with a relatively dense black population has there been some limited residential dispersal from enumeration districts of high concentration to those of lower concentration (these patterns are analysed in some detail by Brown (1984)).

A variety of case studies completed during the late 1970s and early 1980s confirms this generalization, providing ample (though not always easily comparable) evidence of the extent of segregation *within* the major British cities between groups defined according to colour or birthplace[5] (little research has focused on urban Scotland). While comparisons using common indices are fraught with difficulty, there are at least two broad generalizations which merit attention.

First, indices of segregation (ISs)[6] show that black people (whether migrants or not) are on average more clustered than either UK-born or immigrant whites. Early evidence of this is apparent from Woods's (1975) research in Birmingham, which (using units larger than enumeration districts but generally smaller than wards) shows that immigrants born in the New Commonwealth were substantially more segregated than the Irish-born in both years (by as much as 20–30 points in 1961, rising to 30–40 points in 1971), and more segregated (by 15–20 points) than other UK-born residents in 1971.[7] Similarly, in Coventry, while the ward-level IS for residents born in the UK or the Irish Republic ranged from 8 to 14 in 1971, the figure for New Commonwealth migrants as a whole was 52, reaching 59 and 70 for Indians and Pakistanis, respectively (Peach et al. 1975). Even these broad statistics point to the very marked lack of residential integration experienced by the black population in urban Britain. However, the IS is scale-dependent and other analysts have shown that segregation is much more intense at the level of enumeration districts or streets. Cater and Jones's (1979) study of Asians in Huddersfield and Bradford, for instance, shows that while the ward-level ISs (in 1971) exceeded 55 in both cities, the indices were over 20 points higher when calculated at street level.

The most comprehensive analyses of intra-urban segregation based on the 1981 census continue, because of the delay in obtaining more sensitive tabulations, to rely on birthplace data (see Rees and Birkin 1984). Based on this indicator, levels of segregation at the borough level among five major NCWP-born populations in London are between 7 and 26 points higher than for the English-born (ranging from 31.4 for Indians to 50.3 for Bangladeshis).[8] In Leeds, at ward and enumeration district level, the discrepancies are even more marked, with the IS for those born in England standing at 26.9 (by ward) and 32.5 (by enumeration district) in contrast to figures in the range 43–78 (ward) and 62–79 (enumeration district) for NCWP-born groups. The same pattern is maintained in Bradford where, with the exception of those born in East Africa, black migrants experience segregation at levels at least 10 points higher than those experienced by the English-born.

The patterns of segregation that might be inferred from these data are sustained elsewhere in the census, confirming this first generalization that black people, immigrant or otherwise, are more segregated than the white population. In London, the ward-level IS for people living in households headed by someone born in the New Commonwealth or Pakistan is 42 (Husbands 1987), and black people comprise at least 20 per cent of the population in five inner (and two outer) London boroughs. In Birmingham, by the early 1980s, as much as 40 per cent of the population of the city's inner core lived in households headed by a person born in the NCWP (Cross 1986), and there are six wards in which 45 per cent or more of the residents are black. Overall, there are eight districts outside London (Birmingham, Blackburn, Bradford, Leicester, Luton, Sandwell, Slough and Wolverhampton) where black people comprise 10 per cent or more of the total population.

A second generalization about the intra-urban distribution of the black population relates not to the intensity of segregation but to the extent of residential separation between black and white households. There are differences not only in how segregated various populations are, but also in *where* within a city that clustering occurs among one group relative to another. The 1982 PSI survey shows how marked these differences are, indicating that 43 per cent of Afro-Caribbeans and 23 per cent of Asians, but only 6 per cent of whites, live in the inner city zones of London, Birmingham and Manchester. It is rare among studies based on the last two sweeps of the census to find indices of dissimilarity between whites and blacks (whether they are immigrants or UK-born) falling below 40 when calculated for wards or any smaller unit. Robinson (1986) illustrates this on a year-by-year basis in Blackburn, showing that at no time between 1968 and 1984 did the ward level IDs between Asians and non-Asians fall below 50. Effectively, in most known urban analyses almost half the population would have to move between wards, and much higher proportions would have to move between enumeration districts, to achieve complete residential integration.

On the whole, with a few exceptions,[9] studies in the North find Asians both more segregated than Afro-Caribbeans and more dissimilar from whites in their residential pattern.[10] In Bradford, for instance, Rees and Birkin (1984) estimate that 56 per cent of Indians compared with 44 per cent of those born in the Caribbean (but only 15 and 17 per cent of those born in the Old Commonwealth and the Irish Republic) would have to move to achieve the same spatial dispersion as their non-immigrant (mainly white) counterparts. Similar observations have been made in the Midlands.[11] Even where there has been a small decline in the value of Asian:White IDs this appears to be a function of the increasing size and internal sorting of the Asian populations rather than an indicator of their increased opportunities in the city-wide housing market. Indeed, this trend has often been accompanied by an *increase* in spatial isolation (measured by $P\star$)[12], decreasing the prospects for inter-group contact.[13]

Only in the south do Asians appear to be less segregated and less dissimilar from the white population than the Afro-Caribbeans.[14] This trend is most marked in London. In 1971, ward level IDs between residents born in England and Wales, and those born in India, Pakistan and the Caribbean, were 38, 49 and 51 (this last figure varied among the West Indian island groups from 57 for Jamaicans to 44.5 for those originating in Trinidad and Tobago (Peach 1984)). By 1981, indices of segregation by borough were, though very marked for Bangladeshis (50.3), still somewhat lower for Indians and Pakistanis (31, 35) than West Indians (38) (Rees and Birkin 1984).

There is, to summarize, considerable and consistent evidence confirming a fairly high degree of residential dissimilarity between Britain's black and white populations at a variety of spatial scales. There is no simple link between segregation and time of arrival in the UK, and no gradual decline of segregation over time as traditional (and as we shall see political) models of immigration, dispersal and 'assimilation' once predicted. Regional and intra-urban segregation encapsulates a variety of modern as well as historical processes, which are 'increasingly separating blacks and whites into two domains' (Cross 1986: 9). Despite the limited residential dispersal of West Indians associated with their movement into council housing (Lee 1977; Peach and Shah 1980), and notwithstanding some 'suburbanization' among an emerging Asian middle class (Phillips 1981; Ram and Phillips 1985), the majority of evidence confirms Rex's (1986b) observation that segregated cities have become a British norm.

Segregation: fact or value?

In itself, the existence and persistence of residential segregation need not necessarily be of concern. The empirical fact of residential differentiation *need* not be better or worse than the empirical fact of residential homogeneity. There is, furthermore, sufficient scope within these empirical 'facts' to infer that at least part of what we measure as racial segregation is, if not positively desirable, then at least relatively benign by international standards. Two such arguments have been particularly prominent, and I shall discuss them in turn.

The first is based on the discovery that a considerable amount of intra-community segregation occurs within, as well as between, the Asian and Afro-Caribbean populations, which could be taken to imply that residential differentiation is primarily a legitimate expression of cultural preferences. Peach (1984) has shown that among West Indians in London there is a tendency for Jamaicans to cluster south of the Thames, while other islanders live to the north. Phillips (1981), Ram and Phillips (1985), Robinson (1981) and Sims (1981) similarly identify substantial residential 'sorting' among Asians according to national, religious and linguistic criteria.

In part, this intra-group segregation reflects the practice of chain migration, which both confirms that there *is* an important cultural basis for segregation, and helps explain why initial patterns are perpetuated over time (Banton 1972; Desai 1963). This spatial sorting can also be interpreted as an index of the social distance between groups with a single continental origin – a distance which gained spatial expression when early migrants moved home following the arrival of dependents (Robinson 1986). It cannot therefore be denied that some aspects of intra-community residential differentiation are authentic expressions of cultural variety and preference. I shall, however, advance one theoretical reason and two empirical observations to suggest why studies of intra-group sorting cannot be used to legitimize value-neutral interpretations of the racial dimension of residential segregation.

At a theoretical level, such an approach conflates the construction of race with the expression of culture. The latter may account for many small-scale features of the residential mosaic, but the former must be analysed less as a predictor of shared aspirations than as a contested product of the broader political and economic processs structuring residential space. This is not, of course, the same as saying that racialised minorities can never share a sense of cultural unity (insofar as the expression of culture can be interpreted as a form of resistance, black consciousness itself might, in part, be seen as a consequence of racist exclusionism). However, the point here is that intra-group sorting as an expression of cultural preference is not the same object of analysis as *racial* segregation, since the latter, linking the practice of residential differentiation with the process of racial categorization, refers to the clustering of a variety of different cultural groups (perhaps 'united' only by their common experience of colour discrimination) within a limited segment of urban space.

At an empirical level, it is clear that, notwithstanding the significance of cultural variety, the intensity of intra-community segregation is generally less than that between Asians or West Indians and whites. According to Peach (1984), while ward level IDs in London *between* five Caribbean island groups and the indigenous ('white') population varied (in 1971) between 45 and 57, the highest *within-group* value was 41 (Jamaica:Trinidad and Tobago) and only three others exceeded 35 (Guyana, Jamaica and Trinidad/Tobago against 'other Caribbean'). Likewise, among Asians, despite very marked spatial sorting, Sims's (1981) research in Birmingham and Manchester and Robinson's (1981) surveys in Blackburn show that intra-community segregation is again less intense than that separating Asians from whites.[15]

More significant still than the discovery that 'racial' segregation is more intense than the residential expression of cultural variety, is the critical observation that, despite the considerable amount of residential mobility involved in intra-group sorting, there has been relatively little expansion of Afro-Caribbean or Asian residential space into the 'white rings' of suburbs that characterize the major cities. Even if black people prefer segregation, it is hard to understand why they should pursue this in the more run-down segments of the housing stock, rather than in areas where they could secure the symbolic and economic benefits associated with suburban life (this is a paradox explored by Ward and Sims (1981) and Cross (1985)).

A second observation that has tended to allay immediate fears about the consequences of racial segregation in Britain is that such segregation appears to be less intense and less entrenched than its counterpart in the North American ghetto. This second mitigating factor is noted by a variety of commentators, including Husbands (1987), Jones (1976) and

Peach (1979a). None of these is complacent but all feel that, potentially at least, the higher degree of residential mixing in Britain augurs well for domestic race relations.

It is undoubtedly true that, at some spatial scales, indices of dissimilarity between black and white urban residents in Britain are less – by as much as 20 points – than in the USA (although given the lack of comparability of area units, it is hard to interpret the significance of this). However, the extent, meaning and consequence of such differences have been questioned by Cater et al. (1977), Jones and McEvoy (1978) and Jones (1983). These authors argue that segregation in British cities *is* often intense, albeit on the scale of enumeration districts or streets. That the scale is small, they argue, 'is a reflection of the comparatively small size of the coloured minority populations [in Britain] rather than of any particularly enlightened community attitude towards interracial housing' (Cater et al. 1977: 305). Although these assertions have attracted some criticism (see, for instance, Jones 1977; Peach 1979a, b), it is hard to dismiss altogether the evidence that in some urban areas Britain's black population is sufficiently segregated to develop the basis of a relatively separate community life.

I acknowledge the force of some (though by no means all) of the arguments which highlight the optimistic face of residential segregation. This book, however, is not written either as an attempt to specify the extent to which residential patterns express cultural heterogeneity or to examine the intensity of social segregation in Britain relative to some international standard. I shall argue instead that both these issues are ultimately less important than a third empirical observation – that concerning the *configuration* of segregation in Britain relative to the organization of the major markets, institutions and systems of resource distribution. For irrespective of (though linked with) its cultural import, and notwithstanding an irresoluble controversy over its absolute or relative intensity, the character of residential segregation is also, and I believe fundamentally, an expression of racial inequality. The remainder of this chapter introduces the empirical evidence supporting such a view, arguing that the disproportionately disadvantageous residential circumstances of black people reflect, first their position in the labour market, secondly their treatment within the housing system and finally the relatively independent effect of location on both employment and housing opportunities.

Although some of Britain's most deprived urban areas (including Glasgow, Belfast and Tyneside) have very few black residents, enumeration district by enumeration district, black people are disproportionately likely to live in the country's most deprived and disadvantaged neighbourhoods

(Brown 1984). They occupy the older, poorer parts of the housing stock, they live in parts of cities where urban decay is most pronounced and they cluster where services – from education and health care to crime prevention and victim support – are in greatest need but shortest supply. These inner zones and middle rings of the major cities accommodate the majority of black people but only a minority of whites, and while the social and demographic profile of the latter makes them disproportionately eligible for assistance for a range of 'special' needs (related to age, health or disability), black people's population profile reveals no such bias. *Their* disadvantageous position reflects, rather, systematic inequalities dispensed by the interaction of the labour market with the housing system.

The weak labour market position of black people in Britain is now well documented, and low socio-economic status alone would be sufficient to constrain many black households to areas of social and housing stress. Black migrants and their children are generally more likely than whites (migrant or otherwise) to be out of work (see Barber 1981; Cross 1983). This is as true in the 'prosperous' South as it is in the depressed regions of Yorkshire and the North-West, and a recent summary of national and local analyses found that unemployment rates among black workers are consistently at least twice those experienced by whites, irrespective of their qualifications and language skills (Newnham 1986). These discrepancies are particularly marked for younger workers. Among 16–24-year-olds the 1985 LFS indicates that one-third of Afro-Caribbeans and half the Pakistani and Bangladeshi Asians, as compared with only 17 per cent of whites, are unemployed (irrespective of where they were born). More generally, it appears that in periods of high unemployment black people are much more vulnerable to redundancy and underemployment than are whites (Field et al. 1981) and that during the phase of economic restructuring between 1971 and 1982 the most precipitous decline in manufacturing occurred in the industrial categories where black workers traditionally clustered (Cross 1986; Field 1986).

When *in* employment, black people typically occupy lower status jobs than their white counterparts and work for a lower average wage (see Brennan and McGeever 1987; Cross and Johnson 1989). According to Brown (1984), 35 per cent of Afro-Caribbean men, 40 per cent of Asians (including almost 70 per cent of Bangladeshis) but only 16 per cent of whites are employed as semi- or unskilled manual workers. (As might be expected in view of the lower status of women's work generally, the discrepancies are somewhat less among female workers, although black women are still over 10 per cent more likely than whites to work as semi- or unskilled labour.) For migrants, this status difference is not related to the length of time they have been resident in Britain, and it seems more likely to reflect racial discrimination than cultural adjustment. Field (1986) states that black males earned 10–15 per cent less than whites in the early 1980s – a discrepancy which had not diminished over the previous decade, and one that is not explained by differences in socio-economic status (indeed, it is among manual workers that the earnings gap seems to be widening). This evidence vindicates Fevre's (1984) argument that 'the jobs which Blacks do are peculiar in that their pay seems to be unrelated to the level of labour demand in these occupations. Excess demand is not translated into higher pay. Thus Black workers sell their labour *as if the labour market did not exist; indeed it does not exist for Black workers since they suffer discrimination'* (pp. 161–2).

Economic marginality must, in itself, constrain the locational options of black households, regionally and within cities; certainly during the major phase of primary migration, the labour process exerted a powerful independent influence on where immigrants lived. As noted earlier, during the 1950s both the volume of West Indian immigration and the destination of migrant workers were a function of labour demand in Britain. Black people were attracted to those regions with high labour demand in a range of low status industries that were unable to retain a sufficiently large white workforce. These migrants formed a 'replacement' workforce, taking up marginal jobs (and therefore living in marginal areas) vacated by whites who were advancing, socially and spatially (through inter-regional or intra-urban migration), in an expanding economy (see Peach 1965, 1966b, 1968, 1978–9).

The relationship between immigration and labour demand is less marked for Asians (and complicated by substantial refugee migration) but once they were in Britain their destinations, too, were largely controlled by employment opportunities. It was primarily their dependence on traditional industries and low status services that led to their over-representation in the Midlands and the North (see Robinson 1980b, 1986). These patterns were not a function of the skill-status of migrants, but a consequence of the kinds of opportunities that were available to them in a restructuring and racially discriminatory job market. Crucially, Asians were a supplementary rather than a replacement workforce, finding employment in already contracting industries in positions vacated by (white) women, or in jobs which (because of legal and social barriers) female labour could not do (notably night shifts). C. Harris (1987) illustrates this with the example of the wool textile industry in which Asians were performing at night the kinds of tasks assigned to women in the day, but without receiving the same opportunities that women had to move into more skilled operative positions. Thus, as Fevre (1984) observes, 'the division of labour was established on a three-cornered basis with White men retaining the best jobs but with White women and Asian men working *separately* in the remainder. While the sexual division of labour remained, an additional element became apparent with the recruitment of Asians: *the division of labour now had a racial basis*' (pp. 80–1).

Whether as a replacement or a supplementary workforce, black labour helped delay the demise of many traditional industries, allowing entrepreneurs to increase productivity without raising wages. During this period, the circumstances in which migrant labourers – and subsequently their families – lived varied considerably, reflecting regional differences in the interaction of housing opportunities with labour market conditions. Ward (1987) has developed a typology of regions to account for this, contrasting, for instance, the multi-occupation and overcrowding forced on immigrants moving to expanding industrial areas (where there had been little white out-migration) with the relatively low pressure exerted on the housing system by those moving to then-stable traditional industrial areas (who were able to move into properties vacated by upwardly mobile whites). Despite these differences, and notwithstanding the variable responses of the local authorities or the contrasting aspirations of different cultural groups, Ward and many others have observed that black people in all regions occupied the worst segments of the housing stock. Economic marginality had something to do with this, but so too did direct and institutionalized racism in the housing system

The racially discriminatory operation of parts of the housing system is well documented in studies carried out in the 1960s and 1970s (Karn 1982; Lomas 1975; McKay 1977) and is discussed in more detail in chapters 3 and 4. Discrepancies in the housing quality of white and black households are consistently found in all sectors of the housing system and cannot always be explained simply by income differentials (Clark 1977). Black people have always been under-represented as the occupants of detached and semi-detached homes, more likely than whites to occupy pre-war properties, and disproportionately likely to have to share their homes or live at above average densities. At the end of the 1970s, the National Dwelling and Housing Survey (1979) showed that almost a quarter of Asian households and 15 per cent of Afro-Caribbeans, but less than 10 per cent of whites were sharing basic amenities. In contrast, less than one-third of black housholds but almost two-thirds of whites lived in homes with at least one room above the current bedroom standard. By 1982, over half the white households but just a quarter of blacks lived in detached or semi-detached houses, half the whites as compared with 60 per cent of Afro-Caribbeans and 74 per cent of Asians lived in dwellings built before 1945, and only 3 per cent of whites but 16 and 35 per cent of the Afro-Caribbean and Asian communities, respectively, lived at densities exceeding one person per room. Black people are two or three times more likely than whites to live in homes without gardens, 15–20 per cent more likely to lack a washing machine and, if Afro-Caribbean, 5 per cent less likely to have central heating. These discrepancies persist to a more or less marked degree across all tenures, and during the present decade the typical black family has remained restricted to patches of pre-war terraced housing in the older, inner areas of Britain's largest cities, within the confines of the major metropolitan regions (Brown 1984). This can scarcely be considered an expression of black people's preference and it is significant that whereas well over half the white population claim to be very satisfied with their present home (and neighbourhood), only two-fifths of the Asians and one-third of the Afro-Caribbean community share this sentiment.

The form of segregation expresses racial inequalities in the dispensation of housing as well as in the organization of labour. These markets and institutions do not, however, operate independently and while at one level residential segregation may be seen simply as a reflection of the labour process, at another level segregation – because it encapsulates location – may itself be regarded as a factor actively constraining access to better housing, welfare and employment opportunities. This latter role has become particularly crucial given the spatial organization of Britain's economic restructuring over the past fifteen years (a topic addressed by Massey and Meegan (1982) and Massey (1984)).

Changes in the location of employment opportunities and in capital investment have meant that the pattern of regional and intra-urban segregation, which was shaped by labour demand and augmented by overt and institutionalized bias in the housing system, has itself become a factor perpetuating racial disadvantage. Labour shedding has hit those occupations and areas traditionally associated with migrant labour, but spatially and 'racially' selective inertia within the housing system has denied black households access to more buoyant sectors of the economy.

This is illustrated at the broadest, regional, scale by Robinson (1986) who shows how, between 1961 and the 1980s, employment opportunities in the growth regions attracted white workers from a variety of locations while black people remained over-represented in areas of slow growth or decline. Within northern England, the regions with the largest black populations – Yorkshire and Humberside and the North-West – experienced a more dramatic fall in employment opportunities than did the North; likewise, in the centre of the country, the West Midlands fared worse than the East Midlands or East Anglia; and the South-East lost more jobs than the South-West. Moreover, although unemployment rates vary considerably from region to region, black workers seem in every case more vulnerable than whites (Brown 1984). This discrepancy is particularly marked in the North-West, where 40 per cent of Afro-Caribbean and 32 per cent of Asian males but only 17 per cent of white males were unemployed in 1982, and the West Midlands, where the three corresponding figures were 34, 32 and 19 per cent).

Similarly, at an intra-urban scale, the past 30 years have witnessed a marked decline in the ability of inner city residents to secure inner city jobs – a difficulty which, simply by the nature of residential segregation, affects a larger proportion of the black than the white labour force. Additionally, the inner cities themselves have lost jobs – in all categories of employment – at a greater rate than have suburbs, small towns or rural areas. As Cross (1985: 7) has observed, 'the areas of cities most vulnerable to decline are precisely those where minorities were initially forced to congregate and where more recently they have sought to consolidate their communities'. Testifying to the force of this statement, employment fell by 55 per cent among residents of the inner cities between 1951 and 1981 (this compares with falls of 7 per cent in the outer estates and 15 per cent in free-standing cities, and an increase of 20 per cent in towns and rural areas). These same areas have lost employment in manufacturing industries at an accelerating rate since the 1950s, culminating in a loss of 37 per cent between 1971 and 1981 (when the national average was a decline of only 25 per cent). In the same period, employment in the private services fell by 6.4 per cent in the inner cities while it rose by 14.4 per cent nationally, and similar trends – a change of −7.4 per cent in the inner cities and of +7.7 per cent nationally – occurred in public service employment.

These spatial discrepancies in the reorganization of the economy are an important factor underlying black people's disadvantageous position in relation to jobs, housing and locational amenity. It is striking, for instance, that in inner London, Birmingham and Manchester the discrepancy between black and white people's unemployment rates is not that marked, standing at 26 per cent, 19 per cent and 23 per cent for Asians, Afro-Caribbeans and whites, respectively, in 1982 (Brown 1984). The problem is that these three inner urban areas contain one-fifth of all Asians, two-fifths of all Afro-Caribbeans and merely 6 per cent of all whites. (Outside these centres, however, discrepancies in employment patterns *are* more marked, with unemployment among the three populations standing at 19, 26 and 12 per cent in 1982).

Set against accumulating evidence that segregation inhibits black people's full participation in the British labour market (and therefore in the many other opportunities associated with a regular wage) the research of Aldrich et al. (1981), Cater and Jones (1987a) and McEvoy (1987) on

Asians' role in the retail sector contains a tragic irony. These authors argue that the future of this one relatively successful arena of black enterprise is crucially dependent on *preserving* a segregated population of Asian consumers if it is to be adequately protected from potentially destructive competitors in the wider retailing economy.

In conclusion it seems that, for a variety of reasons (but most crucially because of the interdependence of the housing and labour systems) as the 1980s draw to a close, segregation is proving to be not a dwindling legacy of immigration history but a potent indicator of contemporary socio-economic change. Just as there are leading and lagging edges to the economy as a whole, so Hamnett and Randolph (1986) refer to leading and lagging edges of residential restructuring, the latter representing areas where the housing market acts as a drag on the ability of the labour force to respond to employment restructuring. This creates a situation in which 'people are effectively trapped by the housing market in areas of employment collapse' (p. 228). The regions and neighbourhoods in which black people live are a prime example of this, accounting for Brown's (1984) observation that such populations remain confined to those same 'specific localities, parts of the housing stock and corners of the economy' that they have occupied for more than thirty years, and which show few signs of economic regeneration (p. 323).

Despite Field's (1986) optimistic comment on black workers' limited access to professional and managerial posts, labour markets are not, on the whole, characterized by racial integration but rather by increasing geographical and occupational separation (see Cross 1986). This is reflected in, but also sustained by, a process of residential differentiation in which the salience of race is undisputed. Black people have effectively been left behind as 'the great processes of technological change that initiated the demand for less skilled labour have now guaranteed its redundancy as production shifts out of the large conurbations to the small towns, suburbs and overseas' (Cross 1983: 6).

So far, much of the literature on race and racism has (properly) emphasized labour history as a driving force in the constitution of race and in the reproduction of racism in modern Britain. However, as Cross (1985: 1) points out, powerful though migrant labour theory might be, 'it can hardly be applied unchanged to communities that are neither labouring nor migrating'. In the search for alternatives, scholars have tended to underestimate the potency (symbolic as well as material, political as well as economic) of housing and residential space in the racialization of social inequality. Yet, notwithstanding the traditional assumption that labour markets lead housing supply and demand, it is increasingly apparent that housing systems posess an autonomy of their own, capable of constraining as well as expressing the labour process, and structuring access to welfare services, social opportunities and a range of other life chances. This gives residential differentiation a unique role in the constitution of race and in the reproduction of racial inequality. In the remainder of the book, I shall explore this role, beginning in chapter 3, which shows how the relative segregation of Britain's black and white populations developed in a legislative vacuum, at the intersection of housing, urban and anti-discrimination policy.

Notes

1 The 1981 census contains no 'ethnic' question and the 1986 sample census was cancelled. The best census estimate of the size of the black population is therefore based on a classification of individuals according to the country of birth of the head of household, as enumerated in 1981. The advantages and limitations of this kind of estimate are assessed by Rees and Birkin (1984). One major drawback is the inability to count East African Asians living in households where the household head was born in South Asia.

2 When announcing the decision to omit an 'ethnic question' from the 1981 census (largely due to 'grass roots' opposition during final testing of the question in Haringey in 1979), the Secretary of State for Social Services emphasized the government's increasing reliance on voluntary surveys such as the LFS for its information on minority groups. Other such sources include the General Household Survey (which has contained an interviewer assessment of respondents' colour since 1970 and a question on self-ascribed 'ethnic' affiliation since 1983) and the National Dwelling and Housing Survey (which asked an 'ethnic' question in 1977 and 1978, but whose findings are now somewhat dated). None of these national surveys over-sample in ways likely to boost the representation of black people, who therefore form only a small proportion of respondents.

3 The LFS is undoubtedly the best supplement to the census. Its merits are discussed by OPCS Population Statistics Division (1986) and Saggar (1985/6). This survey has effectively carried an 'ethnic' question since 1981 (the version used in 1979 proved unsuitable), and has been conducted annually since 1983. Just under 4 per cent of the 150 000 respondents identify themselves as other than 'white'. The survey elicits self-assessed 'ethnic' identity and so offers an important supplement to the geographical classifications produced from the census. It also provides the only comprehensive source of information on the number of children born in the UK to UK-born black parents. So far the rate of non-response to the 'ethnic' question has been less than 2 per cent.

4 Intercensal comparisons are fraught with difficulty. The 1961 census relied on individuals' birthplaces, and may have under-enumerated West Indians by as much as 20 per cent (Peach 1966a). As much as one-third of the Indian-born population enumerated in this census was white (the children of diplomats and

members of the armed services). The same question was used in the 10 per cent sample census of 1966, although birthplace categories were aggregated and could distinguish effectively only Old and New Commonwealth migrants. The 1971 census included a survey of *parents'* birthplace, providing a much better inferred measure of the size of the black population (not least because it could be constructed (a) to exclude children born overseas to parents born in the UK and (b) to include the UK-born children of immigrants from the New Commonwealth and Pakistan). Nevertheless, as many as 30 per cent of Pakistani-born residents and 15 per cent of those born in the West Indies may not have been enumerated (Peach and Winchester 1974). In 1981, parents' birthplace was omitted and the categorization outlined in note 1 was introduced. The two most recent census estimates are therefore not directly comparable.

5 In addition to a variety of single city surveys, which are patchy in coverage, scattered in space and time, rarely comparable and increasingly dated, there are three major studies completed in 1966, 1974 and 1982 by the Policy Studies Institute and its predecessor, Political and Economic Planning. The earliest (Daniel 1968) is the least comprehensive, focusing on just six towns in England and concentrating on the extent and effects of racial discrimination. The later studies aimed for national coverage, although neither included Scotland, and the 1974 study excluded people living outside the main areas of 'immigrant' settlement (its report is contained in Smith (1977)). The strength of the later surveys is their broad scope (examining disadvantage as well as discrimination) and temporal comparability. Nevertheless, even the most recent study (Brown 1984), which is probably the best ever source of information on Britain's black population, surveys only 0.3 per cent (5000 individuals) of black people resident in this country.

6 Indices of dissimilarity (IDs) and segregation (ISs) measure the degree of conformity in the distribution of two population groups among a set of areas. The ID measures the amount of spatial separation between any two mutually exclusive groups. The IS measures the amount of clustering of one subpopulation relative to that of the population as a whole. Each index ranges from 0 to 100 (from complete integration to complete separation at a given spatial scale). They are calculated as follows:

$$ID_{xy} = 0.5 \sum_{i=1}^{n} \left| \frac{x_i \cdot 100}{\sum_{i=1}^{n} x_i} - \frac{y_i \cdot 100}{\sum_{i=1}^{n} y_i} \right|$$

$$IS_{ty} = ID_{ty} \bigg/ \left(1 - \sum_{i=1}^{n} y_i \bigg/ \sum_{i=1}^{n} t_i \right)$$

Where x_i = size of population x in area i
y_i = size of population y in area i
t_i = population total in area i
n = total number of areas ($i = 1, 2, 3, \ldots n$)
x and y are mutually exclusive.

Both indices are scale-dependent and sensitive to the boundaries, spatial arrangement and number of sub-areas used (see Woods 1976).

7 In 1971, the IS for those born in Ireland was 23, Britain 41, the West Indies 56 and India/Pakistan (then including Bangladesh)/Ceylon (Sri Lanka since 22 May 1972) 69.

8 This represents an increase in segregation of 5–7 points over 1971 for Asians, a stable pattern for West Indians (whose IS, at 38, is still 3–6 points higher than that of any Asian-born group except the Bangladeshis) and a decrease for whites.

9 In Leeds, for instance, the ID by enumeration district between Indians and England-born residents was, at 62, 10 points less than for West Indian-born residents in 1981 (Rees and Birkin 1984).

10 This may partly reflect differences in the absolute size of the different populations. Although the ID and IS are theoretically independent of population size (this, indeed, has been their major attraction), when any one population is small relative to the number of sub-areas used, some distortion can occur.

11 In Nottingham, Husain (cited in Jones 1983) compared the British-born population with its West Indian and Asian counterparts, and found ward-level IDs for 1971 reaching 51 and 64 respectively. Similar discrepancies were observed in the same year in Birmingham (Woods 1975), although the smaller scale (amalgamated areas) gave IDs of 60 and 72 for the two black populations relative to 'whites'.

12 $P^\star$ is an index of isolation given by the formula:

$$x \, P^\star \, y = \sum_{i=1}^{n} (x_I/X) \, (y_i/t_i)$$

Where x_i and y_i are the numbers of groups X and Y in a given sub-area, and t_i is the total population of the sub-area. If $X = Y =$ black people, $P^\star$ measures the proportion of black residents found in sub-areas where the average black person resides (i.e. it specifies the average amount of residential isolation). The computation and interpretation of $P^\star$ is discussed by Lieberson (1981).

13 In Blackburn, for instance, in 1968 the average Asian lived in a ward where Asians constituted just 5 per cent of the population; by 1980 such persons lived in wards where almost a third (31 per cent) of residents were Asian.

14 In Oxford, Peach et al. (1975) found that census tract IDs comparing Asian and British birthplace groups were as 'low' as 43, while the value for West Indians reached 47. Similarly, in Slough, Unsworth (1985) calculated the ward-level ISs for Indians and Pakistanis, respectively, as 'just' 34 and 29 in 1981 (although she points out that this does not preclude over 70 per cent of each group clustering into only eight or nine enumeration districts).

15 In 1976 intra-group IDs, at a ward-level, reached 45 between Sikhs and Hindus in Manchester and 52 between Sikhs and Muslims in Birmingham, but at the same time the IDs separating Asians and whites exceeded 60 and 70 for the two cities, respectively. In Blackburn, enumeration district IDs in the late 1970s ranged from 42 (distinguishing East African Indian Muslims speaking Gujerati

from those of similar origins speaking Kutchi) to 69 (distinguishing this latter group from East African Hindus speaking Gujerati), but while 12 of the 15 intra-community indices Robinson (1981) examined exceeded 50, none matched the Asian:white ID of 73.

3 The Legislative Framework

Ought we continually to allow immigrants to arrive, and freely gravitate towards areas of their choice, almost certainly to areas of highest concentration?

W. F. Deedes, 24 July 1968

Studies of residential segregation rarely consider the role of central government in a systematic way. Likewise, at this national level, the politics of race rarely draw analysts beyond the critical see-saw of immigration policy and race relations legislation. This seems logical, since most centrally dispensed housing and urban policy makes no explicit reference to the interests of black people, while local government bears all practical responsibility for meeting housing needs and promoting racial equality. Nevertheless, I shall argue here that, in Britain, national legislation has been influential in determining the location and quality of black people's housing opportunities, and that this has built the foundations on which racial segregation is erected. To understand how, it is necessary to pay less attention to Governments' stated aims and expectations than to the unanticipated outcomes of a series of legislative decisions implemented in the name of economic necessity and political expedience.

The most fundamental, yet least appreciated, facet of residential differentiation concerns its link with the production of the built environment. It is at the point of production that the characteristics of the housing stock – its quality, quantity, cost and location – are determined. While obviously subject to fluctuations in the national and international economy, housing production has been variously controlled or 'enabled' by Governments, both through the distribution of supports and subsidies to the building industry and by attempts to stimulate demand (see Ball 1983, 1986). In Britain, housing production costs have been relatively high, even in the public sector (which has always relied on private contractors); the stock is steadily ageing (almost 30 per cent of homes now pre-date the First World War); and modernization is not keeping pace with the decline in housing conditions (see Malpass 1986). Reflecting a history of booms and slumps in production, the housing stock is not only highly spatially differentiated in terms of its quality and condition (see Dickens et al. 1985), but is in relatively short supply. Average annual completion rates for the early 1980s indicate a 30 per cent shortfall below the housing requirements predicted by the Government in 1977. Housing is, then, a scarce resource of uneven availability, serviceability and desirability, and given only the vagaries of production, residential patterns are bound to express (and confer) inequalities of some kind. However, my immediate interest is in how these inequalities have become aligned with (and so reinforce) *racial* disadvantage. This, in turn, requires an account of how mainstream public policy and strategies for managing the economy have together impinged on the pattern of housing consumption.

I begin by outlining a series of housing policies which have effectively (if apparently unintentionally) denied black people full access to the welfare and property rights associated with state-subsidized housing (whether these subsidies support public renting or owner occupation). These unanticipated but unmistakably iniquitous consequences of seemingly 'aracial' decisions flow partly from an assumption that the disadvantage and discrimination experienced by black people is adequately addressed by other areas of legislation. The second and third parts of this chapter – a critique of urban policy and a note on race relations legislation – show why such an assumption can rarely be justified.

Housing policy

In a given period, housing policy may be regarded as a product of both ideological struggle (usually over the relative merits of public and private ownership) and economic contingency (an influential determinant of the amount and targeting of public expenditure). While the character and relative importance of these factors varies over time, their consequences are cumulative. To capture this, the discussion which follows expands a chronology sketched in Smith (1987: 29–32) rather than examining the impact of policy on a tenure by tenure basis. Tenure issues *are* important to the black population, but the inequalities its members experience persist across the tenure divide. Therefore, before considering how access, allocation and exchange is managed in the different segments of the housing system (a concern of chapter 4), I concentrate on the legislative mechanisms most broadly responsible for the racial differentiation of residential space. The most significant of these are: first, the decision not to link housing with immigration policy after the 1939–45 war; secondly, the shift from comprehensive redevelopment to *in situ* renewal which was signalled by the 1969 Housing Act; and, finally, the (misnamed) 'commodification' of housing which was given unprecedented impetus in the Housing Act of 1980.

After the war

Housing production slumped during the war years, large portions of existing stock were damaged or destroyed, and post-war governments were faced with an acute housing shortage, a growing population and an urgent demand for migrant labour to reconstruct the economy. Both the Labour and Conservative Parties identified massive investment in public housing as a solution to the problems caused by this widespread general need for shelter, and both were committed to completing the programme of slum clearance initiated in the 1930s. As a consequence, public housing became a cornerstone of the post-war welfare state, as symbolized in the 1949 Housing Act which enlarged the statutory eligibility for public housing beyond the 'working classes'. As a welfare right, state subsidized housing was seen as a key means of offsetting in kind the inequalities in income and wealth that are routinely generated within a capitalist economy. The welfare state embraced the ideals of equality and integration. It sought to unite society and to extend the rights of citizenship throughout the class structure. However, decisions made towards the end of the 1940s were to deny black households their fair share of housing as a welfare resource, and it is at this point that racial categorization and residential segregation first became aligned.

The Nationality Act of 1948 afforded all members of the Commonwealth the full set of rights and privileges associated with British citizenship. Migrants from the New Commonwealth were, in law, placed on the same social, political and economic footing as Britons born in the UK. Despite (perhaps because of) this, when 'non-white' immigration, particularly from the Caribbean, was (reluctantly) encouraged to assist with post-war reconstruction, Britain, unlike her European neighbours in France, Germany and Switzerland, never attempted to coordinate housing and immigration policy. (A comprehensive summary of the coordination of labour migration in Western Europe is given by Castles and Kosack 1985.)

This *laissez-faire* stance proved controversial since in the context of a housing shortage it offered no lead to (and imposed no penalties on) the many local authorities who (on a variety of pretexts but most notably via

L. I. H. E.
THE BECK LIBRARY
WOOLTON RD., LIVERPOOL, L16 8ND

residence requirements) refused to house black people. Even by the mid-1960s only 6 per cent of the overseas-born black population as compared with 28 per cent of Irish migrants and one-third of the English-born had been accommodated in this sector, despite black people's lower than average incomes and greater apparent need (see Rose et al. 1969). Governments were equally reluctant to encourage employers to provide accommodation, even though such provision is not unprecedented in Britain and was widely practised on the continent. Throughout this period politicians' chief concern was to assure a predominantly white electorate that their main priority was to protect the jobs and well-being of the 'host' community. This sentiment reverberated throughout the labour market and housing system.

De facto exclusion from the public sector coupled with low incomes and, in some cases, financial obligations to families overseas, left post-war immigrants with two main housing options. First, they could enter the privately rented sector. This kind of accommodation has been declining in quantity and quality since the rent and mortgage restrictions Act of 1915 (it accounted for 90 per cent of the stock in 1914 but just 9 per cent in 1984). Even now, the majority of the privately rented stock dates from before the First World War. By the late 1950s, private renting was increasingly a residual tenure for the white majority, but provided the main source of shelter for migrant labourers, accommodating 74 per cent of West Indian households by 1961. They lived largely in the so-called 'twilight zones' of the inner city, which Rex and Moore (1967) have so vividly described. In seven London boroughs studied by Davison (1966) in 1961, 79 per cent of black people (compared with 63 per cent of the 'English') were private renters. Even in 1966, 62 and 31 per cent of black people in the London and West Midlands conurbations, respectively (as compared with 31 and 16 per cent of whites), remained in that sector (Rose et al. 1969). However, rent controls, controls on multi-occupation, the rising costs of repairs (due to ageing properties and inflation), tax concessions to owner occupiers and a growing public sector (together with a series of Rent Acts and the Housing Acts of 1961, 1964 and 1969) steadily discouraged private landlords. Black tenants found themselves competing for an increasingly scarce resource and facing exploitative rents, overcrowding and shared, substandard amenities (see Karn 1982).

A second option for black migrants, and one which became increasingly popular between about 1958 and 1964, was house purchase. Those moving on (or excluded) from private renting and still denied a council home usually had access only to cheap properties in inner city neighbourhoods that were either scheduled for slum clearance or blighted by short leases (see Paris and Lambert 1979). The 'attraction' of such properties was their cost: they could be bought outright or with short-term high interest loans by people disadvantaged in the labour market and discriminated against by conventional lending procedures. Although there are a variety of (cultural and pragmatic) reasons why Afro-Caribbean and, more often, Asian migrants moved into owner occupation at this time, a major underlying factor was their sustained, if ill-founded, ineligibility for a home in the public sector. By the mid-1960s, 33 per cent of black Londoners and 60 per cent of those in the West Midlands were home owners, while only 4 and 8 per cent respectively, had secured a council tenancy (Rose et al. 1969). Looking at a wider range of local authorities, Smith (1976) suggests that the public sector housed as few as 1 per cent of black households at this time.

Ironically, because the incomes and needs of this new class of low income owner occupiers were often more consistent with public renting than ownership, they were also to prove ineligible for a second public subsidy on housing consumption – tax relief on mortgage interest, introduced in 1963. This subsidy was not at first very helpful to black buyers, whose incomes were often too low to be taxed. It was not, moreover, available on 'unconventional' loans (a particularly important source of housing finance for Asian migrants). This second restriction also applied to the option mortgage scheme (a government subsidy which allowed building societies to give low income buyers savings on mortgage repayments as if they were above the income tax threshold). This could have been (and sometimes was) a considerable help to black purchasers before it was made obsolete by a progressive lowering of the threshold for tax liability and by unanticipated rates of house price inflation (which took owner occupation beyond the reach of those with very low or insecure incomes).

Broadly, then, a lack of coordination between immigration and housing policy in the post-war years helped exclude black Britons from access to housing as a welfare service, and allowed the market to generate a pattern of residential segregation confining black households to the inner and middle rings of a limited range of large British cities. Black people were prominent among those identified by Hall et al. (1973) as losing out in the urban restructuring that followed the war. They gained neither the welfare benefits of subsidized renting nor the economic perks of subsidized ownership. Nevertheless, for legislative purposes, the view prevailed (as it does today) that *general* solutions to housing problems can benefit black people in the same way, and to the same extent, as they benefit whites.

The 1965 White Paper[1] on 'Immigration from the Commonwealth' insists that 'the *sole* test for action in housing fields is the quality and nature of housing need without distinctions based on the origin of those in need' (para. 37, p. 10, my emphasis). Although this was the year in which race relations legislation first reached the statute books, few recognized that racially discriminatory definitions of need were already excluding black people from the share of welfare rights to which they were legally entitled. Government strategy, albeit more by omission than commission, had already helped establish a link between residential segregation and racial inequality in housing that would endure for more than 30 years. Yet, while direct government intervention was felt by the main political parties to be inappropriate and unnecessary, towards the end of the 1960s decisions were made which inadvertently ensured that neither rehousing associated with slum clearance nor overspill into the New Towns would offer black households an alternative to the neglected inner city.

From redevelopment to renewal

Slum clearance and comprehensive redevelopment was initiated in 1930 by the Greenwood Act. The ideal survived the war and was supported by politicians as an effective and expedient means of improving the urban environment and meeting housing needs. Between 1958 and 1968, following the Housing Repairs and Rents Act (1954), slum clearance decanted some 160 000–180 000 people per year from inner city slums and rehoused them in the public sector in new peripheral estates and high rise flats. However, for reasons discussed below the majority of those removed were white, and in many cities the process intensified the 'racial' dimension of residential segregation.

Black families were excluded from rehousing during the main period of slum clearance for a number of reasons. Several local authorities (especially the London boroughs) denied their responsibility to offer rehousing to tenants of the furnished rental sector, where many black migrants still lived (see Daniel 1968; Hiro 1971). Black owners, on the other hand, were often living in areas blighted by the prospect of compulsory purchase but not scheduled for immediate clearance; they were, in effect, queuing for rehousing behind the predominantly white working class who occupied the central city slums. Finally, even those relatively few black households who did live in active clearance areas were often passed over in the rehousing process and so 'effectively corraled into the remaining area of suitable private housing' (Smith and Whalley 1975: 82). Flett's (1984) analysis of this process in four clearance areas in Manchester showed that Asian residents were between 10 and 40 per cent less likely to be rehoused than average. By one process or another, therefore, the so-called 'middle ring' Victorian and Edwardian apartment houses and terraces were by the mid-1960s accommodating the majority of black households, while a broad cross-section of the white population had been more widely dispersed into new public sector stock.

Had the process of slum clearance and rebuilding continued, many black households must soon have gained access to newer council properties in a wider variety of locations. For by the late 1960s it was formally acknowledged that the black communities lived, on average, in the poorest segments of the housing and urban environment. At this point, however, long-accumulating pressures urging housing policy to relinquish comprehensive redevelopment in favour of gradual *in situ* improvement finally came to a head. The house condition survey of 1967 revealed that, in England and Wales, 1.8 million dwellings were unfit (the figure had not been expected to exceed 800 000 and some thought it would be as low as 250 000). A massive repairs problem was exposed, even in houses not scheduled for demolition, and it was obvious that slum clearance would need a massive injection of resources to continue (see English et al. 1976). In the event, concerns about public expenditure added to existing opposition to the scale, organization and social consequences of redevelopment to bring the era of slum clearance to an end (see Bassett and Short 1980: 122).

It is worth noting that although this decision owed much to public opinion and economic contingency, for some the timing of the policy shift seemed more than fortuitous. Reginald Freeson alluded to a further pressure for change when he asked Parliament about the extent to which 'redevelopment plans are being held up by local authorities because they do not wish to accept responsibility for rehousing immigrants living in twilight zones of major city areas' (HC1965/6, 725, 239).[2] Although his allegation was dismissed as unfounded, subsequent research has detected at least an element of truth in the charge (see Daniel 1968; McKay 1977; Rex and Moore 1967; Smith and Whalley 1975).

Intentionally or otherwise, the *timing* of the shift away from comprehensive redevelopment and mass public housing provision had the consequence of sustaining a marked over-representation of the black population within the poorest segments of the housing stock in the least desirable areas of the major cities. The timing was doubly unfortunate in that it coincided with the increasing accessibility of the public sector to black households (especially Afro-Caribbean migrants, who were beginning to meet local authorities' residence requirements). By 1974, 4 per cent of Asian and 26 per cent of West Indian households had been allocated a council home (Smith 1976) – rising to 10 and 50 per cent respectively in 1978. However, with the end of the redevelopment programme and an increasing preference for renovation over new building, the dwellings immediately available to new tenants consisted of either old stock acquired through compulsory purchase or the newer, centrally located (high rise and deck access) flatted estates. Both sets of options simply extended the existing pattern of social segregation (although in a few cities, such as Liverpool, black tenants were also to become segregated in the difficult-to-let estates of the periphery, neither introduced black tenants to council properties of above-average standard. Even now the legacy of this disproportionate availability of inner city public renting can be seen: overall, 46 per cent of Afro-Caribbean and 19 per cent of Asian households are council tenants, but in the inner areas of the major cities, the proportions rise to 59 and 42 per cent respectively (these figures are taken from tables constructed by Brown (1984)).

The Government could not have been unaware of the consequences of its radical change of policy. Politicians had always hoped that dispersal would solve a range of problems associated with 'racial segregation', but before 1969 they had always claimed that residential integration would be achieved through the normal operation of mainstream housing programmes. As late as the Parliamentary session of 1964/5, MPs were reassured (in a vein now known to be mistaken) that no special provision for 'immigrants'' housing needs was required, since migrants would benefit with everyone else from the overspill schemes (HC1964/5, 712, 35). By 1969, this illusion had faded. The Cullingworth Committee, reporting in that year, suggested and supported state intervention to secure dispersal, and the first experiment – a centre-led regional-scale dispersal strategy – was initiated following the arrival of 27 000 Ugandan refugees in 1972. This scheme is assessed by Bristow (1976, 1978/9) and Robinson (1986).[3] For a variety of reasons, largely related to under-resourcing and bad planning, it failed to prevent Ugandan Asians from settling in existing Asian-dominated zones, and the majority of refugees ended up in the same kinds of poor environment as other black Britons. By 1975, while still supporting the principle of dispersal, central government formally devolved responsibility for its implementation to the local authorities, which according to the new White Paper on 'Race Relations and Housing' (Cmnd 6232) were expected to formulate a 'balanced view' on it.

By this time, however, the shift to renewal had introduced new constraints on the management and allocation of the existing housing stock; Peter Shore was about to announce new urban policies designed to *stem* dispersal from the cities; the political centre had begun to undermine local autonomy with respect to a range of social, educational and housing issues (the consequences of which are explored in chapter 4). Moreover, policies associated with the revitalization initiative itself began to work in opposition to the dispersal 'ideal'. It is not surprizing, therefore, that Rex (1986b) identifies the policy change of 1969 as 'the basis for ghetto formation' (p. 120). The inner city was certainly to benefit from the new area-based improvement initiative, but the Housing Acts of 1969, 1971 and 1974, which brought about the demise of redevelopment and secured the prominence of rehabilitation, put in place an 'alternative' housing system from which 'the whites, who could gain much easier access to suburban housing tended to flee, leaving the inner cities to become increasingly black and Asian ghettos' (Rex 1986b: 120).

The new era of housing policy introduced an area-based approach to neighbourhood improvement which, because it was directed towards the worst environmental conditions, was, in the larger cities, targeted on areas where the majority of the black population lived. This selectivity was achieved by bending improvement grant assistance (enhanced by the 1971 Act) towards General Improvement Areas (GIAs) (provided for in 1969) and Housing Action Areas (HAAs) (designated with social as well as environmental goals in mind after 1974). Since the 1975 White Paper on 'Race Relations and Housing' fully expected the HAAs in the major conurbations to house significant numbers of black people, this new approach seemed promising (except in Scotland, where the concept of Housing Action Area differs, referring to larger zones which are defined only according to environmental criteria). In practice, the achievements of the improvement initiatives were limited: area-based housing rehabilitation has been criticized for its slow pace of implementation, for the often-prohibitive financial demands it places on residents and for its tendency to concentrate on 'cosmetic' rather than structural renovations (see Short and Bassett 1981; Paris and Blackaby 1979). In short, although some significant improvements have been made, there is little evidence that the area-based approach practised throughout the 1970s was able significantly to reduce the racial inequalities associated with residential segregation. Short and Bassett (1981) suggest that property values (and dwelling quality) underwent a relative decline in some of the designated areas. On the other hand, there is every indication that other policies interacted with the renewal initiative to add to the over-representation of black households in these least desirable portions of the housing stock. Two developments noted by Rex (1981a) deserve particular attention.

The first relates to the activities of the Housing Corporation, set up in the Housing Act (1964) and expanded in 1974 to promote the work of housing associations (whose role is discussed at greater length in chapter 4). Against a background of both decreasing subsidies for council renting and a loss of council stock through sales, housing associations have provided a significant outlet for the relatively large proportion of the black (particularly Afro-Caribbean) community who find they must rent (see

Niner 1984). Flexible entry rules often make such properties more accessible to black people than council housing and although the associations' capital spending is largely dependent on the Housing Association Grant (from the Housing Corporation), grant-assisted GIAs and HAAs have offered important incentives for housing association conversions. Indeed, under the terms of the 1974 Housing Act, local authorities were advised to use housing associations in HAAs to attract public funds to such areas directly from central government. Since it is those associations relying on grant-assisted rehabilitation, rather than those expanding through new building, that tend to be most available to black people (see Niner 1985), the promotion of housing association activity has, in some areas, helped to intensify residential segregation, especially among Afro-Caribbeans.

During the early 1970s, the targeting of local authority mortgage finance had a similar effect. Council loans were available for the older, cheaper properties of the inner cities, into which building societies were loth to invest (see Williams 1977). Such mortgages were deliberately allocated 'down market' in an attempt to extend owner occupation (Merrett (1982) and Malpass and Murie (1987) discuss this strategy). Smith (1976) shows that as many as a third of black owner occupiers relied on this source of finance during the 1970s, and they usually had to use it to acquire properties in the cheapest segments of the housing stock in areas where the black population was already statistically over-represented.

The timing of the shift from redevelopment to rehabilitation played a decisive role (directly and indirectly) in reproducing a pattern of segregation which expressed not only black people's marginal economic position, but also their limited access to (and, subsequently, their subordinate position within) an important welfare service – public housing. The organization of the rehabilitation initiative went hand in hand with an opening up of the least desirable segments of the public sector to black households, initiating a trend which Jacobs (1985) condemns as 'the British road to apartheid'. Although both processes obviously sustained segregation, and while neither did much to reduce racial inequality, Labour's new Green Paper 'Housing Policy – A Consultative Document' (1977, Cmnd 6851) reiterated the conviction that black people's housing needs are best met through the assistance a general housing programme can offer to all deprived groups. In principle, this is an ideal worth aspiring to; in practice, the 1980s paint a quite different picture.

Commodification, residualization and diversification

Qualitative and locational changes in the availability of council housing and grant-assistance for home improvements are both part of a wider strategy adopted by all post-war governments to increase the range and availability of owner occupation. This process has accelerated in the past decade, extending home ownership at the expense of both private and public renting (the policy framework in which this has occurred it outlined in some detail by Crook (1986)). Thus, whereas in 1953 only 28 per cent of the country's housing stock was owner occupied, the figure had reached 54 per cent by 1976, 59 per cent by 1982 and now stands at 65 per cent.

Black households have participated in this shift to varying extents. Asians, who have always found owner occupation more accessible than public renting, now have ownership levels much higher than average (72 per cent in 1982). Afro-Caribbean households, who tended to qualify for, and accept, council tenancies earlier, remain under-represented as owners (41 per cent in 1982) and over-represented as public renters (46 per cent in 1982 as compared with 30 and 19 per cent for white and Asian households, respectively).

Owner occupation was stimulated by the introduction of tax relief on mortgage interest in 1963, by the 1972 Housing Finance Act, which encouraged movement away from the rented sector,[4] and by a range of initiatives culminating in the shared equity and starter home packages introduced to stimulate 'low cost' home ownership. It was not until 1975, however, that the financial resources committed to housing policy, which had risen steadily since 1960, were first cut back sharply in real terms.[5] In 1977 the Labour Party's Green Paper 'Housing Policy – A Consultative Document' endorsed plans for a continuing reduction of public investment in housing, and when a new Conservative Government introduced the 'right to buy' (for local authority tenants) in the 1980 Housing Act, the most decisive step yet was taken away from state provisioning in kind towards state-subsidized ownership. For the first time, moreover, the merits of home ownership became linked with a vigorous ideological commitment to reduce state intervention, cut taxes and stimulate individual initiative.

Since 1979, housing has been at the leading edge of Conservative Governments' attempts to reduce public expenditure. Since housing is the *only* public service in which state spending has significantly declined, the symbolic importance of the rise in owner occupation is enormous (in practice, of course, the state subsidy has simply been switched away from capital investment through local authorities and towards tax relief on mortgage interest). Between 1979 and 1984 direct public expenditure on housing decreased by 55 per cent in real terms (Crook 1986), and by 1987 over 1 million council homes had been sold under the 'right to buy'. In the absence of significant new building (completions in the early 1980s had fallen by more than 75 per cent from the level in the 1970s) local authorities' housing stocks have been contracting absolutely as well as proportionately throughout the 1980s. In a climate unfavourable to the private landlord the early 1980s was dominated by an extension of owner occupation at the expense of council renting. The two main trends are popularly (though not strictly accurately) termed 'commodification' and 'residualization'. These are considered in turn, insofar as they have a bearing on the life chances and residential opportunities of the black population.

Commodification   Owner occupation is currently the most heavily subsidized segment of the housing system, receiving preferential treatment 'both as a form of housing provision with respect to housing in other tenures, and as an investment good with respect to other assets' (Maclennan and O'Sullivan 1985: 11). Between 1983 and 1985 tax subsidies to owner occupiers exceeded public expenditure on all other services put together (by more than a million pounds), and the total cost of mortgage interest tax relief increased from £1450 million in 1979/80 to £3500 million in 1984/5 (Karn et al. 1986b).

Since we know that a significnt proportion of the black (especially Asian) population initially chose or was forced (as the private rental sector contracted) to buy rather than rent from local authorities, a superficial glance at the above statistics might imply that the process of commodification would at last be a policy inadvertently working for, rather than against, black households in their struggle for space and resources. However, the fact that the most dramatic extension of owner occupation took place against a background of high unemployment, high interest rates and declining real incomes (the very circumstances least conducive to such a process) gives some cause for concern at the lower end of the income scale, where, as a consequence of their position in the labour market, black owners are over-represented.

The relatively neglected theme of low-income owner occupation has become an increasingly important focus of study in recent years (see for instance the papers collected by Booth and Crook (1986)). Socio-economic differentiation within the owner occupied sector was marked even in the late 1960s when rapidly rising land and building costs prevented low income groups gaining access to suburban greenfield sites (see Ball 1983; Rees and Lambert 1986). If anything, social polarization between the upper and lower ends of the market has increased with the extension of owner occupation. Moreover, in some of the major cities it is becoming apparent that this polarization is aligned with racial inequality and expressed in the form of residential segregation (see Johnson 1987a). The factors most obviously encouraging this are related, respectively, to the housing finance system and to the consequences of differential house price inflation. Both these influences merit attention.

First, it can easily be demonstrated that state subsidies to owner occupiers are not distributed equitably. Ermisch (1984) shows the extent to which such subsidies favour higher rather than lower income groups. It is only in the lowest income decile that owners receive less subsidy than council tenants. Thereafter, the relative advantage of owner occupiers over tenants increases with income, and even those low income owners who *are* advantaged relative to council tenants lose out relative to higher income owners. Black households are disadvantaged in the housing market at one level, therefore, simply by their below average median incomes. This is overlaid by *de facto* discrimination in the allocation of housing finance (discussed more fully in chapter 4) and by the fact that the distribution of housing subsidies has a spatial dimension which works to the disadvantage of the inner cities, where the majority of black buyers live (see Rees and Lambert 1986). Finally, subsidies associated with the process of commodification itself are also skewed, in that the discounts associated with council home sales are calculated in proportion to length of tenure. Black people's eligibility for discounts will therefore have been limited by their initial exclusion from the public sector, making the costs of moving into owner occupation proportionately higher for them than for longer-standing white residents. This is compensated, to an extent, by the higher discounts given on flatted properties, but as we shall see in moving on to consider the differential gains to be made through house price inflation, flats have proved least amenable to purchase and yield lower potential capital gains than houses.

It is the potential for owner occupied dwellings to store and accumulate wealth that secures the appeal of home ownership to the public, and that has tempted observers to use tenure as an index of socio-economic differentiation within the housing system. Smith (1976), however, shows that for the majority of black people home ownership does not mean better housing conditions or the possession of an appreciating asset. The reasons are discussed in some detail by Cater and Jones (1987b) but perhaps the most considered account of the significance of ownership for black people is provided by Ward (1981, 1982).

At a national scale, Ward (1981) shows that the ability of black people to take advantage of the commodification of housing, and of the capital gains associated with this, varies geographically. This reflects the uneven pattern of economic change and urban development in post-war Britain. In London, where both Asian and Afro-Caribbean labour has been required in all sectors of the local economy (i.e. where black workers do not merely continue to serve as 'replacement' manual labour), Ward argues that, notwithstanding existing differences, there is at least the *potential* for black people to fare as well as their white counterparts in gaining access to the 'wealth creating' sector of the housing market. In a northern city like Bradford, on the other hand, economic development has been sluggish, the housing stock has undergone little reconstruction and since the (predominantly Asian) minority labour force still fills a marginal 'replacement' role, they have few possibilities of substantially increasing their assets through owner occupation. Nationally, therefore, the increasingly well documented polarization between the top and bottom ends of the owner occupied housing market affects the black and white populations differently. Notably, in the north (and parts of the midlands) where rates of owner occupation among black people (especially Asians) peak, house price inflation is sluggish and least applicable to the kinds of properties such communities own. (Brown (1984) shows that 91 per cent of Asians are owner occupiers in West and South Yorkshire, as compared with 57 per cent of white households. The corresponding figures in inner London are 34 and 27 per cent.)

Similar generalizations can be made at an intra-regional and urban scale. A study by Karn et al. (1986a), for instance, identified a downward spiral of house conditions and a (relative) depreciation of house prices across a broad spectrum of inner city properties, but found such trends most marked in Asian-dominated areas. Properties in Housing Action Areas (whose very definition often hinged on an over-representation of black households) have also tended to fall in value relative to those in other areas, even *within* the inner city. Indeed, between 1975 and 1979, house prices in two Asian-dominated inner areas of Birmingham fell from 43 to 36 per cent of the regional mean (see Johnson 1987a). A similar pattern has been observed in Bradford where, between 1974 and 1984, house prices in nine inner city wards (those where the Asian population is most likely to live) rose at just 256 per cent (just below the retail price index) whereas suburban house prices increased by more than 300 per cent. Cater and Jones (1987b) show that the average dwelling purchased by Asians between 1980 and 1984 cost less than the amount by which the typical detached house of a white owner occupier would have appreciated in that same period. This stagnation of the housing market in some of the main areas of residence of the Asian and Afro-Caribbean populations is no doubt exacerbated by the withdrawal of local authority mortgages (which had previously helped keep the market buoyant in otherwise financially unattractive locales), and is likely to be sustained by a growing problem of repairs (which according to Karn et al. (1986b) is particularly acute in the pre-1919 terraces which house a substantial proportion of Asian owners). This line of argument has recently been criticised by Saunders and Harris (1988), yet their data also indicate that, even controlling for period of purchase, and without considering the cost of maintenance and repairs, Asian owners make smaller proportionate capital gains on their homes than do whites.

This brief review suggests that some owners (including a disproportionate number of black households) are effectively trapped in properties whose use values are limited by their poor condition, and whose exchange values are depreciating relative to those of other dwellings in the same city or region. Differential rates of house-price inflation – within cities as well as between regions – suggest that such households will find it increasingly difficult to realize their capital gains from home ownership. Additionally, the greater availability of both accumulated and inherited wealth to those who have lived longest in the owner occupied sector will work to sustain the inequalities between black and white owners across generations. The 1982 PSI survey discovered that while 39 per cent of white borrowers raised their deposits from the sale of another property, only 12 per cent of black buyers had such assistance. This reflects both black households' recent entry to the housing market and their larger than average family size (causing inheritances to be fragmented between siblings). These factors will become less important in the future, but for the purposes of securing entry to the wealth creating sector of the owner occupied housing market, this may well be too late.

Residualization Throughout the early 1980s, the corollary of commodification has been a relative and absolute decline in both the size and the overall quality of the council rented housing stock. At the same time, there has been a progressive concentration within that sector of low income and benefit-dependent populations. The significance of this process of 'residualization' has been hotly debated (see Clapham and Maclennan 1983; English 1982; Malpass 1983) but the evidence discussed by Bentham (1986) and by Forrest and Murie (1983) leaves little doubt as to its pervasiveness. Many black households, however, appear to be trapped in the public sector *irrespective* of their degree of benefit dependency. There may, then, be a process of racial categorization as well as a socio-economic differential dividing those who buy their council homes from those who continue to rent. Few published surveys are as yet sensitive enough to document the extent of this,[6] but from our understanding of the broader trends associated with residualization the consequences for black people may readily be deduced. What follows is an attempt to flesh out a framework first suggested by Ward (1982).

The process of residualization is associated with a pattern of council house sales that has been spatially as well as socially discriminatory. Maclennan and Ermisch (1986) point out that as many as 85 per cent of dwellings sold from the public sector have been houses rather than flats, and that their characteristics imply that only a small proportion of sales have occurred in the inner city. Murie's (1986) assessment of the distribution of sales during the first three years of the 'right to buy' policy confirms this suspicion: most sales have occurred in the affluent suburbs, rural districts and New Towns (see also Lawless and Brown 1986).

This geography of sales has important implications for the residential options available to black tenants who live predominantly in inner city estates. The council homes most suitable for purchase (and most amenable to capital accumulation) are located on selected suburban estates and, for reasons already outlined, are almost exclusively occupied by white households. The more centrally located deck access flats and maisonettes, which house the majority of black tenants, are less appealing, least likely to be bought and, even when purchased, least able to accumulate wealth.

As the council sector dwindles the prospects for mobility among those black people who remain as tenants, and who are already disproportionately concentrated in the inner city, are increasingly limited. Their opportunities to transfer into higher quality properties are constrained by a trend in housing policy which 'amounts to little more than an "abandonment" of the worst public stock to a future of further decay' (Maclennan and O'Sullivan 1985: 35). Spatial mobility within the public sector is effectively restricted to a narrow range of relatively undesirable inner urban destinations. Black households had few enough opportunities to transfer into higher quality properties early in their 'career' as tenants, since the better transfer properties tended to go to whites who, because of their longer tenancies, had spent longer on the transfer list (see Simpson 1981). Now that the better parts of the stock have been sold, the transfer system may, even if used as part of a vigorous equal opportunities policy, only be able to offer alternatives which reproduce existing patterns of segregation and, in doing so, sustain racial inequality.

In short, recent trends in housing policy – manifest in the related processes of commodification and residualization – have encouraged not only socio-economic but also *racial* polarization within and between the major segments of the housing system. Just as black migrants' role as a replacement labour force underpins black Britons' current economic marginality, so their initial exclusion from housing as a welfare right and their subsequent role as 'replacement' incumbents of that right (filling the older, poorer vacancies that white tenants had refused or transferred out of) underpins their current difficulties in the private housing market. What, then, is likely to be achieved through the provisions of the new White Paper 'Housing Policy: The Government's Proposals' (Department of the Environment 1987a, Cmnd 214) and the 1988 Housing Act.

Diversification and the 'independent' sector The latest phase of neo-Conservative housing policy is characterized by continuity and innovation. It is consistent with earlier policy in that the 'race dimension has barely entered into discussions about the forthcoming housing Bills at all' (Government advisor, cited by Platt (1987: 4)), and its consequences for black people are once more likely to be unanticipated rather than planned.

The White Paper is unequivocal in its commitment to the further extension of owner occupation and expects to achieve this through continuing tax subsidies, an increase in shared ownership and a provision for tenants to speed up public sector sales.[7] A further impetus for the continued sale of council homes, however, will come from the removal of the cost-floor rule which had previously prevented tenants in homes built, acquired or improved since 1974 from receiving the full discount on their purchase. This may benefit black tenants in some flatted developments, but for the most part it confirms the trend towards selling off those better parts of the public housing stock within which black people are least likely to live.

A more encouraging development is a renewed commitment to assist owner occupiers with home repairs. Following a luke-warm reception for the 1985 Green Paper (Home Improvements – A New Approach', Cmnd 9513), details of the new proposals remain sketchy. The indication is, however, that GIAs and HAAs will be replaced by some other kind of designated areas and that grant entitlement will be determined less by the extent of housing disrepair than by 'a straightforward test of household resources' allowing grants to be based on 'incomes and savings' (p. 7). Given that a broad cross-section of the black population lives in the oldest and poorest segments of the nation's housing stock, this lack of collective commitment to coping with the effects of what is, at root, a crisis of housing production is disturbing. Again it suggests that, for a given income group, the average black household will be expected to invest more in maintaining its home than the average white household, and for less potential capital gain.

A third, more innovative, element of the new policy package is a determined attempt to stimulate what is euphemistically termed the 'independent' sector of the housing market. This will occur directly by removing rent controls on new private lettings, and indirectly, by giving council tenants the 'right to transfer' their tenancies to other landlords (probably commercial interests, housing associations or tenants' cooperatives). It will also be achieved by demanding greater private investment in the housing association movement, and by the break-up of large council estates under the auspices of a set of Housing Action Trusts (which appear to be the housing equivalent of the Urban Development Corporations, and are discussed in greater detail by the Department of the Environment (1987c)).

An increase in private renting could, of course, be helpful (in revitalizing and utilizing neglected parts of the housing stock, in providing short-term accommodation prior to ownership, in increasing the mobility of labour and so on). On the other hand, the provisions of the Race Relations Act have always been difficult to police in this sector and the extent of discrimination is difficult to monitor. The only safeguard against a possible rise in direct or indirect racism in the revitalized privately rented sector was announced in June 1988 (DoE News Release 14). It extends to the Housing Action Trusts and the Housing Corporation the duty local authorities already have under Section 71 of the Race Relations Act (1976) to prevent racial discrimination and promote equality of opportunity. It is too early to say whether this will include sufficient resources to implement systems of 'ethnic' monitoring and secure an anti-racist lettings policy.

Greater tenant control could also be a welcome move (although the current proposals appear to regard it primarily as a means of displacing local authorities in order to speed up property sales). However, a recent paper on the implementation of 'Tenants' Choice' (Department of the Environment 1987b) contains no assurance that new landlords will be required to guard against the rising tide of racial harassment on council estates, and observers have already expressed concern that the new tenancy arrangements could provide an opening for those who wish to maintain exclusively white residential zones. It remains to be seen whether the statutory backing now given to CRE codes of practice in housing will be a sufficient deterrent.

In summary, it is clear that since at least 1945 the housing policies of national governments have, by determining the kinds of locations most available to black people, provided a framework in which residential segregation helps to reproduce racial inequality. For the most part, this is the unanticipated consequence of policies initiated primarily to manage the post-war economy. It is also the product of decisions informed by a belief that black people's interests can best be served by treating them like everyone else (although the same reservations have not been expressed in catering to the special needs of other hitherto neglected groups such as older or handicapped people). If this reasoning is correct, the undesirable consequences of housing policy (rooted in those factors which prevent black people benefiting from housing policy on equal terms with white people) should be dealt with either by *general* attempts to combat urban disadvantage or by legislation developed *specifically* to eliminate racial discrimination. The next section considers policies associated with the first plank of this argument; my final remarks consider the efficacy of the second.

The Urban Programme and a policy for the inner cities

By far the largest proportion of public finance targeted towards the urban areas in which black people live is allocated via mainstream economic and housing policy. Nevertheless, during the past twenty years, a series of distinctively 'inner city' policies have emerged, whose symbolic importance far outstrips their financial base. Concern over successive 'race relations' crises has provided an important impetus for such policies, and the initiatives discussed below represent one of central government's key concessions to the need to combat racial disadvantage.

There are at least two generations of urban policy directed towards the general problems of the so-called inner city (a label which has become synonymous with areas housing a majority of black people and a proportionate minority of whites). The achievements of such policies in the context of urban management generally are widely reviewed elsewhere (see Lawless and Brown 1986; Rees and Lambert 1986; Short 1984; Stewart 1987a). My interest here concerns the extent to which these initiatives have succeeded in alleviating racial inequality: is it possible, by tackling general disadvantage, to secure for black people adequate access to housing (and, indeed, to a wide range of other economic and welfare rights)?[8] The key questions in looking to urban policy to break the link between segregation and inequality concern, first, whether or not urban policy discriminates in favour of the *areas* in which black people are most likely to live and, secondly, whether or not the initiatives involved are effective in improving the life chances of black *individuals*. I shall explore these issues by looking chronologically at the major phases of the Urban Programme and related inner city policies.

The 'traditional' Urban Programme, 1968–77

The Urban Programme was announced by Harold Wilson, Labour leader and Prime Minister, in May 1968 during a major speech on race relations and immigraton which was given shortly after Enoch Powell's highly emotive outburst against contemporary immigration policy. The initiative was launched amid rising concern about urban deprivation at a time when the size and distribution of the black community was becoming a scapegoat for the 'rediscovery' of poverty in urban Britain. A precedent for tackling such deprivation on an area by area basis was set in the Plowden and Seebohm reports; a precedent for making special provision for some sections of the black population is built into the provisions of Section 11 of the Local Government Act of 1966.[9] However, the first phase of the Urban Programme confirmed the Government's preference for area-based rather than group-targeted positive discrimination, and urban policy has since been driven by a search for the most efficient way to draw geographical boundaries around social deprivation.

As originally conceived, the Urban Programme was to channel Government funds, via the Home Office, to areas with acute housing, educational, health and welfare needs. The enabling legislation is laid out in the Local Government Grants (Social Needs) Act of 1969. This allowed local authorities to bid for grants amounting to 75 per cent of expenditure on their own projects (which attracted the bulk of such funds) and on any voluntary projects they wished to support. In practice, the majority of the early Programme was devoted to education (especially nurseries), broadening only later into a wider range of social schemes. From the beginning, however, there was an ambiguity concerning the precise role of the Programme in catering to black people's needs.

On the one hand, the Government was clear that its commitment to positive discrimination referred to areas not groups. Merlyn Rees's written answer to questions about the targeting of funds stated unequivocally that 'the presence of immigrants is not the only factor, though it is an important one, in determining the existence of areas of special social need for the purposes of the Act.' On the other hand, politically and pragmatically, race relations has been consistently at the Programme's core. As Sills et al. (1983: 34) point out: 'In the ritual composition of indicators which has been the regular precursor to each reincarnation of urban aid, the numbers and spatial distribution of ethnic minorities in inner cities have been key elements.' Legislators were cautious in admitting it, but most observers agree that, symbolically, the traditional Urban Programme wa a gesture of positive assistance to immigrant communities and, as such, could be invoked as the 'tender' counterpart to Government's 'tough' stance on immigration control (see Gibson and Langstaff 1982: 144).

In practice, any implied commitment to advancing the interests of either immigrants or the black community very quickly dissolved.

Edwards and Batley (1978) show how an early concern with specifically racial disadvantage petered out as the policy was put into place. Government officials were wary both of being over-generous towards black people (so risking hostility from the far Right and from a white electorate) and of over-stating their concern with racial disadvantage (so encouraging those who erroneously identified a causal relationship between New Commonwealth immigration and urban degradation). Such equivocation undoubtedly impinged on policy implementation and, by most accounts, limited its achievements.

Sivanandan (1986) has condemned the Programme as a scheme developed primarily for the white working classes and he alludes to an entrenched hostility among British politicians towards programmes for black minorities. (Young (1983) provides a more general discussion of this attitude and MacEwen (1987) identifies a similar complacency at the level of central government in Scotland). Even the initial plan to target projects on 'areas where immigrants settled' was 'progressively weakened with the growing recognition by officials that positive discrimination in favour of immigrants carried with it its own political difficulties' (Edwards and Batley 1978: 46). In the event, only one Government circular (phase 12 of the Programme) referred explicitly to the requirements of black people (its aim was to encourage self help) and just 5 per cent of Programme funds were allocated to projects dealing with racial disadvantage. The Programme was announced to allay fears about social unrest, but the policies it spawned rarely addressed race-related issues directly (a problem illustrated by Higgins et al. (1983)). In typical 1960s style, the Programme focused resources on *areas* of special need; it showed little inclination to explore the relationship between general deprivation and the kinds of disadvantage encountered by black people.

The mid-1970s did, however, bring an increasing propensity to target urban policy more carefully on the most deprived urban areas, and Edwards and Batley (1978) show that Home Office officials had begun to resurrect their initial concerns about racial inequality and to phrase them in a more explicit form. This was the culmination of an era of experimentation in the organization of 'area-based' positive discrimination, which included a series of specially commissioned investigative reports (notably the Inner Area Studies) and witnessed the birth (in 1973) of an Urban Deprivation Unit in the Home Office (to conduct research and coordinate the work of Government departments). Experiments in local involvement and service coordination were launched, including the politically contentious Community Development Projects and the short-lived Comprehensive Community Programmes, but it was increasingly recognized that only the Urban Programme was far-reaching enough to have even the potential to impinge on the overall well-being of the black population.

Ironically, it was at this point that the emphasis of the Programme was changed, and that responsibility for guiding it was taken out of the hands of the Home Office. This shift was a response to various valid criticisms – that the Programme was merely a symbolic palliative, that it was constructed hurriedly with little thought for the economic roots of social unrest and that its provisions made scant impact on the process of industrial restructuring that lies at the core of Britain's 'urban crisis'. It is unfortunate that, in an attempt to reduce these shortcomings, the Programme's awakening concern for racial equality was, for a time at least, eclipsed by the wider concerns of environmental management.

New policies for the inner cities, 1977–88

In 1976, the Government announced a major review of the Urban Programme which culminated in the 1977 White Paper 'Policy for the Inner Cities' (Department of the Environment, Cmnd 6845) and the Inner Urban Areas Act of 1978. From this point onwards, the Programme was to combine its earlier emphasis on the social origins of deprivation with a drive towards economic, industrial and environmental regeneration. In response to the demands of a deepening economic crisis, responsibility for the Programme was moved from the Home Office to the Department of the Environment (a parallel shift occurred in Scotland: the details are outlined in Clapham and Smith (1988)). Whatever else the new changes signalled, they meant that central guidance for the Programme would no longer come from the department with formal responsibility for race relations. Rather, they would issue from a department which had been condemned, only two years earlier, by a Select Committee on Race Relations and Immigration for a negligible ability to respond effectively to the needs of black people.

The 1977 White Paper acknowledges the presence of 'ethnic minorities' in just three short paragraphs, placing them alongside economic decline, physical decay and social disadvantage as a dimension of the inner city 'problem'. No special policies for the minority groups were announced and the Paper denies any responsibility for racial discrimination or its effects (the arena, it claims, of the Commission for Racial Equality, which came into operation during the same year). In an assessment of the new initiative, Stewart (1987b: 7) is in no doubt that 'one of the basic justifications for the policy was the fear of racial tension and a subsequent loss of social control'. The Home Office did, therefore, retain a minor role in the Urban Programme in an attempt to secure the representation of black people's needs. Its efficacy was blunted by a lack of staff and local knowledge, and by the general complacency regarding racial inequality that stretched across the policy arena. At the turn of the decade, Young and Connelly (1981) noted that 'Home Office participation in the traditional and enhanced Urban Programme is largely a matter of form' (p. 137); in assessing urban policy more generally, these authors conclude that 'the claim by one civil servant that issues of race were "on the back burner" may serve as a motif for our entire study' (p. 154).

The enhanced Urban Programme had become part of a much broader and better funded strategy for inner city revitalization, and to this extent it had greater potential to improve the quality of life of a majority of black people. The 1978 Inner Urban Areas Act created a hierarchy of area-types for priority assistance which favoured the inner rings of the major cities. The bulk of funds channelled through the Inner Areas Programme was directed, in progressively decreasing amounts, towards seven Partnership authorities, fifteen Programme authorities and fourteen other designated districts.[10] Resources from the traditional Urban Programme continued to be allocated in response to competitive bidding from the remaining local authorities, and a 10-year funding commitment helped to resolve past uncertainties about Government's plans for the future of the inner cities. Schemes sponsored under the enhanced Programme were expected to be innovatory, and individual projects were regarded as seed money to encourage the 'bending' of resources from mainstream budgets (as well as to attract private investment). Both these features could, theoretically, have increased the relevance of the new policies to the black population.

In practice, Cross (1982a) finds little evidence that the early operation of the enhanced Urban Programme significantly reduced racial inequality. He shows that, contrary to conventional wisdom, the area targeting of the Programme did not serve the interests of the majority of the black population: at that time as many as 60 per cent of black people were living *outside* the Partnership and Programme authority bounds. There appeared to be no relationship on a local authority by local authority basis between the proportionate size of the black population and the allocation of Programme funds and, as a consequence of the way in which increasing priority was afforded to economic and environmental concerns, 'by 1980, black groups with an interest in social and community projects were at risk of being squeezed out of the urban programmes' (Young 1983: 291). The systematically iniquitous consequences of this are apparent from research in Birmingham which indicates that black organizations fare worse than their white equivalents in attracting funds. In 1980–1, black voluntary organizations received less than 4 per cent of what they bid for (the average grant being £7000), while other applicants were given 20 per cent of the funds they requested (with an average grant of £17 000) (see Cross 1982a). In their 1980/1 annual report the Birmingham Community Relations Council point out that only 10 per cent of Programme funds were allocated to voluntary bodies, and that no commitment to the needs of the black community was apparent in plans to spend the remaining 90 per cent.

The wider currency of these trends is confirmed in a review published by the Department of the Environment (1980) itself, which shows that only 9 of 54 sampled projects benefited 'ethnic minorities' directly (although in a further nine projects black people formed a significant proportion of the client group). By 1980 it was clear that, despite rhetoric to the contrary, the enhanced Urban Programme was not affording particular priority to the challenge of racism. This is reflected in the 1980 guidelines for evaluating the Programme which identified the two *fundamental* criteria for evaluating projects as 'ameliorating special need' and 'operating in a deprived area'. The less enigmatic and, arguably, easier to operationalize criterion of 'assisting ethnic minorities' was the last of five additional 'desirable' aims (Department of the Environment 1980).

As the decade advanced, the ideological preferences of a new Conservative Government dictated a further reorganization of urban policy priorities; and widespread civil unrest in the inner cities, in 1981 and 1985, demanded renewed commitment to the problems of racial disadvantage. Unfortunately, the aims of British neo-conservatism have not always been sympathetic to the pursuit of specifically racial equality and the tension this causes is well illustrated in the evolution of urban policy during the 1980s.

In the panic following the riots of 1980 and 1981, a Home Affairs Committee identified the Urban Programme as the major vehicle by which central government could support local authorities' attempts to combat racial disadvantage. Indeed, in Stewart's (1987a) opinion, 'there can be no doubt that the fear of social disorder, and its association with the needs and demands of black people has been a major factor in sustaining central government interest in inner cities policy' (p. 134). Accordingly, new ministerial guidelines were issued to the Partnership and Programme authorities in July 1981 containing an instruction to ensure that 'the special needs of minority groups are recognised and catered for' (Department of the Environment 1981). Sir George Young was given special responsibility for race-related issues within the Department of the Environment and, in a flurry of activity, over 200 new 'ethnic projects' were approved for 1981/2. The targeting of resources and their relevance for minority groups were reassessed in a study commissioned by the Department of the Environment (Stewart and Whitting 1983) and financial commitment to the 'ethnic projects' was scheduled to increase from £8 million in 1981/2 to £15 million in 1982/3 and £29 million in 1983/4. Although not all the findings of the evaluation were accepted, and while it was already clear that the Government saw public expenditure as only a small part of the resources required for urban revitalization, between 1980/1 and 1985/6 'ethnic' projects increased their share of Urban Programme resources from 3 to 12 per cent (Department of the Environment 1985). This was a direct consequence of the Department of the Environment's increasing willingness to address a problem labelled 'racial disadvantage' and to recognize the importance of tackling it through projects linked to mainstream housing, employment, education and social policy (Department of the Environment 1984).

This increased commitment within urban policy to the specific needs of black people has taken place against a background of an expanding Programme.[11] Public spending on the initiative rose from £39 million in 1978/9 to a peak of £320 million in 1984/5, and has steadied at £317 million more recently; over 12 000 individual projects are supported. As a consequence of this expansion the one facet of urban policy that seems to have been designed to target those areas in which black people live has, in this respect, succeeded. Of the 20 'largest ethnic settlements' identified by Robinson (1986) from the last census, only four are not now designated as Partnership or Programme authorities. Since the majority of the 36 000–41 000 jobs created (at a cost of £58 million) through the Programme by 1984 went to *local* males, there is at least the possibility of direct benefits being experienced by black individuals (see Department of the Environment 1986). Recently, however, the enlargement of the Programme has been coupled with a change of priority which does not necessarily augur well for black Britons.

The trend now is not merely to complement the social aims of the traditional Urban Programme by building in certain economic priorities, but rather to direct urban policy almost exclusively towards the goals of industrial regeneration and wealth creation.[12] The idea is not so much to use public funds to guide the 'bending' of mainsream public policy as to stimulate private investment (see Hambleton 1981; Stewart 1983). The persistence of this emphasis was guaranteed following the investigations of the House of Commons Committee on Public Accounts (Department of the Environment 1985), which indicated that the most successful Programme projects are economic or environmental, while social schemes are (and, by implication, should increasingly be) part of the 'normal' responsibilities of local authorities. As a consequence, economic schemes increased their total proportion of Urban Programme funds from 29 to 34 per cent between 1979/80 and 1985/6, at the expense of social schemes, with a share falling from 51 to 43 per cent (and with funding often at, or near, an end) (see Department of the Environment 1985). While these latter schemes have always proved most sensitive to the needs of black people, only one of the Department of the Environment's ten categories of economic development projects contains even a passing reference to measures designed to benefit minority 'ethnic' groups (this category is labelled 'miscellaneous'). More disturbingly still, responsibility for urban policy seems to be drifting away from the Department of the Environment and towards the Departments of Employment and Industry, whose interests are central to the Government's new 'Action for Cities' (launched on 7 March 1988).[13] This may mean that care for the inner cities is again slipping away from a department evincing concern for black people's disadvantage and towards departments whose willingness to confront racism remains to be confirmed.

Overall, the Urban Programme and its associated array of inner cities policy may have failed to combat racial inequality for the following reasons. First, the resource commitment is relatively small (£2 billion were spent on the Programme between 1979 and 1987) and even against a background of expansion its emphasis has gone against changes in mainstream funding, which decreased the resources available to the inner cities by as much as 50 per cent between 1975/6 and 1985/6 (Lawless 1986). Secondly, black people have suffered from the targeting of policy towards *areas* rather than groups. Even as a method of combating general disadvantage, area-based positive discrimination is suspect (on moral as well as pragmatic grounds), but as a policy intended to meet black people's needs it has proved particularly contentious. Finally, black people are hit hardest by the decision to shed central responsibility for the social dimension of urban policy. This social responsibility has become the mandate of local government at a time when reductions to the Rate Support Grant make it difficult for them to 'bend' resources in line with existing Urban Programme priorities, let alone offer new or continuing funding for the kinds of projects that have traditionally assisted black community groups.

Racial discrimination and spatial disadvantage

So far, this chapter has shown how black people's marginal position in the division of labour is expressed in, and compounded by, their experience in the housing and urban environment more generally. Through the housing system, racial inequality has been exacerbated, first by racialized minorities' limited access to housing as welfare and subsequently (and as a consequence) by their limited opportunities to use housing to store wealth. This process has encouraged the spatial concentration of black people into areas where their life chances and material well-being depend crucially on the success of other policy initiatives.[14] The Urban Programme was, symbolically, a unique attempt to bend mainstream policy towards race-related problems, but its impact was limited by its poor overall coordination and its variable commitment to the problem of racial disadvantage. Ultimately both housing and urban policy assign responsibility for securing the conditions for achieving racial equality (in the general distribution of economic and welfare resources) to the tightly circumscribed arena of anti-discrimination legislation.

The Race Relations Acts are the one area of policy in which Governments explicitly recognize the difficulties that black people experience, and much is expected of them. Unfortunately, this legislation was passed relatively recently (in 1965, 1968 and 1976) and has developed incrementally. The main Acts were never coordinated with the development of housing or urban policy, and even a brief examination of their timing exposes a fundamentally limited ability to confront many of the problems that black people have faced. First, attempts to outlaw racial discrimination were systematically excluded from the statute books throughout the period in which segregation was initiated. Even the 1965 Act, which outlawed incitement to racial hatred and racial discrimination in public places, explicitly omitted responsibility for discrimination in employment and housing! It was not until 1968 – well after the marginal housing position of black people had been established – that the Act was extended to cover these crucial areas.

A further eight years were to pass before the concept of *indirect* discrimination was recognized. This means that until 1976 the law was unable to challenge practices that discriminated against black people not explicitly on the grounds of colour, but on the basis of some other social, economic or demographic attribute more characteristic of black people than of whites (either because of their migration history, or because of a history of discrimination). This new Act came too late to prevent black people's exclusion from the public sector by indirectly discriminatory residence requirements (by the early 1970s, many black – particularly Afro-Caribbean – households had already fulfilled this entry condition). It was, in many cases, too late to guard against institutionalized racism in housing allocation (an area where the pervasiveness of indirect discrimination is now amply demonstrated), but it *was* in time to allow the 1977 White Paper to outline a new policy for the inner cities that explicitly declined to make special provision for racial disadvantage.

Even had the advent of race relations legislation been timely enough to deal with racism institutionalized in the implementation of housing and urban policy, its potential effectiveness in guarding against entrenched discrimination must be questioned. Responsibility for enforcing this legislation in Britain has, with successive Acts, been entrusted virtually exclusively to, first, the Race Relations Board, then the Community Relations Commission and (currently) the Commission for Racial Equality (CRE). Each body has acquired substantially more powers than its predecessor but even today the CRE's legal role is limited to investigating cases and complaints about racial discrimination (and, as Grubb (1987) shows, even here their efficacy is being hampered by the courts). This artificial distinction between race relations and mainstream policy, and the restriction of the former to a small, poorly resourced enforcement body, is quite out of step with developments in the USA, where the body equivalent to the CRE is a very minor part of a much larger set of policy initiatives.

Cross (1982b) provides an accessible and informed account of why the effectiveness of anti-discrimination legislation in Britain has been so limited. He probes beyond conventional attacks on the diversionary role of the Commission for Racial Equality and on this body's mismanagement, poor leadership and ineffective targeting of resources. The problems, he argues, are much more deep-seated than this. They relate to the lack of coordination of anti-discrimination measures between policy areas, to a poorly specified and weakly enforced law and to acute under-resourcing. These conditions, he concludes, are all symptoms of the inescapable fact that 'the promotion of racial justice appears to be low on the list of central government priorities' (p. 86). It is significant (and disconcerting) that against a background of cuts in the budget of the CRE, and at a time when central intervention in local housing systems and urban environments was beginning to reach unprecedented heights, the Race Relations Act of 1976 assigned exclusively to local authorities a major new duty to promote racial equality.

The achievements of the local authorities are considered in the next chapter. It is clear from *this* chapter, however, that central governments' own success in combating racial inequality has so far been limited. The nature and timing of housing policy has had the little publicized and largely unanticipated consequence of sustaining racial segregation; urban policy has failed to alleviate racial disadvantage; and, contrary to legislators' stated expectations, the laws against racial discrimination have not been able – and in their present form probably never could be able – either to tackle the roots of racism or to place black people on an equal footing with whites as the beneficiaries of housing and urban policy.

Such a conclusion could be mistaken as grist to the mill of the 'New

Right', whose key arguments against state intervention are that it fails to achieve its aims and has undesirable unanticipated consequences. In fact, the most striking feature of the legislative history of racial segregation in Britain is that undesirable consequences arise where policies are not drawn tightly enough, where their aims are insufficiently explicit and where scope for discretion is too wide. The evidence here makes an argument for more, not less, intervention, urging decision-makers to anticipate the disadvantage that public policy can confer on black people and to strengthen the provisions of the race relations legislation.

Society's ultimate goal must, I believe, be to dispense with any policy or practice that differentiates populations according to spurious racial criteria (this is not, of course, the same as arguing for the removal of cultural variety or the denial of national histories). Currently, however, *seemingly* aracial policies appear only to exacerbate black people's disadvantage. For the past 40 years, central governments have been issuing policies that are 'colour-blind' not 'race-neutral' and if the future is to see a reduction rather than a widening of racial inequality, legislators may have to allow 'race enlightened' (or anti-racist) criteria to impinge on the dictates of economy and ideology in the development of mainstream housing and urban policy. Given a history of accumulating disadvantage, it is hard to see how else it will be possible to secure adequate access for black people to the full range of employment, property and welfare rights to which they are entitled.

Notes

1 White papers are government policy statements published for the information of Parliament before the introduction of a Bill (these are usually preceded by Green Papers – consultative documents which effectively test the plausibility and feasibility of possible policy initiatives).
2 This refers to Parliamentary Debates in the House of Commons (Hansard). The format is year, volume number (fifth series before 13 March 1981 and Volume 1000, sixth series thereafter) and column position (this is also relevant to citations in chapter 5).
3 The dispersal policy was managed by the Uganda Resettlement Board, which had been allocated a limited number of public and privately rented dwellings to encourage refugees to settle away from established Asian communities. Bristow (1976) argues that because insufficient dwellings were provided, the process was slow. The consequence was that a large proportion of refugees made their own arrangements and while 38 per cent did follow the pattern of dispersal, the large majority – 62 per cent – moved to traditional inner city areas.
4 This Act replaced housing subsidies with means-tested rent and rate rebates; it

instituted 'reasonable' (market-related) rents in the public sector; and it curbed the building of new council housing (see Rees and Lambert 1986: 134).

5 This was partly related to the sterling crisis of the mid-1970s. The pound was saved by a loan from the IMF that was granted only in return for cutbacks in state borrowing – which draws attention to the importance of viewing housing policy in the much wider context of national and international economies, as well as in terms of its relationship with other areas of social and economic policy.

6 The most recent PSI survey, conducted before the bulk of council sales had been completed, detected only a tiny proportion of respondents who had changed tenure between 1977 and 1982, except to form new households.

7 The White Paper outlines arrangements allowing those council tenants who encounter unnecessary delays in buying their home to begin paying their rent to a deposit holder (rather than to the local authority) to be used as savings towards the eventual purchase price of the dwelling.

8 An early indication of the faith placed in this assumption is apparent from Rex's (1986b) account of his tenure as a member of the housing panel of the National Committee for Commonwealth Immigrants in 1966. His request for provisions to combat racial discrimination in housing allocation was met with proposals for coping with general problems in *areas* of 'special housing need'.

9 Section 11 of the Local Government Act allows local authorities to claim 75 per cent of the salary costs of workers appointed to meet needs created by the presence of 'substantial numbers of immigrants from the Commonwealth', whose settlement has taken place in the past 10 years. Labour's attempt to update this provision to serve the needs of the large proportion of the 'ethnic' communities who are not immigrants was lost to the 1979 general election. Modifications passed in 1982/3 have extended its scope slightly, and assistance is now available in areas where migrants have been settled for over a decade, and where they comprise less than 2 per cent of the population. The majority of expenditure (over 80 per cent) has been on education and, symbolically at least, it has always been eclipsed by the Urban Programme.

10 The original Partnership authorities are Birmingham, Hackney and Islington (these received individual status in 1982), Lambeth, Liverpool, Manchester/ Salford, Newcastle/Gateshead and Docklands (which later became an Urban Development Corporation). The Programme authorities were Bolton, Bradford, Hammersmith/Fulham, Hull, Leeds, Leicester, Middlesbrough, North Tyneside, Nottingham, Oldham, Sheffield, South Tyneside, Sunderland, Wirral and Wolverhampton. These were joined by Blackburn, Brent, Coventry, Knowsley, Rochdale, Sandwell, Tower Hamlets and Wandsworth in 1982.

11 Following the phasing out of the traditional Urban Programme (announced in May 1986) there will be 45 Programme authorities in 1987/88, including 15 of the 16 'other designated districts' (Ealing is the only one to remain) and adding seven authorities that were previously reliant on the traditional Urban Programme.

12 Virtually all the urban policy initiatives of the 1980s have been orientated towards the wealth creating sector. These have included the creation of Urban

Development Corporations, Task Forces, Enterprise Zones and City Action Teams (to coordinate the work of Government departments in specific areas) as well as the establishment of the Financial Institutions Group, Business in the Community and, more recently, 'Elevenco' (a combination of the 11 largest civil engineering and construction companies to seek out inner city sites for private development). These all represent attempts to harness private to public investment, voluntary to statutory involvement, in the task of urban revitalization. In assessing some of them, Jacobs (1986) finds no new or pressing commitment to the principles of anti-racism or racial equality.

13 The twelve initiatives redeployed public spending to establish a new Urban Development Corporation (in Sheffield) and an expansion of the one in Merseyside, new City Action Teams in Leeds and Nottingham, special funds, grants, loans and infrastructure to encourge private sector investment, help for the unemployed and measures to control crime and fear.

14 Most recently, analysts have suggested that the Community Charge or Poll Tax will disproportionately penalize black (especially Asian) households. A report by the London Research Centre for the Association of London Authorities (1988) indicates that household size, location of home and type of dwelling all determine whether households will be better or worse off under the new system. On all three counts, black people are expected to fare worse, on average, than whites.

4 Access, Allocation and Exchange: the 'Race Relations' of Housing Consumption

It is nobody's fault that people from overseas are content to live in conditions different from those sought by white people.
                                        Eric Fletcher, 22 November 1957

A review of the major policy events sustaining segregation has exposed a crucial ambiguity in the state's responsibilities towards racial inequality. On the one hand central government is a fundamental arbiter of black people's access to living space (and to the package of resources associated with this); on the other hand, formal responsibility for the geography and well-being of black Britons has been devolved to the local authorities. This tier of government was charged to formulate a 'balanced view' on the wisdom of dispersal by the 1975 White Paper (Cmnd 6232). It is required to make arrangements to 'eliminate unlawful discrimination' and to 'promote equality of opportunity and good relations between persons of different racial groups' by Section 71 of the 1976 Race Relations Act, and it is expected to fulfil a 'particular responsibility to tackle the problems of racial disadvantage' by the Department of the Environment (1983: 1).

In principle, this decentralization of responsibility is welcome as an acknowledgement of the variable circumstances in which discrimination occurs and as recognition of the value of local initiative. In practice, however, there are grounds for suspecting that this trend is less a gesture of faith in the integrity of local democracy than evidence of the continuing marginalization and peripheralization of the race issue that is so eloquently exposed by Bulpitt (1986). This pessimistic interpretation is supported by the following observations.

First, it is striking that, before the mid-1970s, local government had given the political centre no reason to think that it would be interested, let alone successful, in pursuing racial equality. During the late 1950s and early 1960s, when local government had a relatively high degree of fiscal and political autonomy, it did very little to cater to the needs of black people. Discussing that period, McKay (1977: 96) concludes that 'many local governments (in areas of high immigration many of them labour controlled), behaved as though blacks did not exist'. Even the written evidence of the Ministry of Housing and Local Government to the Royal Commission on Local Government in England (1967) did not mention the needs and aspirations of black people, despite paying considerable attention to the housing needs of numerous other special and disadvantaged groups. For at least two decades, therefore, local authorities sustained the tradition of central government and made scant attempt to intervene to improve the living conditions of its black rent- and rate-payers.

Secondly, by the close of the 1970s, central intervention in local affairs had removed many of the options for securing racial equality that were once available to local government. This has been particularly true with respect to the manipulation of the housing stock. Since 1978, local authorities have been required to produce detailed housing plans to allow central government more systematic control over public spending. In this respect, local autonomy has been replaced with central sovereignty in a way that exacerbates urban stress generally (Maclennan and O'Sullivan 1985). In the past decade, the local authorities have found it increasingly difficult to tackle their now clearly defined mandate to pursue racial justice because of a growing financial dependence on Whitehall and a steady loss of local political autonomy.

It is, nevertheless, at a local level that the intersection of central constraints, private institutions and public bureaucracies variously shape the social relations of housing consumption in which racial discrimination in one guise or another plays an important role. Exploring each segment of the local housing system in turn, this chapter monitors the accumulating effects of both complacency and impotency on the part of local governments, showing how these two sets of constraints have helped to limit black people's access to a proper share of the economic and welfare benefits embedded in the housing environment. Paying particular attention to the points at which disrimination occurs in local housing systems, the discussion exposes a further set of mechanisms responsible for sustaining the link between residential segregation and racial inequality.

Private renting and the 'independent' sector

Around 90 per cent of dwellings were privately rented before 1919 but since then this tenure has shrunk dramatically in absolute and relative terms. Although the standard of accommodation provided by private landlords has steadily deteriorated since 1945, such lettings offered a key point of entry into the British housing system for post-war migrants from the New Commonwealth and Pakistan. This itself required black people to live in the oldest and poorest segments of the housing stock, usually in buildings constructed before 1919 and often without the exclusive use of basic amenities. It also meant that they had to rely on a form of renting where, in the absence of explicit sets of allocation rules, there is maximum potential for direct racial discrimination by landlords – a practice which remained quite legal until 1968. Indeed, the Milner Holland Committee, reporting in 1965, found that only one-third of all private landlords in London would consider letting their property to a 'coloured' tenant (Milner Holland 1965).

Today, with potentially powerful legislation in place, there are still enormous problems in identifying and policing racial discrimination in the privately rented sector. The CRE has had to limit itself to 'assisting individual complainants who are seeking redress in the courts' and to conducting 'periodic investigations where there is strong prima facie evidence of systematic discrimination by particular agencies and their landlord clients' (CRE 1980: 1). Two such investigations have been completed but, as a more recent report by Boga et al. (1986) shows, these can only have exposed the tip of the iceberg.[1] Even in 1982, as many as half the West Indians and a third of the Asians surveyed by Brown (1984) claimed to have experienced direct discrimination in obtaining their home.

One consequence of a history of discrimination in this tenure sector is the emergence of a dual rental market in which, by 1975, hardly any white tenants were renting from black landlords and less than 15 per cent of black tenants rented from white landlords. The early PEP reports indicate that even during the 1960s only about a third of Afro-Caribbean tenants and a mere 15 per cent of Asians had ever felt able to apply for accommodation from a white landlord. The effects of this are now less far-reaching than they were, since, with the exception of Bangladeshis, black people are under-represented in the privately rented sector (see table 5). Nevertheless, the complacency of the major landlords and agencies (best exposed by Boga et al. (1986)) is disturbing in the light of the Government's housing plans.

According to Karn (1982) the experience and expectation of discrimination has helped to intensify segregation by discouraging black tenants from seeking a move up-market (into properties owned by white landlords in better areas). 'Solutions' to the problem of racism in the privately rented sector have not therefore flowed from legislation or from attitudinal change on the part of whites; instead racial discrimination has been

Table 5 Tenure patterns in the 'independent' sector[a]

| | Private renting | | | |
	Furnished	Unfurnished	Total[b]	Housing association
White	2	7	9	2
West Indian	3	3	6	8
Asian	4	1	6	2
Indian	4	1	5	2
Pakistani	4	1	5	1
Bangladeshi	8	2	11	4

[a] Entries are row percentages where n is the total number of households in each subpopulation.
[b] Discrepancies with the sum of furnished and unfurnished percentages are caused by rounding.
Source: Brown 1984, p. 56

avoided by individuals opting for a restricted range of landlords and for a correspondingly restricted pool of accommodation.

Avoidance strategies bring their own problems, most notably by effectively reducing the availability of accommodation within an already limited, and relatively low quality, stock of housing. Doling and Davies (1983) have explored some of the consequences of this in Birmingham, where they discovered a significantly lower propensity among black than white tenants to use the Rent Acts to obtain fair renting agreements. Some black tenants (renting from resident landlords) cannot, of course, make such appeal (and black tenants are more likely than whites to live in these circumstances). Others, however, are fearful of landlords, unaware of the legislation protecting them and dare not challenge high rents when accommodation is perceived to be scarce. Racial inequality is exacerbated, it seems, by the weakness of legislation which assumes that 'even in a situation of housing stress, combined with class and racial tensions, tenants are still able to apply for protection, freely and without fear of adverse consequences' (Doling and Davies 1983: 492);.

Within the privately rented sector, black tenants have, for all these reasons, always secured accommodation of lower than average quality, in which they must live at higher than average densities, for larger average rents than their white counterparts (see Bovaird et al. 1985). A GLC survey completed in the early 1980s indicates that the average black tenant paid £34 per month more than the average white tenant, but was almost twice as likely to be living in accommodation of 'very poor' condition (cited in Boga et al. 1986). Private renting is also a refuge for growing numbers of the homeless (and, in London especially, a rising proportion of these are black families), who are accommodated in squalid bed and breakfast hotels while they await rehousing by local councils. In London, the number of people housed in this way tripled between 1983 and 1986; in some boroughs these tenants face long periods living in sub-standard, overcrowded and unhealthy surroundings (Bonnerjea and Lawton 1987).

Relatively little systematic or comprehensive research has been completed on the problems of racial discrimination in the privately rented sector in recent years. Boga et al. (1986) use a range of survey material collated for the London region to expose the need for reform in the following services (very few of which currently operate systematic monitoring or anti-discrimination procedures): Housing Aid Centres (which provide the most comprehensive range of services for private tenants), Tenancy Relations Officers (appointed to deal with disputes between private landlords and their tenants), Environmental Health Officers (whose responsibilities for enforcing health and housing standards allow them to force landlords to make essential repairs), local authority legal services (especially in relation to tenants' rights under the Rent Acts) and Rent Officers (who can supply criteria for setting fair rents). Local authorities inspired by their duties under the 1976 Race Relations Act could, therefore, exert considerable pressure on the private rented sector to promote racial equality. Whether these powers remain available to them, and whether they are actively wielded, will become an increasingly crucial issue if the rented sector expands in the way the Government predicts.

Since the mid-1970s, the traditional role of the private rented sector has been partly absorbed by an expanding housing association movement. Although they are small in absolute terms, housing association lets are disproportionately significant for some black households. Publicly funded (through the Housing Corporation) but privately administered (by local management comittees), the associations (which number more than 3000) now accommodate about 2 per cent of all households, 8 per cent of Afro-Caribbean households, 4 per cent of Bangladeshis and 3 per cent of Hindu families. Despite the relatively scanty documentation of housing associations' policies and practices towards black people, it is obvious that their significance for racialized minorities is considerably greater than their small contribution to the property market suggests. Their relevance to the black population is enhanced because their tenancies (for reasons outlined in chapter 3) are often geographically concentrated in metropolitan districts and in the inner areas of cities (matching the distribution of the black population as a whole), their operations (centrally financed through the Housing Corporation) account for an increasing proportion of all public activity in housing and they are legally able to cater to particular groups. This targeting can (in some circumstances) favour black people. Between April 1985 and 1987, 27 black housing associations were established in England and Wales, and there are plans for a further 25 over the next five years (which could play a significant role in providing employment as well as housing opportunities for black people). In 1986, the Housing Corporation appointed its own 'Race and Housing' adviser, set aside £1.5 million for newly registered black associations and allocated £100 000 p.a. for three years to encourage the participation of ethnic minorities in the housing association movement (part of which is earmarked for training black housing association directors).

In 1982, the Housing Corporation consulted the CRE and issued an equal opportunities policy, alerting housing associations to its belief that 'because minority groups are over-represented amongst those in most urgent housing need, special initiatives to assist those minority groups are likely to be necessary'. Subsequently, the National Federation of Housing Associations (NFHA) published two documents containing equal opportunities guidelines to be adopted wherever the catchment of a housing association has a minority population exceeding 2 per cent (NFHA 1982, 1983). It is encouraging that, even in the early 1980s, over one-third of the member associations had instituted some system of 'ethnic' monitoring of their allocations. It is less encouraging that Niner's (1984) investigation of three large urban housing associations who had tried to follow the NFHA guidelines (and had also implemented 'ethnic monitoring' systems to chart their progress) revealed only one with apparently non-discriminatory practices. A second discriminated against black applicants in terms of allocation criteria, waiting time, choice and type of dwelling allocated; the third assigned black households in disproportionate numbers to homes in racially segregated areas of poor environmental quality. Some of the same problems were uncovered in the CRE's (1983) enquiry into the Collingwood Housing Association, where informal judgements exercised by housing managers were working against the interests of black tenants, and where information about the availability of tenancies was not adequately advertised to the black population. (Other problems relating to allocations, monitoring and liaison with local authorities are listed in the CRE report.)

The situation in Scotland is even more difficult to gauge since it was not until April 1985 that Scotland's housing associations (which tend to be smaller and have a more distinct geographical base than their counterparts in England and Wales) were alerted to the Housing Corporation's concerns about *their* activities, in a circular (HC22/85) which 'reaffirms the commitment of the Housing Corporation to combating racial disadvantage in those areas of housing activity for which we have a responsibility'. Not surprizingly, little research has yet been completed in this area, and Lear's (1987) recent survey is the first of any significance, though the preliminary results of a more intensive study in Glasgow indicate that black people are under-represented as tenants of, and applicants to, housing associations, and that this partly reflects the low priority attached to attracting black households (Daghlian and Dalton 1988). Lear's work shows that in Central Clydeside black people receive a proportion of housing association lets that is lower than might be predicted from their presence in the population (more than 1 per cent of the population is black; between them they received 0.58 per cent of properties allocated). This survey was sent to all the Scottish associations and of the 24 urban associations that replied only two had any black committee members (numbering three in total) and only two had a black director. The majority (71 per cent) had not adopted an equal opportunities policy and a review of the routine allocations procedures currently in place suggests there is considerable scope for indirect discrimination in the Scottish system.[2]

A distinctive feature of the housing association movement has, nevertheless, been an insistence by the Housing Corporation and the National Federations on pursuing the goal of equal opportunities within a flexible and adaptable framework of housing provision. Both centrally and locally, this segment of the housing system has been well enough coordinated to tackle direct and institutionalized racism in a systematic way. Whether this will be maintained in the future remains to be seen. The Government now classifies housing associations as part of the 'independent' (by which it means private) sector (see Department of the Environment 1987a, d). There are plans to raise an increasing proportion of the associations' costs from rents and private investment, and it is expected that 'a growing proportion of the [Housing] Corporation's programme will be funded on a mixed basis using private finance' (Department of the Environment 1987d: 4). Currently, 80 per cent of the Housing Corporation's Approved Development Programme is concentrated on the inner-cities (Niner 1987), but the commercial sector has not usually been noted for its interest in these zones or, indeed, for its attention to the anti-racist cause. It is disturbing that the new proposals come without clear details on how the principle of equal opportunities is to be guaranteed, although it is encouraging that the Housing Corporation will have a statutory duty to avoid discrimination.

Owner occupation: choosing an asset or forced to buy?

Although owner occupation is increasingly regarded as both the 'ideal' and the 'normal' tenure for most households, chapter 3 showed that black people are among those least likely to benefit from the extension of home ownership. As the privately rented sector contracted, the movement of Asians and, to a lesser extent, Afro-Caribbeans into owner occupation was not therefore associated with a process of suburbanization or gentrification. Rather, it was associated with life in run-down environments, in homes of below average quality and at a point on the housing 'ladder' where owners receive less subsidy, and accrue fewer amenities, than do their counterparts in the public sector. This is especially problematic for Asians who, as we saw earlier, have higher rates of ownership than either the white or Afro-Caribbean populations (with the exception of Bangladeshis, whose rates of owner occupation are, at 30 per cent, lowest of all).

Patterns in the granting of housing finance probably exert most influence on the character of residential differentiation at a local level. I will therefore summarise a range of studies which show how building societies' bureaucratic responses to a changing economy have worked to exclude black buyers from the better parts of the housing stock either indirectly – as a consequence of their low incomes and rates of labour force participation – or directly through discrimination in the mortgage market (factors discussed more fully by Karn (1977) and Karn et al. (1985)).

Cater's (1981) study in Bradford is unusual in examining the impact of a property boom on the availability of mortgage finance to Asians. His work refers to a period in the early 1970s when building societies attracted massive investment and so increased the availability of loans by adopting more flexible lending criteria. In Bradford, this opened up the inner ring housing market to marginal (often black) buyers and brought suburban living within the reach of middle-income whites. The result was accelerated outmigration by whites, increased black owner occupation in the inner areas and an intensification of 'racial' segregation. This also secured the viability of a new generation of Asian estate agents whose role will be considered below.

Other authors have concentrated on the effects of fiscal restraint and housing shortage on building society activity, and have shown that it is more difficult under these circumstances for black people than for whites to obtain finance for house purchase (see Brown 1984; Stevens et al. 1982). Karn (1982) shows that, when funds are limited, mortgage refusals discriminate against black buyers. She observes that the policy of not lending to non-savers is more often waived for whites than for blacks and that stereotyped beliefs about area preferences 'steer' buyers so as to sustain existing patterns of segregation.)

In the early 1970s, acknowledging the limits to building society lending, local authorities as well as clearing banks and finance houses were beginning to intervene to support inner city housing markets. Council mortgages (encouraged since the 1959 House Purchase and Housing Act) became particularly important for black buyers, considerably widening their access to 'conventional' housing finance. (A recent CRE (1985b) inquiry, however, suggests that, for no obvious reason, Asians receive smaller loans than whites (relative to the size of their request) – a factor again restricting the range of properties for which they can bid.[3]) At the same time, loans from finance houses, which had been freely available for cheap pre-1919 properties (i.e. those within the financial grasp of the black population) were qualified by high interest rates, short repayment periods and punitive clauses to safeguard investments. This means that black borrowers have tended to pay more for their credit, as well as receiving less tax subsidy, than higher income owners with more expensive homes.) These disadvantages persisted following the collapse of the fringe banks in 1974/5, when informal loans from friends and relatives, and personal (5–7 year) loans from clearing banks became increasingly important (especially to Asians, who still had limited access to council housing).

According to Karn (1982: 46), the dependence of black owners on these alternatives to conventional lending has sustained their very marked concentration in the metropolitan inner cities. Yet even following Governments' attempts throughout the 1970s and during the 1980s to encourage financiers to lend down-market, black buyers still find access to conventional loans restricted. The CRE (1985b) has shown that between 1977 and 1981 in Rochdale, 75 per cent of white owners but only 50 per cent of blacks relied on building society mortgages. In Birmingham and Liverpool such finance is used by between 12 per cent and 45 per cent of Asian owners, as compared with 80 per cent of all buyers; in two studied areas, 86 per cent of black owners had been refused at least one 'conventional' mortgage application (Karn et al. 1986a).

There are at least two possible explanations for this continuing difference, quite apart from direct and overt colour discrimination. White households' greater eligibility for conventional loans could be accounted for by their (possibly) greater willingness to invest with building societies. However, Stevens et al. (1982) have shown that in Leeds, even in the most mixed areas, white buyers receive preferential treatment from building societies irrespective of their status as savers. Alternatively, the discrepancy could be related to the character of the properties chosen by prospective buyers. Karn et al. (1986a) suggest that this is not the case on a regional scale, finding building societies more willing to lend to slightly more affluent white buyers in Liverpool than to poorer Asians in Birmingham, even though the properties in the North-West were inferior to those in the West Midlands. Nevertheless, CRE investigations indicate that, at an intra-urban scale, property characteristics may provide the basis for indirectly discriminatory lending procedures. In Rochdale, factors related to dwelling age, type, condition and location were more than likely than income to be given as a reason for refusing a mortgage to black people (CRE 1984b). Asians *were* more likely to be rejected than whites on grounds related to savings and incomes (the proportions were 21 and 12 per cent) but the bulk of refusals related to property characteristics (this accounted for 27 per cent of white and 46 per cent of Asian refusals).

Assessing the grounds for these clearly discriminatory lending patterns, the CRE found no rational economic motive for building societies' reluctance to lend on cheap properties, on properties without front gardens or on properties in certain (improvement and action) areas. But because black buyers are more likely than whites to require access to such properties, the withholding of mortgages was found to be indirectly discriminatory, and therefore illegal. It is hardly surprizing in the light of such evidence that many black householders still avoid applying for 'conventional' mortgages because of the apparently high risk of failure (Karn et al. 1986a).

Building society activity (and inactivity) has probably been most decisive (directly or indirectly) in sustaining the 'racial' dimension of residential segregation at a local level in the private sector. The discriminatory practices involved appear to develop as a consequence of local branch discretion rather than because of procedures embedded in overall society policy (Housing Monitoring Team 1982; Stevens et al. 1982). This form of institutional racism is most difficult to eradicate since it may not be sensitive to central directives and policies. On the other hand, since it has been demonstrated that many of the notions underpinning indirect racism in mortgage lending are economically inefficient, in an essentially commercial enterprise, reforms effected through training policy and local codes of practice could initiate far-reaching change.

The character and location of property available to black buyers may also be influenced by the practices of the 'exchange professionals' – estate agents and solicitors – whose involvement in housing transactions is expected to increase the success of low income groups seeking mortgage finance (see Karn et al. 1986b). As early as the mid-1960s, PEP found evidence of direct discrimination by estate agents against 60 per cent of sampled West Indians (Daniel 1968). In one-third of these cases, black buyers were deliberately steered away from 'white' neighbourhoods. Other strategies are more subtle, such as sending property details later to black purchasers than to whites, thus affecting the odds of competing for any particular dwelling. These kinds of tactics raise the search costs incurred by black households, reduce their effective choice and may increase the price paid for a home (by as much as 5 per cent according to Fenton (1984)). Concern remains as estate agents continue to limit black buyers' residential options (most recently by impeding access to the 'gentrified' districts of London (*Independent*, 13 May 1988, p. 2)).

One corollary of this is that many Asians (and to a lesser extent Afro-Caribbeans) now avoid using intermediaries in property transactions. Cater (1981) estimated that informal transfers may have accounted for up to 50 per cent of the Asian to Asian transactions recorded in his Bradford study. This involved the simple exchange of the lowest priced dwellings in the least desirable areas.

Although there are many reasons why individuals might prefer not to use estate agents (including cultural preferences as well as institutional barriers), Fenton (1977) shows that attempts to minimize the anxieties associated with discrimination and racism may be particularly important. In behavioural terms, this often means searching through local social networks and agreeing informally on a sale. An alternative avoidance strategy, again noted among black buyers, is to deal only with a vendor from one's own cultural group. This practice may signal the beginnings of a dual owner occupied housing market operating alongside that already observed in the private rental sector.

In Bradford, Cater (1981) found that Asians who purchase their homes through white estate agents account for only a small proportion of property transfers to Asians (even here, the sales concerned usually involve cheap, old properties located in Asian-dominated areas). Asian estate agents therefore deal with the majority of Asian purchases where an intermediary is used. According to Cater, their practices are encouraging the development of a split market, since they sell at prices well above the inner city norm for a given property type (usually terraced houses) and above those asked by white agents operating in the same area. Moreover, although Asian vendors aspire to promote certain 'good' residential areas for their Asian buyers, they in fact 'operate in a predominantly residual market, selling dwellings for Asians to Asians, and thus helping to reproduce the present pattern of ethnic residential segregation' (Cater 1981: 176).

The operation of the housing finance system, the practices of property developers and exchange professionals, and the development of an informal housing market all mean that black households are over-represented among those least likely to receive the financial subsidies and psychological benefits associated with home ownership. Because of the quality, condition and location of their dwellings, black owners must also bear the physical hardship and economic consequences of the growing repairs problem in this part of the private housing stock. Even so, there is evidence that black owners have less opportunity to use public subsidies to improve their properties than do their white counterparts.

Rex and Tomlinson's (1979) survey in Birmingham's inner city showed that although over a quarter of owner occupiers (and almost one-third of West Indian respondents) had applied for an improvement grant, the success rates for West Indians and Asians were 26.2 and 35.4 per cent, respectively, compared with 69.4 per cent for white owners. The 1982 PSI survey also showed that although a higher proportion of black than white owner occupiers apply for local authority improvement grants, only 45 per cent of surveyed West Indians (in contrast with 65 per cent of Asians and whites) were successful in obtaining them. Taking into account the evidence of those who had not applied for a grant, and in view of the generally poorer housing conditions of black owners, Brown (1984: 80) concludes that the improvement grant schemes are not benefiting some of those who need them most. The reason may not be direct discrimination but the fact that 'information on the terms of eligibility, the application procedures and the types of work covered is inadequately targeted towards ethnic minorities'.

This all implies that black owners must make a proportionately higher investment of personal savings than whites in order to acquire basic amenities and a tolerable level of comfort. Oc's (1987) study of Housing Action Areas in Leicester, Bristol and London suggests that this level of investment is beyond the means of many black residents. Johnson and Cross (1984) show further that even where Asian owners now have relatively low levels of housing need (defined in terms of basic amenities) this is frequently accounted for by their relatively high expenditure on property improvement.

In some respects, the issue of who uses grants and why may be of marginal concern for the future of much of the inner city housing stock. The costs of improving large tracts of properties are becoming prohibitive given residents' limited financial resources and the relatively small size of the improvement grants themselves. (Karn et al (1986a) show that by far the greatest proportion of expenditure on repairs and maintenance – between half and three-quarters – comes from household savings; improvement grants contribute less than a fifth of resources used). Today, many properties in these more run-down areas would not sell for more than the initial costs of purchase and improvement. There is, it seems, a 'valuation gap' – notably in the north and parts of the midlands – which may deter people from improving in future and which condemns many black owner occupiers to homes that are depreciating in relative, if not absolute, terms. The 1987 White Paper offers little consolation here, relinquishing any collective responsibility for repairs, and indicating that improvement grants will be related not to house condition but rather to ability to pay.

As in the privately rented sector, there is evidence among owner occupiers not only that social and economic policies can have the unanticipated outcome of reinforcing segregation, but also that local institutional practices tend to inrease the probability of this being coupled with relative disadvantage. Despite local authorities' mandate to eliminate racial discrimination and promote equal opportunities, they have virtually no power to intervene in the expanding owner occupied sector. If central government's faith in the self-regulating capacity of the market is not well placed, then the owner occupied sector of the housing system will continue to be instrumental in the reproduction of racial inequality.

Council housing: uneven rations of a scarce resource

The overall improvement in black people's housing conditions over the past 15 years is accounted for in large part by their access to the public sector. By 1982, 41 per cent of West Indian households and 53 per cent of Bangladeshis (though only 19 per cent of Asians overall) had secured a council tenancy, as compared with somewhat under a third (30 per cent) of white households. This tenure shift also explains the limited amount of desegregation, particularly of Afro-Caribbeans, that was observed between 1961 and 1971.[4] Nevertheless, a recent survey of British social attitudes showed that only 21 per cent of black respondents, as compared with 36 per cent of the population as a whole, find council estates pleasant to live in; this, as the authors note, is just one contribution to the 'growing evidence that the council estates on which ethnic minorities are concentrated *are* the most unpleasant of council estates' (Jowell and Airey 1984: 91). In England and Wales this impression is confirmed by the most recent PSI survey, which indicates that, even controlling for number of council homes lived in, time of allocation and households characteristics, black tenants live in smaller, more crowded homes than do their white counterparts, tend more often to be allocated flats (rather than houses) and their flats tend to be located on the higher floors of multi-storey blocks (Brown 1984).

Even in the public sector, where homes are supposedly allocated according to 'need' rather than ability to pay, black people have received the least desirable tenancies and are clustered in the more run-down and difficult-to-let parts of the council rented stock. This pattern is confirmed in all the recent CRE investigations (the details of which are discussed below). In the past this disadvantageous position reflected local politicians' assumptions about the exclusionary desires of a (majority) white electorate. Today, racial inequality persists despite many local governments' commitment to the principles of anti-racism. The policies and practices which have sustained residential segregation during both these phases, to the relative disadvantage of black people, are outlined below.

Access and eligibility

Daniel (1968) showed that even after living in Britain for as many as five or ten years, immigrants from the New Commonwealth rarely registered for council accommodation because they believed their eligibility could be questioned. Other research has shown the truth of that perception. It is therefore worth considering at greater length how black people were so effectively, and for so long, prevented from exercising their rights to receive subsidized shelter.

Initially, there is no doubt that such exclusion was pursued deliberately. In a rare historical case study of the local politics of race, Rich (1987a) detects an explicit attitude of 'containment' among Birmingham's councillors even during the 1960s. In 1966, for instance, the Birmingham Borough Labour Conference openly rejected a proposal to allocate council houses on new estates to black applicants. Other exclusionary strategies were more veiled, appealing to the wisdom of the formal rules governing housing allocation (particularly residence requirements which afforded white households privileged access to welfare rights – and ultimately to economic benefits – simply because of their longstanding local connection). Whatever the stated rationale, councillors in the mid-1970s had a strong interest in trying to ensure that the procedures for gaining a good quality council tenancy were more favourable to the main body of their electorate than to the black minority (see Ward and Sims 1981). Rex and Tomlinson (1979) go as far as to claim that Birmingham (which retained a five-year residence requirement until 1977) systematically exaggerated the number of 'native' whites requiring accommodation specifically to avoid rehousing black families. Similar evidence of exclusionary practices for political gain is discussed by Haddon (1970) and Hiro (1971). The effectiveness of such practices can hardly be in doubt when it is considered that, during the mid-1960s, white households were 26 times more likely than their black counterparts to secure a council home.

Although local politicians in the major cities are now likely to regard black voters as an electoral asset, the legacy of past antipathy still infuses a range of bureaucratic procedures regulating entry to the public sector. This is true for each of the three common entry points: rehousing following clearance (or, more recently following 'decanting' to allow improvements or modernization); rehousing from the conventional waiting lists; and rehousing due to unintentional homelessness.

Chapter 3 showed that during slum clearance in the late 1960s the majority of new council properties were reserved for the mainly white occupants of clearance zones. Where clearance spilled over into the 1970s, it did offer rehousing opportunities for some black families but only for a brief period. Today black people are often *more* likely than whites to be 'decanted', owing to their marked over-representation in those poorer parts of the existing stock where repairs and renovation are most urgent (CRE 1984b). However, since new building in the public sector is at such a low ebb, their prominence on the 'decant' lists does not promise a move into new or high quality dwellings. Thus, the impact of public spending cuts has been particularly severe for black tenants, who are disproportionately likely to continue to live in properties in greatest need of repair and modernization.

Black households are also at a disadvantage when seeking housing through the general waiting lists. This is because a number of indirectly discriminatory rules exist (in addition to the residence requirements that have already been mentioned) and are routinely applied as housing departments attempt to keep their waiting lists down to a manageable size. These rules include the following. (a) Owner occupiers tend to be excluded, on the assumption that they are already adequately housed. This has discriminated against Asians, who, as owners, are over-represented in the most severely deteriorating parts of the private housing stock. (b) Points systems have afforded less favourable treatment to unmarried ('common law') couples. In the past, this has been regarded as a factor unjustly excluding a disproportionate number of Afro-Caribbean partnerships. (c) Owing to a shortage of large dwellings, joint or extended families have been required to split up to obtain public housing. This rule has discouraged many Asian families from applying to the council. (d) Persons from separated families have not been allowed to register, even though they anticipate the arrival of dependents from overseas. These rules all help to explain the delayed entry of black people into the public sector, and also account for the later and lesser entry of Asians than of Afro-Caribbeans.[5]

The other key route into council housing is through homelessness. As the council stock dwindles, and homelessness increases, this route is becoming increasingly significant in the major cities, and may now account for a much larger proportion of allocations than do the waiting lists. Of the black people sampled in the CRE's (1984a) enquiry in Hackney 46 per cent were homeless, and Phillips's (1986) study of council house offers in Tower Hamlets found that 37 per cent of Asians' offers, as compared to 4 per cent of other offers, went to homeless people.

Local authorities have a responsibility to house homeless people under the 1977 Housing (Homeless Persons) Act. To benefit from this – to receive a council home or to be placed in bed and breakfast accommodation at public expense (which is increasingly the norm, especially in London) – applicants must be deemed unintentionally homeless. Pressures on the housing stock have drawn increasingly tight boundaries around this definition. Early in 1987, the London Borough of Tower Hamlets threatened to evict 44 Bangladeshi households (12 of whom *were* made homeless), arguing that because they left their homes in Bangladesh voluntarily the council has no obligation to house them. An appeal court ruling to the contrary[6] has left the decision substantially unchanged (*Independent*, 7 June 1988). In November 1987 a second London Borough, Camden, announced plans to repatriate some Irish tenants under the provisions of the 1986 Housing and Planning Act, and suggested that, in principle, such a move could be extended to homeless Bangladeshis (*Guardian*, 13 November 1987, p. 1). These examples illustrate the danger that in attempting to control a crisis of homelessness local authorities, bound by their obligations under the Homeless Persons Act, will develop racially exclusionary practices to minimize their managerial and financial difficulties.

Although the critical research of the early 1970s prompted many local authorities to adopt equal opportunities housing programmes, subsequent investigations reveal continuing discrimination at all points of entry into the housing system: black people are still unfairly excluded from parts of the stock whether they apply via general waiting lists, because they are homeless, because they require a transfer or by qualifying as 'decants' from properties undergoing demolition or refurbishing (CRE 1984a, 1985a; Phillips 1986). Even now the evidence is that black households are not eligible for the same rights to shelter as their white counterparts. They may manage to secure a place in the queue for public housing (indeed, in 1982 a higher proportion of black than white applicants remained on the waiting lists) but as local authorities stocks diminish this offers no guarantee of accommodation. As a welfare benefit, access to state-subsidised shelter continues to be racially differentiated.

Allocation and transfer

Research completed over the past 15 years indicates that it is not merely at the point of access that black people are disadvantaged in public housing. Racial inequalities are also sustained by the processes of allocation and transfer. The tendency for black households to receive the worst quality properties and to be concentrated into certain estates – usually those of the poorest quality in the inner areas of cities – is widely reported. As a welfare right, therefore, black people's housing circumstances have been qualitatively as well as quantitatively inferior to those experienced by whites.

The earliest thorough accounts of how housing departments discriminate against black tenants when allocating their properties were completed in the mid-1970s by Valerie Karn and her colleagues working in Birmingham, and by members of the SSRC's Research Unit on Ethnic Relations based on casework in Manchester and Birmingham. Henderson and Karn (1984, 1987) offer a penetrating account of how black people's disadvantage in council housing arises at the intersection between bureaucratic expedience and discretionary judgements. These authors show that although finely tuned procedures are adopted by local authorities in an attempt to grade applicants according to their need for housing, it is only through an additional informal grading of tenants' 'respectability' that an effective system for rationing homes – a scarce resource of variable quality – can be sustained.

Using a variety of examples, Henderson and Karn (1984) demonstrate how racial stereotypes (as well as images of class and gender) become associated with scales of distinction and disrepute, which are in turn translated into offers of better or worse tenancies. A 'common sense' association of black people (as well as of women and the lower classes) with opprobrium provides some working criteria by which to meet management imperatives (these being let to homes quickly, while avoiding conflict, discontent or resistance from the (white) majority of tenants and applicants). As a consequence of giving the worst homes in the worst areas to households who fare badly according to a number of subjectively assigned qualitative criteria (such as housekeeping standards), public housing is allocated according to hierarchical rather than egalitarian principles and the 'geographical segregation of West Indians and Asians and the poorest white families in the private sector is being repeated and reinforced in the public sector' (Karn 1981: 21). This pattern of reinforcement is neatly exposed by Flett (1979), whose study of allocations in Greater London, Manchester and Birmingham (where the majority of black tenants are housed) revealed in all three centres a net suburbanization of white households and an increased concentration of black people in inner city neighbourhoods. Such trends are inevitable in MacKay's (1977: 182) opinion as long as the public housing system 'continues to be geared to the "respectable" working class rather than to the economically marginal or to a black population largely unloved and possibly feared by many white public housing tenants'.

This pattern does not seem to have altered markedly in recent years, despite local governments' generally greater commitment to anti-racist principles. This is apparent from Phillips' (1986) study of over 5000 offers made to GLC tenants in the London Borough of Tower Hamlets between 1983 and 1984 (1000 of the offers were made to Asians, mainly Bengalis). Despite specific guidelines to the contrary, the segregation of Asian tenants was clearly being reinforced by allocations procedures which effectively steered applicants towards areas dominated by their own ethnic group, often irrespective of any stated preference. This made it much more likely that Asians would be offered older properties, without gardens and without central heating. Although anti-racist guidelines had removed the discretion associated with dubious practices like the grading of housekeeping, subjective judgements continued to infuse the allocations system with bias against black householders (such judgements were based on whites' supposed antipathy towards Asians' cultural practices, as well as on ostensibly benevolent concerns about the perceived risk of racial attack).

The same kind of conclusions emerged from the CRE's (1984a) investigation in Hackney. This study was not able to compare the quality of properties allocated in such detail, but it did confirm that black people still tend, irrespective of household composition, to receive flats rather than houses and older rather than newer properties. Like the other studies cited in this chapter, the Hackney enquiry did not have access to information on applicants' incomes – a factor that Clapham and Kintrea (1986) argue is generally an important determinant of the quality of council homes achieved. It does, however, contain information which might be seen as controlling for the effects of income. According to Clapham and Kintrea (1986), income influences public sector allocations because it enables less desperate (more wealthy) households to refuse offers and so wait until a 'suitable' (good quality) tenancy becomes available. In Hackney, however, nearly all applicants whether black or white, accepted their first offer. Here, 'ability to wait' could not have been a key factor introducing racial inequality into the allocation process (though it *is* interesting that black people were more likely than whites to accept the first offer because they felt they had no real choice and believed they would not have fared better by waiting).

The related CRE (1984b) investigation in Liverpool, which adopts a 10-

year reference period, includes a wider range of measures of housing quality, and still finds marked racial inequalities on almost every count.[7] This study exposes a factor other than income which may account for the differential ability of black and white households to 'bargain' for better quality council properties. Here, the best offers were secured by those households who had made representations to the council through advocates such as councillors and social workers. Significantly, only 13 per cent of black applicants as compared with 36 per cent of whites had secured such representation. This limited bargaining power, coupled with black people's apparently lesser knowledge of the extent and availability of the council stock, meant that their 'choice' of area of residence was 'easily directed through offers of accommodation by housing staff' (CRE 1984b: 67). Informal stereotyping of a kind mentioned earlier meant that black applicants tended to be 'steered' towards existing areas of black settlement in the worst parts of the housing and urban environment. Survey evidence suggests that this is an active rather than passive process: as many as a quarter of black applicants (but only 12 per cent of whites) believed that council allocations were unfair because residential 'choice' was so tightly controlled by housing managers.

The disadvantage conferred by housing allocation procedures appears to be exacerbated rather than offset by the transfer system. Karn's (1981) research in the mid-1970s shows that white applicants receive a disproportionate number of available transfers and are over-represented among those allowed to move into newer houses. This privilege reflects their longer average tenure as council renters, which allows them more time to 'prove' their suitability for better homes (by maintaining standards, paying rent promptly and so on). Although the later study in Liverpool (CRE 1984b) found that black people, by then, had a higher likelihood of securing a transfer than whites (reflecting their greater absolute need for rehousing), 40 per cent of black transferrers compared with only 21 per cent of whites were allocated poor or average quality stock, and almost one-half of the white transferrers but less than one-third of blacks received 'excellent' properties. These differences were not related to household characteristics, and were maintained whether or not tenants had stated their area preference. Nationally, too, black tenants are now more likely than whites to be awaiting transfer to better parts of the housing stock: the 1982 PSI survey indicates that one-quarter of black tenants (compared with one-eighth of white tenants) remain on the transfer lists. Given the pattern and rate of council house sales discussed in chapter 3, their prospects of securing a better home must be slim.

Dispersal versus equality

This review of the local housing system indicates that racial disadvantage is conferred by a spectrum of markets and institutions as they dispense homes (and locations) according to both need and ability to pay. Barriers in access to mortgage finance and to the tax subsidies associated with ownership are paralleled in the public sector by disadvantage at the points of entry to, allocation of and transfer within a diminishing stock of council housing. These processes all help to reproduce the racial inequalities that are expressed in, and moulded by, residential structure.

Local government has intervened in two ways in attempting to develop fairer systems of access to the range of urban resources that is indexed by location. The first, 'dispersal', came as a mandate from central government in 1975 (although experiments had often been taking place before that time); the second, anti-racism, is local authorities' own response to the 1976 Race Relations Act and is more often resisted than assisted by the political centre.

By the end of the 1960s it had formally been acknowledged that public housing, which is allocated according to criteria other than those dictated by the market, provided a unique opportunity to extend to black people the right not just to better homes and neighbourhoods, but also to a range of the other goods and services that are differentially distributed over space. In the wake of the Cullingworth Committee recommendations, a number of local authorities began to build dispersal policies into their systems of council house allocation. Cullingworth had supported this strategy on the condition that it could be implemented in accordance with the wishes of the black population.[8] However, in the absence of central guidelines, dispersal policies became 'little more than a rather vague and general attitude' among housing managers (Smith and Whalley 1975: 92), and the outcomes were less than satisfactory. Flett (1979) shows how, despite attempted dispersal in Greater London, by 1976 70 per cent of black families housed by what was then the GLC lived in just four boroughs: Tower Hamlets, Southwark, Lambeth and Hackney. 'Dispersal' had produced a *greater* borough-specific concentration of black households than in previous years! Flett (1979) also provides evidence to show that this reorganization of residential space was not in line with tenants' choices. As many as 31 per cent of black households (compared with 21 per cent of whites) did not get a home in their preferred borough; 53 per cent of black people (but 35 per cent of whites) were given a home outside their preferred area; and 84 per cent of blacks (and 64 per cent of whites) moved to an area where they previously had no friends. Re-sorting occurred without desegregation and, as a consequence of local authority practice, 'whilst blacks were staying in inner London, and in that sense not dispersing, many had lost one of the great advantages of concentration: the support of their own network of friends and acquaintances' (Flett 1979: 187).

Some clues as to why dispersal failed can be gleaned from one of Britain's best documented 'trials' conducted in Birmingham between 1969 and 1975. Here the policy appears to have been less a gesture of unqualified altruism than a pragmatic response to the exclusionary demands of a small group of white tenants. It was precipitated by a petition and threatened rent strike by nine white tenants concerned about the entry of a second black household into their block of twelve maisonettes. Following this incident, a dispersal policy was implemented to ensure that, in future, each black household would be separated by at least five white tenancies. The stated aim of these measures was to break the existing trend towards the concentration of West Indians in the post-war inner ring properties, of Asians in pre-1919 middle ring terraces and of whites in post-war outer city estates.

Not only did this quota policy prove unlawful under the 1976 Race Relations Act (since it denied people homes on the grounds of colour), but it failed to redress the inequalities experienced by black people in the public housing system. Flett et al. (1979) show that, despite the stated intention of disperseal, black people who expressed a preference to live on a 'white' estate were less likely to have their preferences met than were white applicants who requested a 'white' estate. Overall, the preferences of all applicants were most likely to be met when they specified an area in which their own 'racial' group was relatively prominent. According to Henderson and Karn (1987) the net effect of the public housing allocation system in Birmingham between 1971 and 1978 was to reinforce Asians' existing pattern of segregation within the middle ring (of Edwardian and Victorian terraces), and to move the locus of Afro-Caribbean segregation towards the inner core (of flatted estates). The most marked trend of all was the continuing suburbanization of white families; this in itself must have increased the intensity of segregation.

This kind of outcome is only to be expected in the context of a housing shortage and in a situation where black people are over-represented among those in greatest average need. To have succeeded (as a mechanism to promote racial equality) dispersal would have had to offer black tenants privileged access to the better parts of the housing stock – a strategy which local politicians would never entertain. Karn (1981) points out that, irrespective of any stated policy, it is in the day-to-day interests of management that black tenants should sustain demand for inner city properties, despite the poorer quality of such housing. It may be neither accidental nor entirely innocent, therefore, that the dispersal policies observed by Flett et al. (1979) do little to further the interests of black householders.

By the early 1980s, the crude spatial determinism of dispersal had been abandoned by local governments. Local politicians began to recognize that dispersal policies were vulnerable to stereotyped beliefs about the demands of the white electorate, too simplistic to meet the social needs of black tenants and impossible to work in circumstances of resource shortage without denying black people access to much of the housing they might wish to occupy.[9] This change of attitude was consistent with the findings of academics such as Jones (1980), Lee (1977) and Rex (1981a), who all point out the shortcomings of dispersal ideology. It simply diverted attention away from the sharp inequalities of wealth and status that deny black people access to the rewards and life chances dispensed within the housing market. This failing panacea was therefore replaced at a local level by the more comprehensive philosophy of anti-racism (as we shall see in chapter 5, the response of central government was quite different).

Anti-racism is designed to affect all areas of social, economic and institutional life within the domain of local government (Gilroy (1987) and Phillips (1987b) discuss the problems and achievements of such an approach). Municipal (as distinct from 'popular') anti-racism attempts not only to tackle racism within public and state institutions, but also to oppose the very notion of racial categorization and the beliefs that sustain it.[10] In practice, the problem of institutionalized racism has attracted most effort, particularly in those areas of public life over which local government attempts to retain some control (education, social services and housing).

Institutional racism occurs where the 'normal' operation of organizational rules and procedures is racially discriminatory (detailed accounts are given by Phillips (1987a, b) and Williams (1985)). In order to eliminate this deep-seated source of inequality, local governments' anti-racist strategy has advanced along at least three distinct fronts.

First, although a hallmark of institutionalized racism is its detachment from the intentionality of individual managers and administrators, it is argued that some racist practices must be regarded as the product of uncritical rather than unconscious action. The anti-racist movement deals with this through racism awareness training (RAT), which aims to enhance bureaucrats' understanding of the extent to which their own routine activity can inadvertently sustain racial inequality. RAT provides individuals at all levels within an organization with the knowledge or 'enlightenment' they require to check any tendency to work with stereotypes and to challenge informal procedures which appear to have discriminatory effects.

Secondly, since institutional racism refers to forms of racism that are systematically reproduced through an organization's ostensibly aracial practices, it is acknowledged that the source of racial inequality will only be exposed if records are kept, monitored and used to inform policy. Although widely acknowledged as important, this is an area where local authorities have been slower to respond to the anti-racist challenge. Only two of the 40 local authority housing departments that keep race-coded data (Lambeth and Lewisham) produce regular monitoring reports, and a recent investigation of all its members by the Association of Metropolitan Authorities concluded that as a consequence, with respect to ensuring racial equality in housing, 'the majority of authorities have a long way to go in terms of policy and practice, and many have yet to get started' (AMA 1985: 7).

Finally, and most fundamentally, the anti-racist movement offers formal recognition that institutional racism is not a process confined to housing or to any other single system of resource distribution. It is, rather, a pervasive process sustained across a range of institutions – housing, education, employment, health and social services – that have procedures which combine to produce a mutually reinforcing pattern of racial inequality.This acknowledges that virtually all large organizations concerned with the allocation of power and resources develop conventions to distinguish the deserving from the undeserving and the reputable from the debased, in order to help prioritize applicants queuing for goods and services. Virtually all these conventions invoke 'racial' attributes, tacitly or explicitly, as a criterion for exclusion or inclusion in the dispensation of scarce resources. Anti-racism acknowledges this in principle, and the Race Relations legislation gives local authorities a mandate to deal with it in practice.

The anti-racist movement is important because almost all state responsibility for securing racial equality has now been decentralized. However, it is increasingly apparent that local governments have few of the resources they need – fiscal or political – to tackle an interlocking system of racial inequality across a broad front. The *powers* required to pursue the anti-racist goal have instead been gradually concentrated into the hands of central government and, in many instances, passed on to the market. Even the most committed of local authorities may therefore have limited scope to challenge local institutions when they work to augment the racial differentiation of residential space. I have so far offered some evidence as to how this has occurred; chapters 5 and 6 consider *why* it has happened in a society where ideas about race have never formally been invoked to control access to citizenship rights.

Notes

1 These investigations found a breach of sections 20, 21, 30 and 33 of the 1976 Race Relations Act, uncovering evidence of how lettings agencies omitted to provide black applicants with the opportunity to view certain accommodation, failed to let certain properties to black applicants, instructed staff to discriminate against black applicants and assisted their landlord clients to discriminate against potential tenants.

2 At a meeting on current issues in housing management convened by the Scottish Federation of Housing Associations on 9 May 1986 (and attended by the author) it was clear that few of the housing associations represented either catered for or monitored their relationship with the black population. It was, moreover, apparent from the discussion that there are three areas where indirect discrimination against black applicants is almost inevitably occuring: nearly all associations had closed waiting lists (and could not, therefore, be available to new black applicants in the foreseeable future); many required local connections as a criterion for entry (which in practice could exclude people outside a predominantly white Scottish social network and so parallels the discredited local authority residence requirement; it also discriminates against many black people not only because of their status as immigrants but also because of existing levels of social segregation); and many avoid taking on the kinds of properties most suitable for the extended families of the Asian community (i.e. they avoid the larger properties which tend to be in poor repair or are deemed unsuitable for conversion).

3 In a one-year period between 1978 and 1979, Asian and white applicants for local authority mortgages requested more or less the same proportion of the purchase price of their prospective dwellings. However, in the two six-month periods examined, Asians received a mortgage of between 6 and 10 per cent less than they requested, whereas the corresponding figures for white applicants were 4–6 per cent.

4 Their virtual exclusion from public housing in the early 1960s considerably limited the areal distribution of the black population. Even limited admission to the public sector therefore produced a measurable decrease in the intensity of segregation. This is documented by Lee (1977), Peach and Shah (1980) and Robinson (1980c). The dominant process was still a 'piling up' in areas of existing settlement rather than a spread into new areas of the city.

5 Robinson (1980c) offers a different explanation for Asians' late entry to council housing – the unsuitable location of the available stock. He argues that once the location and character of lettings offered socially and economically advantageous alternatives to owning, Asians entered into public renting in greater numbers. Cater (1981) interprets this same surge of applications as a response to the

restricted availability of mortgage finance, which removed the option to buy for a considerable proportion of Asian households.

6 *Regina* v. *Tower Hamlets London Borough Council, Ex parte Monaf and others*, 27 April 1988. The judges ruled that the council had a duty to house the children and should therefore reconsider the decision to evict.

7 This is the most comprehensive of the recent investigations, analysing 5000 lettings between 1971 and 1981, and controlling for a wide range of attributes of both tenants and dwellings.

8 There were, at the time, a number of arguments which could be construed as lending support to the concept of dispersal. West Indians living outside the main areas of black residence in London had better quality dwellings than their more segregated counterparts, even controlling for socio-economic class and demographic variables (Lee 1977). A report by the CRC (1977) found that both black and white people in 'less multi racial areas' were better satisfied with their home and district of residence than people living in 'areas of ethnic concentration'. In political circles, it was argued that dispersal encouraged integration and good race relations, that it was necessary to prevent racial polarization in schools, and it would alleviate racial disadvantage in housing.

9 Thus the emphasis of local authority policy is now shifting away from ideas of dispersal quotas and towards the notion of 'equality targets' as described by Seager and Singh (1984). That is, attempts to break the association between segregation and disadvantage now rely less on eradicating the former and more on alleviating the latter.

10 Anti-racism has been most vigorously pursued in the London region, and included a vast publicity campaign by the GLC which culminated in the designation of 1984 as London's anti-racist year.

5   Political Interpretations of 'Racial Segregation'

We must ask ourselves to what extent we want Great Britain to become a
multi-racial community . . . a question which affects the future of our own
race and breed is not one that we should leave merely to chance.

Martin Lindsay, 5 December 1958

Residential segregation is a medium for the reproduction of racial
inequality. Neither economic development nor the welfare state has
undermined this process. Neither centrally dispensed policy nor locally
sensitive practices have reversed the trend. Central governments have
shaped segregation; the interlocking activities of local bureaucracies have
sustained it. Focusing on the first of these tiers of government – where
most power is now concentrated – this chapter attempts to explain why
nearly every major decision relating to the housing environment of post-
war Britain has directly and cumulatively (if seemingly inadvertently)
contributed to a racially iniquitous division of residential space.

Britain has no domestic history of enforced social separatism on
ostensibly racial grounds. All permanent residents have theoretically equal
claim to the rights of citizenship (even though the right of residence is
itself contentious and divisive). For systematic inequalities to persist in this
context they must be not only reproduced through material forces (related
to the production and distribution of resources, including housing), but
also legitimized by appeal to what is normal, reasonable and tolerable in an
advanced liberal democracy. Only by exploring the processes by which
politicians attach legitimacy to the nature and consequences of public
policy can we begin to appreciate *why*, in a society that portrays itself as
open, just and at times egalitarian, it has been possible for residential
differentiation to become, and remain, an index of racial inequality.

This chapter shows that 'racial segregation' is a politically constructed
problem as well as a policy outcome: it is a symbol in the minds of

legislators as well as the arena in which black people experience urban life. This construction is informed by a sequence of political ideas about race and immigration. At any one time, these images determine (and rationalize) the range of 'solutions' that may be put into effect. By analysing the relationships between problem construction and policy solution, I will show how responses to the official problem of racial segregation have diverted attention from social inequality and given impetus to public policies which, while themselves racially divisive, are rarely pertinent to the effective management of residential space.

The politics of race

The thrust of my argument is that to understand why 'racial segregation' persists it is necessary to encase measurements of residential structure and analyses of the operation of markets and institutions within a broader understanding of the politics of race. Until recently, sociology and political science had paid scant attention to the impact of race-related issues on the development of mainstream public policy (despite a vigorous interest in the segregated arena of race relations and immigration legislation). Solomos (1986a) indicates that even as late as the mid-1980s scholars showed little interest in the political management of race, rarely paid serious attention to the role of racism in British political discourse and hardly ever attempted to trace its impact through to specific policy areas. With a few exceptions (notably in the work of Zig Layton-Henry and Paul Rich and in their edited collection, *Race, Government and Politics in Britain*) this continues to be true.

The most justifiable reasons for this apparent neglect reflect a more general problem of linking political decision making with the belief systems of legislators (or, in this case, of specifying the relationship between racial ideology and policies which are explicitly or inadvertently racially biased). The complexity of such an undertaking is documented by Hogwood (1987). Most persuasively, it can be argued that policy is influenced more by the economy, and especially by the pressures exerted by corporate interests, than by political beliefs or partisan ideals (Dye 1976). Some Marxian analyses of racism, making a causal link between the changing requirements of British capitalism and shifts in policy towards racialized minorities, would also favour this view. McKay and Cox (1979), however, argue that economic factors constrain rather than determine policy outcomes in Britain and therefore do not preclude the intrusion of political ideology into a fairly wide range of legislation. According to Sharpe and Newton (1984) such penetration is likely to be much more marked in Britain, where party lines are sharply drawn in ideological terms, than in the USA, for instance, where ideological distinctions are much less clear cut.

Additionally, it might be suggested that legislative decisions are more sensitive to outside pressures (such as the experience of other countries, the findings of academic research or the weight of public opinion as orchestrated by the mass media) and to the decisions of influential bureaucrats than to the tenor of Parliamentary debate. This view, however, begs the question of *why* some external pressures rather than others are used by politicians to bargain for particular policy ends, and it assigns unsubstantiated innovatory powers to civil servants, whose preference is usually to maintain the status quo. Moreover, for much of the period under discussion there is evidence that Parliament was either remarkably active in its legislative capacity or vociferous in contesting and informing the legislative demands of a Cabinet elite (see Crowe 1980; Schwartz 1980). As Minogue and Biddis (1987) show, it is only in the past few years that the course of British politics can be regarded as being inextricably tied to the Prime Minister's personality (and accordingly, my treatment of the 1980s will focus particularly on the influence of 'Thatcherism' as a distinctively British form of neo-conservatism).

It is important in any analysis of the political process to acknowledge the strength of corporatism, the influence of international and extra-parliamentary political communities, and the vagaries of bureaucracy. There is nothing in this, however, that denies the efficacy of Parliamentary bargaining itself as a factor affecting the scope of policy, the kind of impact that policy can have and, above all, the legitimacy of particular policies as a form of government. Undeniably, political constructions of social problems are sensitive to a variety of economic, bureaucratic and pragmatic constraints, but at the same time the fine tuning of the legislative agenda is acutely sensitive to what Freeman (1979) calls the proximate determinants of policy (such as political styles, partisan ideological debate and the wider belief systems of decision makers). Crucial among these is what I shall term political culture – the historically grounded systems of shared meanings that are routinely negotiated to ease the operation of liberal democracy.[1] Political culture cuts across party ideology to express common (though contested) aspirations regarding the management of state and nation. It cannot, therefore, be mapped directly on to legislation; but it does provide the basis of a Parliamentary 'common sense' which tacitly guides politicians both in defining policy problems and in selecting appropriate solutions.

In an attempt to analyse this 'common sense' in relation to the politics of race, I draw on a reading of Parliamentary debates and proceedings between 1945 anmd 1987, set in the context of contemporary events in domestic and foreign affairs. This approach, which relies heavily on an analysis of political discourse, is favoured on the assumption that, if politicians are correctly viewed not as passive respondents to various outside pressures but as active mediators of these pressures, then 'the language and arguments which policy makers use can be a fruitful source of data on their information, perceptions and values' and policy itself will be more accurately understood as the result 'not only of power struggles or environmental constraints, but of argument, reflection and persuasion' (Freeman 1979: 11–12). Following Freeman, therefore, I regard political discourse as an index of the cultural context infusing those broad governmental strategies in which specific policies and actions are embedded. The perspective this offers on the construction of political problems can, as Reeves (1983) points out, be related not only to decision making but also to the *absence* of decision making which, in the light of chapter 3, is particularly pertinent to the present discussion.

The core of my analysis is restricted to proceedings in the House of Commons (the referencing convention is given in chapter 3, note 2). Because it exemplifies the elective principle, the Commons provides an arena for political bargaining and negotiation which is important for both the construction and the legitimation of policy. Political discourse impinges on policy directly (through the amendment and passing of legislation) and indirectly (by virtue of its relevance to the orientation of select committees and through its ability, via the mass media, to mobilize public opinion). Even more crucially, by exploiting the power of rhetoric and by appeal to personal and constituents' demands and experiences, Parliamentary debate becomes the medium through which Governments win normative support for their legislative programmes. As Miliband (1982: 20) observes, the Commons is the embodiment of liberal democracy in Britain and its proceedings provide 'the absolutely indispensable legitimation for the government of the country'.

In the sections that follow, I shall attempt to show how the politics of race generally, and of racial segregation in particular, have impinged on both the legislative and the legitimizing roles of Parliament. My point of departure is around 1945 although, as Rich (1984/5) indicates, segregationism has infused debate throughout the present century, evincing 'deep historical roots in British political thought on racial and cultural difference' (p. 86). In the post-war years the political problematic of racial segregation has at least three identifiable phases.[2]

The first phase begins in the years 1945–8 as politicians grappled with the delicacies of replacing Empire with Commonwealth and, in doing so, inserted 'racial' issues firmly into the domain of foreign affairs. This period ends between 1958 and 1962 when civil unrest forced race relations on to the domestic political agenda at the same time as a reorientation of foreign policy was moving British interests away from the Commonwealth and investing them in Europe. The next phase therefore opens with the formal application of immigration controls and is characterized by an intensification of racial awareness among politicians and the public, as well as by a see-saw of exclusionist and integrationist policy interventions. This period concludes near the end of the 1970s, following a sterling crisis that curbed public spending and brought Margaret Thatcher to the Conservative leadership (in 1975) and subsequently to the Premiership (in 1979). My discussion of this final period is therefore dominated by the consequences of far-reaching changes in the character and influence of British Conservatism.[3]

For each of these periods in turn, I shall explore three inter-related themes which seem pertinent to the interpretation of racial segregation. First, I examine political conceptions of race, identifying the criteria used to signify racial differentiation and showing how this affects the standing of black people in Britain. Secondly, I consider how these shared ideas have impinged on the legislative process by informing the construction of racial segregation as a policy problem. Finally, I examine the solutions this problem has demanded, locating the impact of housing policy as discussed in chapter 3 within the broader framework of the changing politics of race.

The colonial legacy at the end of an empire

Conceptions of race: the Commonwealth ideal

The post-war Labour Government and its Conservative successor treated black people in Britain almost exclusively in the context of foreign policy and colonial affairs. Nevertheless, politicians' early, hidden fears about the domestic impact of 'colonial' immigrants are clearly documented in the post-war Cabinet papers (see Carter et al. 1987; Harris 1987). From the beginning, this tension between hidden concerns and stated agenda was to create a political ambivalence about the status of black Britons that has never been resolved. At the root of this ambivalence lay, on the one hand, politicians' commitment to the pursuit of a Commonwealth ideal and, on the other hand, the tenacity of stereotypes concerning the cultural backwardness and moral inferiority of 'coloured colonials'.

For strategic and symbolic reasons, politicians throughout the 1940s were eager to place Britain at the head of a united Commonwealth of nations. The vision of a tolerant and accommodating 'mother country' was

L. I. H. E.

THE BECK LIBRARY

WOOLTON RD., LIVERPOOL, L16 8ND

deliberately encouraged throughout the war by the Ministry of Information, in a bid to secure the loyalty of the Caribbean colonies. The threat of communism in Europe also increased the urgency of retaining India under the umbrella of British democracy.[4] Equally, the *imagery* of a Commonwealth, led and nurtured by Britain, was important to sustain national pride as the Empire crumbled and decolonization progressed. Thus paternalistic sentiments, disguising supremacist assumptions, dominate a debate on the Colonial Development and Welfare Bill of 1940 which Malcolm MacDonald (as Minister of Health) claimed would deal with 'everything which ministers to the physical, mental or moral development of the Colonial peoples of whom we are the Trustees' (HC 1940, 361, 1). The significance of these assumptions is evident from statements like that of Ivor Thomas who, as Secretary of State for the Colonies, argued: 'We are at the centre of a great Commonwealth and Empire, and as long as the United Kingdom remains at the centre of that great Commonwealth and Empire our voice will never fail to command attention in the councils of the World' (HC 1946/7, 441, 1424). Even as late as 1949, a Conservative Party statement on 'Imperial Policy' identified Empire as the supreme achievement of the British people and claimed that its demise – *if it came* – would strip the country of resources and relegate the nation to a third class power (see Reeves 1983: 114).

So central was this imperialist ideal, and so inviting, as Deakin (1968: 26) notes, was the 'mystique of a multi-racial Commonwealth bridging the gap between rich and poor nations', that the intrinsic 'Britishness' of colonial subjects, whether at home or abroad, was politically unquestionable. Black people in Britain were to be entitled to all the rights associated with citizenship, and this was affirmed in the British Nationality Act of 1948. Although this Act recognized a distinction between the old independent Commonwealth and the remainder of 'Empire' (to become the New Commonwealth) it reasserted the Imperial ideal that anyone born under the Crown could claim equal privilege as a British subject. The Act did not, therefore, affect black people's rights of entry to, and settlement within, Britain, and once settled they were offered not only equality before the law, but also the rights to vote, to seek employment and to claim welfare benefits. In principle, and certainly for legislative purposes, any material differences between black and white Britons were regarded as a temporary phase of cultural adaptation and not as an index of immutable 'racial' difference.

In practice, however, the tenacity of colonial stereotypes tended to outweigh the lure of the Commonwealth ideal. For the most part, black people were regarded as 'fairly exotic creatures known from books, from Hollywood films, from war-time encounters and from the stories of men who had been to Africa or India' (Banton 1985: 30). They were depicted as 'heathens who practised head-hunting, polygamy, and "black magic"' and as 'uncivilised, backward people . . . illiterate, speaking strange languages and lacking proper education' (Fryer 1984: 374). Educational events like London's Colonial Exhibition of June 1949 (which subsequently travelled to the provinces) carried life-size models of 'colonial peoples' and did little to dispel this ethnocentrism. Politicians often identified distinctions rather than commonalities between black and white Commonwealth citizens, so that when Beresford Craddock addressed a Bill to remove the colour bar from colonial territories, he claimed that 95 per cent of Africans were 'primitive people' whose 'sanitary habits are not all that could be desired', who were often 'riddled with a disease of a very unfortunate kind' and whose view on sexual matters was 'entirely different from the attitude of the general run of Europeans' (HC 1954, 514, 2533). Such deep-seated beliefs created a disjunction between the theory and reality of black peoples' access to civil rights in Britain. This was apparent even in the earliest attempts to solicit migrant labour for the post-war economy.

The depression of the 1930s had produced a social climate hostile to immigration and after the war, despite the acute labour demands associated with industrial reconstruction, all migrant labour was treated with suspicion. *Colonial* immigrants, however, were seen as particularly undesirable. The Royal Commission on Population, reporting in 1949, felt unable to welcome a systematic immigration policy without assurances that (para. 329) 'the migrants were of good human stock and not prevented by their religion or race from intermarrying with the host population and becoming merged with it'. With this in mind, politicians put forward, formally and informally, a variety of reasons why 'coloured colonials' might be particularly unsuitable for recruitment.

Four objections were made 'officially' (these are identified by Harris (1987)): that there was insufficient accommodation to house colonial immigrants, especially if they stayed very long; that the incipient black 'ghettoes' of the port areas would be intensified; that industrialists and trade unions found white labour more fitted to the kinds of jobs available; and, most persuasively, that, because of the privilege of a common Commonwealth citizenship, black workers would be entitled to stay in the UK – and claim the benefits associated with this – even if they became unemployed.

This preference for white workers was also expressed informally, articulating deeply held fears about the ill health and poor educational standards of black migrants and depicting them as 'sufferers from an inefficient, cheese-paring colonial administration which, for years, had failed to embark on social, industrial and welfare programmes . . .' (Dean

1987: 307). Such views punctuated a debate on Colonial Affairs in July 1946, in which G. S. Woods identified the 'native populations' as 'victims of abject poverty, ignorance, disease and malnutrition' whose capacity to work on the necessary scale was seriously in doubt (HC 1945/6, 425, 325). There was even concern in the Home Office that black migrants harboured the threat of communist infiltration (see Harris 1987).

These overlapping worries spawned a range of legally questionable administrative rules and procedures which served to debar prospective migrants even before the development of explicit immigration controls (see Carter et al. 1987). Thus, despite the vigour with which Greenwood's 'Operation Westward Ho'[5] was pursued, black labour was solicited only as a last resort when ex-prisoners of war, Polish ex-servicemen and the European Voluntary Workers' scheme failed to meet demand. It was, moreover, always made clear that the jobs of the indigenous population would not be jeopardized by the volume of migrant labour. Black immigration was therefore only ever perceived as an exceptional and short-lived measure required to stimulate the economy; in Harold Davies's view 'having helped our productivity and output, that manpower or woman-power could go back to the Colonies and be a nucleus of productivity there' (HC 1946/7, 441, 1415).

In the post-war years, therefore, British politicians evinced a more marked racial awareness than is commonly supposed. For strategic and symbolic reasons the distinctions between black and white Britons were presented as cultural (moral, behavioural and malleable), rather than biological (inherent, inherited and immutable) in origin. A social boundary had been drawn but, 'officially' at least, the differences it marked were to be subsumed within, and ultimately eroded by, the ideal of a common Commonwealth identity.

Segregation: a passing phase in immigration history

Politicians were never unaware of the problems facing black people in British cities. The post-war Cabinet is known to have discussed the consequences of discrimination in employment and inequality in housing (Thomas 1982) and in 1949 an Inter-departmental Committee on Colonial People in the UK expressed dismay that Britain now contained a 'measure of segregation comparable to that in other parts of the world' (cited in Rich 1986d: 51). This spatial clustering was known to be accompanied by poverty, poor health and overcrowding, which caused suffering both to the migrants and to those 'English' people destined 'to share unwillingly the existing accommodation with immigrants from overseas' (Eric Fletcher, HC 1957, 578, 752). Accordingly, a statement prepared for publication by the Cabinet in 1955 claimed, 'the most serious problem arising at present from coloured immigration is undoubtedly in the field of housing' (cited by Carter et al. 1987: 7). In response, a small band of left-wing MPs (notably Fenner Brockway and Reginald Sorensen) campaigned for the introduction of anti-discrimination legislation. Most, however, attributed the problems associated with segregation to factors other than racism; when the Race Relations Board was established in 1952 it was expected to deal with foreign rather than domestic affairs.

Throughout the post-war decade, both major parties assumed that racism only occurred overseas and that Britain led the world in promoting good 'race relations'. In one of the few early debates on racial discrimination, on 6 May 1949, Tom Driberg praised Britain's successful record achieved 'by our example and leadership in the world, by our actions in the Colonial Empire and in the United Nations, and also, to a much lesser degree, of course – because it does not arise in such a widespread or acute way – by our administration in this country (HC 1948/9, 464, 1398). The dominant assumption was, as F. W. Skinnard put it, that the 'average person in the ordinary little street in village or town just does not know what the colour bar means. . . . There is not the slightest discrimination nor, indeed, the slightest imagination that there should be discrimination, which is an even finer thing' (HC 1948/9, 464, 1417/8).

Insofar as racial segregation was a problem it was seen as the temporary corollary of a supposedly fleeting period of immigration required to stimulate the economy. It was depicted as a passing phase of cultural adaptation experienced by people who possessed the same rights, opportunities and aspirations as white Britons. If prejudice was discerned at all, it was regarded as a consequence, not a cause, of the conditions in which black people lived. As Eric Fletcher put it, while it is 'nobody's fault that people from overseas are content to live in conditions different from those sought by white people' it is also the case that 'overcrowding is causing colour prejudice. Colour prejudice is not spontaneous in this country – British people are friendly to coloured immigrants – but the degree of prejudice is growing as a result of these housing conditions' (HC 1957, 578, 753).

As a newly emerging problem, racial segregation as conceived by decision-makers in post-war Britain, was undoubtedly beginning to produce some politically embarrassing parallels with the USA and South Africa. It posed a dilemma for domestic policy too, by drawing attention to a persisting housing shortage. Fundamentally, however, it was regarded as a temporary inconvenience associated with a fleeting moment in immigration history. Segregation epitomized the transient problems of adjustment faced by a tiny proportion of the population; the 'solutions' pursued were consistent with this belief.

The policy response: laissez-faire

To the extent that post-war migrants were envisaged as permanent settlers (and many were not) they were expected to be absorbed 'naturally' into the lifestyle and institutions of British society. Beliefs about the superiority of Western and British culture, and about immigrants' free access to the rights of citizenship, encouraged governments to favour an assimilationist model which placed the onus on black people 'to adapt to an English and more "civilised" way of life' (Denney 1985: 56). Although politicians believed that 'if they are all dispersed there would be no great problem to which public attention could be drawn' (Ministry of Labour 1948; cited by Dean 1988), Governments took the line of least resistance and waited for segregation to resolve itself. Dispersal was expected to flow unaided from economic growth, regional development and social mobility (as well as from black people's supposed affinity for heavy industrial jobs away from the main seaports (see Rich 1986a)). Assimilation – the anticipated corollary of this – would follow with little assistance apart from good neighbourliness on the part of whites (HC 1948/9, 467, 1410).

Non-interventionism seemed logical to politicians who often took the view that migrants came on their own initiative and should not be eligible for 'special' dispensation.[6] The option of coordinating immigration was also rejected, to avoid taking responsibility for the welfare and accommodation of 'colonial' settlers (Joshi and Carter 1984). Domestic policy towards black people, rooted in the principle of *laissez-faire*, was therefore little more than a smokescreen of colonial nostalgia hiding the widening rift of racial inequality.

This did not mean that the black presence in Britain was surrounded by a policy vacuum, as some have implied. Rather, it reflected the fact that, throughout the 1950s, immigration and its effects (including segregation) were viewed in the context of foreign (rather than domestic) and colonial (rather than European) policy. This orientation precluded any official recognition of the salience of race (or the effects of racism) within the UK. Politicians were determined not to disrupt negotiations for colonial independence with anything that could be construed as a colour bar in Britain.

Most obviously, the delicacies of foreign (colonial) policy kept the anti-immigration lobby at bay, despite an increasing concern about the rate of migration and the size of the black population. But it also helped to legitimize politicians' reluctance to confront the realities of racial inequality, discrimination and disadvantage. Indeed the Bill introduced by Fenner Brockway in June 1956 to outlaw discrimination (the first of nine such attempts) had to be justified more by its ability 'to exert an influence in territories such as South Africa which now practise discrimination' (HC 1956, 554, 25) than by its relevance to public life in Britain. Even then, the Bill was destined to fail as long as politicians' fears about the impact overseas of building race into British legislation outweighed their suspicions that a *de facto* colour bar might already be in place. It was impossible to intervene to secure racial equality (or even to identify racial inequality) in domestic affairs while decolonization and the task of substituting Commonwealth for Empire dominated foreign policy.

This post-war phase of non-interventionism was decisive for the future of black people in Britain. In the absence of strong government directives, and in the context of politicians' assurances that jobs for the white British public were their primary concern, firms inevitably instituted colour quotas and limited black employees' access to skilled and supervisory posts. Employers felt no obligation to provide accommodation for migrant labourers, and a marginal position in the labour market immediately began to promote racial disadvantage in the housing system. This was not offset by public subsidies being poured into housing at the time. Contrary to the welfare ideal, black Britons received virtually none of the benefits associated with council housing for at least 15 years following the war. This exclusionism was to squeeze New Commonwealth immigrants into the deteriorating remnants of the privately rented sector and into the least attractive portions of the owner occupied housing stock. A legacy of government inaction became the first link in a chain of events tying residential differentiation into the structures of racial inequality.

Constructing 'Little England': the racialization of residential space

Conceptions of race: an indigenous racism

Towards the end of the 1950s political ideas about racial differentiation and the import of segregation began to alter. This change coincided with shifts in public opinion, in the orientation of foreign policy and in the fortunes of the economy. It was to mark the end of an era of presumed racial harmony and the beginning of a moment of conflict and confrontation. In this sense, the 1960s can be characterized above all by what Miles and Dunlop (1987) term the racialization of politics – a process by which race (defined by colour and presumed immigration status) became both the explicit object of political debate and the implicit cause of a range of policy-relevant problems.

Race found its way from the periphery to the centre of domestic policy in the aftermath of the 1958 Notting Hill riots. These disturbances (a wide scattering of incidents spread between 23 August and 6 September) received extensive and inflammatory press coverage. In their wake, arguments were voiced which, for the first time, embedded the notion of race – as a social distinction based on the physical appearance of New Commonwealth immigrants – within the language of domestic affairs. The process is documented more fully by Miles (1984); it signalled what Joshi and Carter (1984) have identified as a transition from colonial to indigenous racism. During the 1960s, intrinsic, immutable differences, indexed by colour, rather than malleable, cultural boundaries or transient distinctions related to immigration history, became the tacit touchstone of political debate. This new imagery was possible not only because of the changing social climate within Britain, but also because of the changing patterns of international relations.

By 1960, Britain had acknowledged the end of Empire and was disillusioned with the Commonwealth ideal. Nationalist movements in Africa, the newly established Republic of South Africa and the lure of the EEC all began to undermine the search for a common Commonwealth identity. By the middle of the decade it was widely recognized that Britain's interests were not only distinct from, but often opposed to, those of the Commonwealth (Rich 1986c); Britain's initial (unsuccessful) application to join the Common Market occurred in the same year that the Commonwealth Immigration Bill received its first Parliamentary airing. The potential arose to treat black people not as equal under the umbrella of common citizenship, but as outside the British political community with only tenuous claims to their rights as British subjects. Black people were no longer a symbol of post-war regeneration but instead became a symptom of Britain's declining world role (see Ben-Tovim and Gabriel 1982).

Economic problems were also high on legislators' agendas during this middle period. Indeed, Joshi and Carter (1984) link the transition from colonial to indigenous racism primarily to public and political perceptions of a gloomy economic future. In 1957/8 immigrants began to appear on the lists of the unemployed and throughout the 1960s the fluctuating fortunes of manufacturing industry (especially the car industry) periodically threw black and white labour into intense competition (both actual and perceived), not only for jobs, but also for housing and a range of other resources and services. Subtly but surely, black people were depicted not as different in 'quality' but as different in kind, distinguished less by their supposed moral inadequacy and more by their threat to the well-being of whites. We must, claimed Selwyn Lloyd, 'accept the fact that we have many thousands of these people here who cannot be integrated or assimilated' (HC 1964/5, 711, 1034). The tenor of debate shifted away from the notion of 'colonial fellow citizens' and towards the imagery of 'coloured immigrants' – that large number of people who, 'however worthy, are alien, have alien cultures, different temperaments, totally different backgrounds and habits and different ways of life' (John Hall, HC 1968, 759, 1320). While individuals' views were many and varied, politicians of every hue appeared to subscribe to the essentially Conservative assumption that 'separate races and the relations they engender will continue to exist indefinitely' (Reeves 1983: 165).

The corollary of this hardening of boundaries around the social cateogry 'coloured immigrant' was an unrealistic faith in the homogeneity and common interests of the white 'races'. This view is epitomized in Bernard Braine's challenge to David Ennals during a debate on the distinctions between the Old and New Commonwealth. Arguing against imposing the same immigration controls on residents in both these regions, Braine queried 'Does the honourable gentleman altogether dismiss the fact that Britons, Australians and New Zealanders are people of one blood and bone?' (HC 1967, 752, 1532). Such imagery, if rarely so explicitly expressed, helped to legitimize the use of colour as an index of race and testifies to the fact that, in England at least, this newly explicit process of racial categorization was to be an important vehicle in the articulation of national pride.[7]

A new dimension was thus added to domestic ideas about the nature and status of black people in Britain. Colonial stereotypes were not displaced by this transition, but were overlaid with new layers of meaning. Assumptions about immigrants' benign cultural and educational inferiority were augmented by fears about the threat black people posed to the material advancement of whites, and politicians did little to refute the popular belief that '"they" could take "our" jobs and live in "our" streets' (Joshi and Carter 1984: 66). The 1960s drew increasingly tight 'racial' boundaries between black and white Britain, and this unprecedented racialization of politics became the touchstone for most other areas of debate. Thus, just as Carter et al. (1987) analyse the political racialization of immigration, and as Cross (1983) and Solomos (1986b) explore the racialization of poverty and of riot, respectively, the section that follows examines the racialization of residential space. This process is directly implicated in the reconceptualization of racial segregation during this second post-war period.

Segregation: from incipient ghetto to insurgent state

As the decade unfolded and a new racial awareness drew attention to the enduring black presence in 'white man's country', earlier images portraying segregation as a passing phase in immigration history crystallized into a vision of ghettoization on British soil. Debating the 1965 White Paper 'Immigration from the Commonwealth' (Cmnd 2739), politicians worried that British cities could face a North American future and, despite well documented arguments over the *number* of black settlers, it was their spatial concentration that created most distress. Public anxieties were not, claimed Selwyn Lloyd, related so much to the proportion (then about 1 per cent) of the population accounted for by these immigrants, as to the 'fact' that 'where they have settled they constitute far more than 1 per cent of the population. They are up to 10 per cent in some towns, and more than that in some areas'. It was, he intimated, the speed and intensity of settlement rather than the size of the black population that formed the crux of the new 'racial' problem (HC 1964/5, 711, 1033–4).

Much contemporary debate was characterized by vivid appeal to personal and constituents' experiences, and such narrative (which should be read for its legitimizing role rather than its objectivity) became a powerful weapon in the struggle to initiate legislative change. Through clever rhetoric, 'the presence with us of a very considerable number of settlers from Commonwealth countries' was mapped on to a 'new and major social problem' to which Frank Soskice addressed the 1965 Race Relations Bill (HC 1964/5, 716, 977). A short leap of imagination from scantily produced facts allowed the problem of race in the mid-1960s to be presented as one which arose 'quite simply from the arrival in this country of many people of wholly alien cultures, habits and outlook . . . who tend to concentrate in their own communities' (Reginald Maudling, HC 1968, 759, 1345).

Building on the 'facts' of spatial concentration, the problem of racial segregation acquired three well polished facets. First, the environmental problems associated with 'immigrant' areas were attributed to the immigration process itself. Secondly, segregation became an index of the pressures on resources and services supposedly exerted by migrants. Finally, the spatial consolidation of the black population was regarded both as a threat to white affluence and as a challenge to that most precious of a nation's resources – it's territory. These are considered in turn.

As early as 1958, the failure of segregated black communities to disperse 'naturally' was interpreted as a sign that they *chose* to remain clustered. James Lindsay, for instance, objected in the Commons to the way that 'coloured people' tended to 'segregate themselves in certain areas' (HC 1958, 585, 1420). Soon, this practice was linked with deterioration in the housing stock, and these migrants (like the Jews who had settled earlier) were depicted not as the victims but as the perpetrators of decay. In Harold Gurden's view, 'Slums now exist in hundreds or perhaps even thousands where previously they could be measured in dozens.' Never, he went on 'was there such filth and such obscenity. The humiliation and degradation of these people are dreadful' (HC 1961, 649, 742). In a similar vein, Selwyn Lloyd referred to the problems besetting 'places where there is residential downgrading of house property, and where there are dormitory conditions in which single coloured men are crowded together in circumstances that shock those living near' (HC 1964/5, 711, 1033–4). Reeves's (1983) analysis of 27 Parliamentary speeches in favour of three post-war immigration bills shows that even 'moderate' politicians sub-scribed to, and sustained, the belief (now known to be erroneous) that immigration and housing deterioration were causally linked. Thus the view that black people *constitute* urban deprivation frequently eclipsed the extent to which they suffered from it, and when the Urban Programme was launched in 1969, 'ethnic mix' was regarded not as a product but as a component of urban disadvantage (moreover, because this was a spatial Programme, the use of such indicators simply reinforced the negative stereotypes associated with distinctively 'racial' segregation).

Concerns about the environmental consequences of segregation were soon overlaid with anxiety about the strain such settlement placed on local services and resources. Despite evidence that migrants made a net addition to the welfare budget (Freeman 1979; Jones, 1967), the image of black people demanding priority treatment at the expense of (and by actively exploiting) whites was sustained across the political spectrum. For Labour, George Rogers argued as early as 1958 that the overcrowding of immigrants into properties 'badly needed by white people' was an important element of Britain's racial problem (cited by Miles 1984: 263). Conservatives, too, condemned black householders who purchased their property 'very often over the heads of English residents and thereby, because of overcrowding, driving out the English people' (Frank Taylor, CACR 1961: 29). Many shared Patricia Hornsby-Smith's sympathy for those 'hard pressed local authorities whose social services have been far outstripped by the influx of immigrants', and few could ignore the electoral implications of her claim that 'if the housing committees allocated their property exclusively on the basis of social need, no white family would get anywhere near an allocation for the next 10 or 15 years' (HC 1971, 813, 118). Black people were regarded both 'as penniless aliens overburdening the housing market' and 'as greedy and corrupt landlords'

(Joshi and Carter 1984: 65), and overall the image of a country hampered by too many 'aliens', crushed into too small a space, demanding too many services and resources, was remarkably enduring.

Finally, it proved to be only a short step from describing racial segregation as an illegitimate drain on services and resources to regarding it as a symbolic threat to the intrinsic character of urban Britain. In its most extreme form, this view gained currency only because of the unprecedented (and so far unsurpassed) intrusion of overt racism into Parliamentary politics. (This third component did, nevertheless, contain elements which, albeit subtly, were to inform a reconstruction of race and segregation during the 1980s.) This shift to the racist Right is discussed by Dearlove and Saunders (1984), Foot (1965) and Jacobs (1986). It gave Peter Griffiths his surprise victory in the 1964 General Election at Smethwick, on the oft-quoted platform 'If you want a nigger neighbour, vote Labour'. Shortly afterwards, boosted by the speeches of Enoch Powell, the appropriation and defence of territory became a vehicle through which racial differentiation, and its expression in residential segregation, was infused with a new surge of patriotic sentiment.

Powell's role in the politics of race has been considered elsewhere by himself and others (Foot 1969; Freeman 1979; Phillips 1977; Powell 1969, 1972). Most authors 'credit' him with giving impetus to the immigration debate and to the repatriation lobby by fixing negotiations concerning the future for black people in Britain around the concept of numbers. But he was also instrumental in creating a vivid image of the *territorial* challenge issued by post-war immigration. He spoke of the 'extending of the numbers and area of the immigrant' (television interview cited in Gordon and Klug (1986: 19)); he referred to the beleaguered English 'made strangers in their own country', finding 'their homes and neighbourhoods changed beyond recognition'; and he described 'the transformation of whole areas . . . into alien territory' (Birmingham speech, 20 April 1968, reprinted in Smithies and Fiddick (1969: 74)). In his book *Still to Decide* he outlined the predicament of a people 'who find themselves displaced in the only country that is theirs', and spoke of the 'Englishman' who, in encountering black immigrants, 'comes face to face with those who will dispute with him the possession of his native land' (p. 209). In his Eastbourne address, he defined black people as 'detachments of communities in the West Indies, or India and Pakistan, encamped in areas of England' – areas from which the 'indigenous' population had been 'dislodged' (cited in Barker 1981: 39). Thus Powell's imagery reaffirmed the salience of race as a principle of social inclusion and exclusion within urban Britain, using it to further his belief that an 'instinct to preserve an identity and defend a territory is one of the deepest and strongest implanted in mankind' (Powell 1969 on BBC TV; cited by Barker 1981: 22).

Although Powell's remarks cost him a career in Edward Heath's government, not only did his vision of white seignority over UK space become enshrined in the patriality clause of the 1971 immigration act, but his mediation between 'respectable' Conservatism and the demands of a more reactionary public proved vital to that Party. So crucial was this latter role that, as Bulpitt (1986: 32) has observed, if Powell had not existed 'it may have been necessary to invent him'. With or without Powell, the cornerstone of a 'new' segregationism (to be discussed in the final section) would almost certainly have been laid.

To summarize, by the early 1960s politicians had ceased to regard segregation as a passing corollary of immigration. It was depicted, rather, as an enduring symptom of post-colonialism and as a symbol of the sustained (supposed) distinctiveness of black Britons. By the early 1970s, this symbol had acquired at least three distinct facets. First, in the absence of 'natural' dispersal, segregation was increasingly viewed as the choice of the segregated, and immigration was assumed to have caused the environmental problems besetting the lower end of the housing market in which black people lived. Secondly, by virtue of their relative disadvantage and deprivation, 'immigrant areas' were regarded both as a drain on the welfare services and as a threat to white people's well-being. Finally, segregation gave spatial expression to a new black presence just as enthusiasm for the Commonwealth ideal had been eclipsed by concern about Britain's uncertain future in the world economy. In a decade and a half, problems attributed to racial differences – once only an external threat to the replacement of Empire by Commonwealth – had become central to domestic affairs and were being portrayed as if they might cast a cloud over the very future of urban life.

While this sketch necessarily oversimplifies the complexity of opinion held by politicians, the most striking characteristic of Parliamentary debate at this time is the broad consensus achieved concerning the existence and character of racial segregation. Most politicians ascribed significance to colour as an index of racial differentiation, linked race with immigration, and defined the immigrant 'problem' not only in terms of numbers but also in terms of *location and visibility*. Segregation (and the poor housing, unemployment, overcrowding and deprivation associated with it) was the consequence of having too many 'coloured colonials' packed into too little space. The associated controversy centred not on whether this view was accurate but, rather, on what the political response should be.

Avoiding the ghetto: remove or disperse?

Once segregation was recognized as a 'problem' that would not go away naturally, legislators across the political spectrum relinquished their *laissez-faire* inheritance in favour of concerted interventionism. This shift reflects a wider re-orientation of the nation's economic strategy (towards a neo-Keynesianism favouring supply-side rather than demand-side management) that remained in place until the sterling crisis of the mid-1970s. This possibility of intervening made the new 'threat' seem manageable, but because of the way in which the problem was constructed, policy solutions brought little reform.

From the moment the immigration debate focused on the number of black people in Britain, as well as on where they were clustered, repatriation was advocated from the far right as the most desirable solution to the race relations problem. Although this rarely appeared on the serious political agenda, there was a time when Home Secretary James Callaghan and his Tory shadow Quintin Hogg seemed determined to surpass the generosity of each other's voluntary resettlement schemes. Retrospectively, and notwithstanding the psychological effect of the repatriation debate on the black population, perhaps the key significance of this dialogue during the 1960s was its role as a yardstick against which the policies that *were* entertained were deemed moderate and realistic.

'Integration' became the touchstone of domestic policy throughout the 1960s and early 1970s. As a liberal alternative to repatriation, integration was endorsed in 1965 both at the Conservative Party Annual conference and in the Labour Party's White Paper on 'Immigration from the Commonwealth'. Despite some debate as to what exactly integration would achieve (its connotations varied from absorption to pluralism), it was generally agreed that it would involve residential dispersal as a means (or consequence) of (a) diluting the problems supposedly associated with immigration and (b) providing black people with access to a fairer share of resources and opportunities. Three strategies were invoked to set this process in motion: immigration controls, race relations legislation and statutory measures to secure desegregation. They are considered in turn.

Tacitly or explicitly, politicians assumed throughout the 1960s that Britain's race relations problem was not so much the fault of white individuals or institutions as a consequence of immigration. Immigration had, some argued, imported a range of race-related problems that were more usually associated with foreign affairs. As a consequence, the fundamental prerequisite for successful 'integration' must be tough immigration control.

The viability of control had, as I have suggested, been considered by the

Attlee Government (an administration which was at least as concerned with the prospects for emigration *to* the Empire as with immigration *from* it). Even during the 1940s, Governments were secretly but explicitly preoccupied with the question of how to prevent black people settling in Britain. The principle of control was therefore widely accepted in Whitehall well before the Notting Hill riots (Ashford 1981; Bulpitt 1986; Banton 1985). But it was not until the end of the decade that the issue could be debated in public; it was not, therefore, until the early 1960s that politicians had to justify their 'new-found' support for a notion so clearly at odds with their earlier Commonwealth ideal. Despite this difficulty, by 1961, following a Party conference at which 38 of the 536 motions were restrictionist, the Conservative Party was openly committed to control, and the first of a series of major Immigration Acts (passed in 1962, 1968 and 1971) was introduced to the Commons. Each of these Acts was to be more discriminatory than the last (as illustrated by Layton-Henry 1984; Marrington 1987; Miles and Phizacklea 1984; Reeves 1983) but my concern here is with the extent to which these measures were legitimized by their expected role in solving the problems indexed by segregation.

Immigration control in the early 1960s could never seriously be justified on economic grounds. Indeed, it was the economic *irrationality* of stemming the supply of Commonwealth labour that made left-wing opposition (spearheaded by Hugh Gaitskell) to the 1961 Commonwealth Immigration Bill so persuasive (see HC 1961, 649, 795).[8] Such opposition failed because these immigration restrictions were not justified by appeal to the fortunes of the economy. Although controls took the form of vouchers to regulate migrant labour, the principle of restriction was won primarily through arguments advanced on social grounds (and the practice, as Peach (1986a) has shown, was more effective in preventing the immigration of dependents than in excluding primary migrants). Immigration policy remained the responsibility of the Home Office rather than that of the Department of Employment and Productivity and its rationale was primarily 'to allow the government time to produce effective integration programs and to give the immigrants and the natives sufficient time to adjust to each other' (Freeman 1979: 56). Such legislation was necessary, claimed its proponents, not only because of the scale and speed of the migration but also 'because of the way in which it was concentrated in certain areas where whole districts changed their character very rapidly' (Maudling, HC 1971, 813, 42–3). As 'Rab' Butler, then Conservative Home Secretary, put it: 'the greater the numbers coming into the country the larger will these communities become and the more difficult it will be to integrate them into our national life . . . there is a real risk that the drive for improved conditions will be defeated by the sheer weight of numbers'

(HC 1961, 649, 694–5). This argument was to be the touchstone for immigration legislation for over two decades.

Immigration control was 'justified', then, as part of a strategy of integration – as a solution to the problems attendant on immigration, as a panacea for the ills associated with racial segregation and as a response to the challenge posed to British institutions by a multi-racial society. The aim, quite simply, was to dilute and disperse the problems of immigrant areas on the pretext that 'unless some restriction is imposed we shall create the colour bar we all want to avoid' (Norman Pannell, *The Times*, 28 August 1958). Controls would assist in defusing social conflict and in building 'a homogeneous society of which all of us can be proud, and which will command the allegiance of everyone dwelling within it' (Quintin Hogg, HC 1968, 759, 1259).

Although it is retrospectively questionable, this dependence on promoting integration by restricting immigration is not hard to understand. In the wake of Notting Hill, politicians convinced that racial discrimination had no part in British life or law were plunged into a dilemma. The rhetoric of tolerance seemed hollow, but the realities of racism had to be denied. Anti-discrimination legislation was still beyond the pale, and to build a racial dimension into mainstream housing and urban policy was unthinkable. For pragmatic politicians, the only viable solution to the problem they had defined was to limit immigration and hope for the best (a best which, by shedding the Commonwealth labour market, might secure entry into Europe).

By the mid-1960s, the goal of integration seemed no nearer, and this provided a convenient point for Labour, under Wilson, to relinquish its electorally unpopular stance against immigration controls. In 1961, Labour had denounced the Commonwealth Immigration Bill for failing to address the problems faced by black Britons. By 1965, the Party had decided that the way to respond was 'to combine tight immigration controls . . . with a constructive policy for integrating into the community those immigrants who are there already' (Crossman 1975: 149). For at least a decade, Roy Hattersley's dictum that 'without integration, limitation is inexcusable; without limitation, integration is impossible' provided the foundation of Labour's race relations policy.

Race relations legislation was first introduced, like the Immigration Act before it, 'to facilitate the absorption of these new immigrant communities into our community as a whole' (Peter Thorneycroft, HC 1964/5, 711, 944).[9] Nevertheless, compared with the swift passage and strong provisions of the Immigration Acts, race relations legislation has always faced equivocation and compromise, and its impact has not been great. As a consequence, the 1965 Act was a much diluted version of the earlier Race

Relations Bill, and Ashford (1981: 239) concludes that it was less a sign of enlightenment than a bipartisan pact 'to do little or nothing'. These new measures did not (and could not) remove the barriers to socio-economic integration sufficiently to disperse black households away from the worst 'spaces' of the economy and the housing system. Nevertheless, in 1968 politicians still agreed that the route to integration lay in 'the dispersal of the great concentration of these people' (Neil Marten, HC 1967/8, 761, 1156). Reluctantly, a third interventionist strategy was entertained – that of residential dispersal through direct manipulation of the housing system.

Solomos et al. (1982) discuss the concept of dispersal as one of a series of packages developed during the 1970s to deal with race relations problems. The concept of dispersal made explicit a belief that spatial engineering could impinge on social processes, and this appealed to politicians as a promising route towards the integration and advancement of immigrants. There was no shortage of suggestions as to how dispersal might be encouraged. Sir George Sinclair pinned his hopes on a national programme of house building (HC 1964/5, 710, 49), Harold Gurden preferred to relocate immigrants 'from overcrowded districts of large conurbations' into overspill areas (HC 1964/5, 712, 35), and Donald Chapman wanted to control immigrants' destinations by an arrangement under the voucher system (HC 1964/5, 713, 2165). When Maurice Foley was appointed in 1965 to coordinate the work of Government departments in the integration of immigrants, it was therefore assumed that dispersal would be high on the agenda.

In the event, despite a broad commitment to interventionism in most areas of Government, legislators were reluctant to introduce special programmes for migrant minorities, especially in housing. The consequence was a decade of equivocation, ending in 1975 when the responsibility for effecting dispersal was devolved to local government. By this time, of course, it was apparent that only fairly dramatic interventionist policies could achieve the desired end: the economy was ailing, primary immigration had been reduced to a trickle, dependents would obviously need to live near their sponsors, and much of the so-called 'immigrant' population was now accounted for by black people born in Britain. All these factors were to encourage local inertia rather than dramatic change in the residential patterns of black households. Moreover, as we saw in chapter 3, in the year that Cullingworth reported (and six years before dispersal was officially sanctioned) Parliament, exemplifying the isolation of race-related legislation from mainstream public policy, had passed a Housing Act which removed the one mechanism which might have allowed dispersal to succeed (in the sense that it might have provided local authorities with the opportunity to couple desegregation with a move towards racial equality).

In short, at the height of interventionism in post-war Britain, the 'problem' of racial segregation was used to justify legislation (most notably immigration controls) which had a minimal impact on residential differentiation. In contrast, intervention through housing policy – then a key source of influence on the social ecology of cities – was avoided until the last moment. Even then, Parliament displaced its responsibilities to local governments only after trends in national housing policy had limited their scope to act. For reasons ranging from benign equivocation to thinly disguised racism, legislators missed an opportunity to address the real problem of segregation – the way in which housing systems confer disadvantage on black people – at a time when their powers to do so were greatest. This left an unfortunate legacy for the market-oriented 1980s.

The euphemization of race and a new segregationism

For almost a decade, British policy-making has been dominated by a Conservative Government supported by a large Commons majority. Since 1979, a reshaping of race-related issues has been important to this Government's success in combining monetarist economic policies with popular authoritarianism to form a distinctively British version of the 'New Right'.[10] Martin Barker (1981) has formally linked the emergence of the New Right with the development of a New Racism and, while acknowledging that the 1980s are characterized by continuity as well as change, I shall argue that recent trends in the politics of race cast new light on the interpretation of segregation.

The New Right in Britain is generally discussed as an amalgam of neo-liberalism and conservative authoritarianism (Barry 1987; Gordon and Klug 1986; Kavanagh 1987; King 1987) and this uneasy coalition structures the present discussion. Elliot and McCrone (1987) make a further distinction between libertarianism (emphasizing the rights of the individual over that of the collectivity or state) and economic liberalism (the basis of monetarist economic policy). However, because libertarianism has been important primarily as an ideological safeguard for individual economic and property rights (and has therefore been aligned closely with the aims of neo-liberal economics), I shall not dwell on this latter distinction.

This emphasis on the role of the Right does not deny that ideas about race have changed across the political spectrum. Yet notwithstanding the anti-racist commitment of some Labour-controlled local authorities, the

Left has made little impression on race-related legislation in recent years (Fitzgerald 1987). Whether by design or by omission, opposition parties have avoided fundamental debate, 'and ended up with platitudes saying they all agreed broadly, but asking the Tory right not to be so nasty' (Barker 1981: 20; see also Fitzgerald and Layton-Henry 1986). Neo-Conservatism therefore sets the terms of modern political debate, reconceptualizing race, redefining racial segregation and realigning public policy. These themes are considered below.

Race rephrased: economic individualism and the ascent of culture

Neo-liberalism, the first element of New Right ideology, is based on a 'rediscovery' of nineteenth-century free market philosophy. Addressing itself to the project of economic regeneration, this movement brought a diverse collection of monetarist policies to post-industrial Britain. Montarism's preferred unit of competition and achievement is the individual (firm or family), and this denies group characteristics, including 'race', any role in public life at a national level. As Home Secretary Douglas Hurd has observed, 'We believe in individualism. We believe in the right of the individual to pile up a good standard of living for himself and his family; we believe that this is natural, right and necessary' (HC 1987, 118, 390). Accordingly, neither race nor racism is recognized as a policy-relevant variable in the economic sphere nor, indeed, in the arenas of housing, health or welfare. Rather, 'step by step, city by city, we are showing that the ladders of opportunity in our professions, in our industries and in our public sector, are open for all to climb' (Hurd, HC 1987, 118, 390).

While the 'ideals' of neo-liberalism recognize the integrity of the individual, they also shift responsibility for achievement (and failure) to individuals. The role of the state is to set markets free, not to interfere with competitors. The principle of individualism is in this context a two-edged sword which can, in theory, be praised for denying the innate reality of races but which, in practice, must be criticized for ignoring the tenacity of race as a *social* construction with real political and economic consequences. Reverence for the market turns a blind eye to systematic inequality, ignores the possibility that ostensibly aracial practices can have racist outcomes and brushes aside the accumulating disadvantage faced by black Britons.

This revival of liberal economics helped secure Margaret Thatcher's electoral success, but it has had social and political consequences which demand legitimation. To fill this role, a second component of the New Right – that of neo-conservative authoritarianism – has proved increasingly important and, through its reconceptualization of race, it may have more far-reaching consequences for black peoples' future.

Social authoritarianism (a revival of the traditional conservative themes of hierarchy and social control) is less preoccupied with the state of the economy than with a supposed demise of morality. It is concerned less with individuals' opportunities in the marketplace than with collective responsibility for social control. Strategies invoked to restore lost social values include a strengthening of traditional institutions (especially the family) and the promotion of law and order. The key to moral renewal, however, is that sense of solidarity supposedly lodged in national pride. This reasoning has inspired the revival of 'one nation' Conservatism, popularizing the view that, in the interests of collective responsibility, 'it is natural to form a bounded community, a nation, aware of its differences from other nations' (Barker 1981: 21). From this perspective, it is 'in our biology, our instincts, to defend our way of life, traditions and customs against outsiders – not because they are inferior, but because they are part of different cultures' (Barker 1981: 23–4).

By replacing the language of race with the euphemism of culture, separatist inclinations appear to celebrate social diversity rather than to impose judgements of superiority. By stressing the reasonable concept of difference rather than the uncomfortable facts of inequality, modern authoritarianism depicts 'cultural' boundaries, even when drawn along 'racial' lines, as benign expressions of identity, not as supremacist assertions of power. Yet, although pervasive, this belief about the morally neutral, socially natural, defence of one's cultural heritage is hard to sustain. Beneath its thin veneer, themes like 'the British nation', 'the British people' and 'British culture' are increasingly (and often explicitly) constructed to exclude black people (see Lawrence 1982: 48). By conflating the idea of race with concepts of nationhood and culture, authoritarian rhetoric preserves the imagery of racial differentiation even within the boundaries of the state.

There are, then, two conceptions of race subsumed in the imagery of Britain's New Right, corresponding with the tenets of neo-liberal individualism and Tory collectivism, respectively. Monetarism emphasizes equal opportunities for individuals in the market place and regards race as insignificant to the concerns of politics and economy. Moral authoritarianism recognizes the importance of cultural differences in the *social* sphere but fosters a popular patriotism which draws social boundaries along racial lines. These ideological perspectives conflict to the extent that one denies the salience of race and the other implicitly celebrates its legitimacy. They coexist partly by virtue of the Conservatives' success in separating the spheres of economic management and social control, and partly because they are characterized by what Reeves (1983) calls 'deracialized discourse' – a language that disguises its reference to race (while effectively denying responsibility for racial inequality).[11]

Together, these views from the Right sustain a political imagery in which race (indexed by colour but referred to as 'ethnicity' or 'culture') corresponds with social differences that are 'real' but do not, in theory, impinge on the (liberal) principle of equal opportunity and relative autonomy for individuals in political and economic terms. A concept of 'different but equal' has reached the realm of reasonable political ideas, impinging on attitudes towards residential segregation and on the tenor of public policy.

In developing such policy, liberal market philosophy and traditional conservative authoritarianism divide their attention between the problems of economic decline and the prospect of moral decay. Both traditions take segregation as part of their remit, and both use it to articulate some key problems of British economy and society. Collectively, they provide a perspective on racial segregation that represents a sharp break with the past. Yet neither advances a solution which furthers the cause of racial justice. The reasons for this are considered below, taking in turn each ideological strand of the British New Right.

Segregation: the view from the market

The complexities of, and contradictions within, New Right economics are examined in recent works by Barry (1987) and King (1987). These authors identify the importance of a mixture of ideas rooted in the liberal influence of Friedrich von Hayek (on Austrian economics and on public choice theory as advanced by London's Institute of Economic Affairs), as well as in the Chicago tradition of neo-classical economics (best known through the writings of Milton Friedman). These approaches share the assumption that free market societies have an inherent tendency to order and justice which is damaged or distorted by state intervention (see Bosanquet 1983). The persuasiveness of New Right economics (which in Britain is dominated by neo-liberalism) therefore rests not only on its faith in the force of the 'invisible hand' (the beneficial consequences of a free market) but also on its fear of what Dunleavy and O'Leary (1987) term the 'invisible punch' (the costly consequences of state intervention).

From a neo-liberal perspective, state intervention is seen as a drain on the economy, demanding increasing levels of public spending and high rates of taxation (both of which, it is argued, inhibit economic initiative.). State subsidies are expected to impede the efficient allocation of resources – a process exacerbated because intervention supposedly has few integral checks and balances, rarely achieves its stated aims and has a wide range of undesirable unanticipated effects. Extending this reasoning, if segregation is a problem, it is less likely to be regarded as the product of systematic discrimination or disadvantage than as a symptom of imperfections in the housing market resulting from over-intervention by the state.

Such over-intervention, moreover, is held to have social and political (as well as economic) consequences. It is regarded as an infringement of individuals' liberty (to reap individual reward for individual effort) and as a disincentive to the work ethic. Intervention is also criticized for affording too much power to vote-seeking politicians, so encouraging the politicization of an essentially 'natural' (or, at least, socially neutral) system of resource distribution. According to this reasoning, if *racial* segregation is a problem, it appears as such not because of racism but because of the politicization of social inequality around the issue of race relations (such thinking explains why right-wing politicians often marginalize the anti-racist movement as an aberration of the 'loony left').

Where 'racial segregation' is defined as a problem caused by state intervention, the logical *solution* is to 'roll back' the state and re-establish the conditions in which markets may function freely. The market is regarded as the most efficient means of promoting economic growth and of distributing goods and services. It is acknowledged that market mechanisms generate some inequality (which is regarded as a necessary stimulus to initiative and drive), but it is argued that free markets contain sufficient integral checks and balances to prevent this becoming excessive. According to this view, housing markets will never want (or be able) to diminish the inherent variety of the residential mosaic; but because individuals theoretically have an equal opportunity to compete in those markets, residential differentiation should never become aligned with *systematic* social inequality. Tackling the problem of 'racial segregation' can, according to this reasoning, be subsumed within more general policies promoting the 'commodification' of housing. Race-specific measures are regarded as economically counter-productive and socially inappropriate.

By extending this line of thought, it is easy to see why a reassertion of market principles is perceived as morally, as well as economically, desirable. Such a move is not only seen as a way of curbing the powers of politicians, and of protecting the market from partisan or factional interests, but also appears attractive as a means of promoting social ends without submitting to collectivist principles. As Barry (1987: 36) shows, the liberal idea of a market 'envisages public benefits accruing *unintentionally* from individual maximisers pursuing their self interest' (his emphasis).

Despite the popular appeal of neo-liberal strategies, it is evident from chapters 3 and 4 that the legacy of a long-established link between segregation and racial inequality is being accentuated rather than ameliorated by the market forces encouraged through current housing policy. Yet even though social polarization in housing is increasingly expressed along 'racial lines', for the purposes of managing the economy segregation remains acceptable (or tolerable) as a phase in the adjustment of market forces. The reasons for (and implications of) this cannot be fully appreciated without exploring the imagery and activity of the second ideological strand of Britain's New Right – social authoritarianism.

The conservative problem: segregation as a symptom of urban malaise

Unlike neo-liberalism, which seeks to diminish the salience of race, popular conservatism has drawn the problem of distinctively racial segregation to the centre of a new campaign against social decline. This reconceptualization has been stimulated by the revival of social authoritarianism (which demands a central role for the state in maintaining public order and social stability), an emphasis on moralism (which seeks to restore traditional religious and moral values), and a move towards exclusivism (arguing against the reduction of inequality and the extension of citizenship rights). Together, these reconstruct the problem of racial segregation round two key facets of a presumed urban crisis: the demise of law and order and the erosion of public morality. Both are examined below.

Segregation, law and order; deriving conflict from diversity 'Racial segregation has been drawn into Britain's law and order debate through a theory of human nature (introduced above) that not only legitimizes social separatism but also portrays conflict as the corollary of diversity. As a consequence of the 'tensions inevitably produced by the inflow of a large culturally and racially distinct minority' (Peter Lloyd, HC 1979, 975, 325), images of segregation now mark the culmination of a longstanding 'race and crime' controversy which began as early as 1958. In that year, Norman Pannel urged deportation for immigrants with criminal convictions. This 'threat' of black criminality was compounded by the scare over illegal immigration in the late 1960s and re-emerged in the popular (though poorly grounded) association between black youth and 'mugging' forged a decade later. However, it is the *territorial* link between a black presence and urban violence that dominates debate today.

In 1980, Enoch Powell warned the Surrey Monday Club of the dangers of 'citadels of urban terrorism' being established in the major cities (*Guardian*, 8 October 1980; cited in Layton-Henry 1986). In the House of Commons, he claimed that black people may comprise as much as a third of the population in such areas and forecast a situation in which the country would be 'unlivable and ungovernable' in the wake of 'civil discord and violence' (HC 1980, 980, 1045). Soon after, at the third reading of the British Nationality Bill on 4 June 1981, Harvey Proctor referred in the same sentence to three decades of mass migrations from the New Commonwealth and Pakistan and to 'the dreadful and inevitable racial strife of which we see evidence weekly, if not yet daily, in metropolitan London and elsewhere' (HC 1981, 5, 1174). In a similar, if more muted vein, Ivor Stanbrook took the floor in a debate on race relations on 10 December 1981 and berated legislators who 'too often ignore the fact that some areas of this country are inhabited by people who are unwilling to accept and openly reject lawful authority' (HC 1981, 14, 1045). The 'respectable' press took a similar view and Brixton became 'the iceberg tip of a crisis of ethnic criminality which is not Britain's fault . . . but the fault of the ethnic community itself' (*Sunday Times*, 29 November 1981).

By 1982, the 'black' inner city symbolized a crisis of public order, prompting William Whitelaw to argue that 'it is in the interests of effective law enforcement for special precautions to be taken in respect of certain premises and localities, which may in some cases be those of the ethnic minorities' (HC 1982, 19, 82). Further outbreaks of civil unrest (discussed more fully in chapter 6) were attributed to the sheer human wickedness infusing the inner city (see Fitzgerald 1987), and there is little doubt that, in the eyes of a range of politicians, 'the 1985 riots helped strengthen the imagery of blacks, and young blacks in particular, as an "enemy within the very heart of British society"' (Solomos 1986b: 28). 'It is,' claimed Harvey Proctor in a speech to the Newham North-East Conservatives in November 1986, 'as though multi-racialism had acted as a catalyst to the growth of crime by destroying the sense of community, solidarity and identity' (cited in the *Guardian*, 11 November 1986). By this time, the Public order Branch of the Metropolitan Police was using 'ethnic mix' to identify housing estates with a high risk of disturbance (*Guardian*, 12 July 1986, p. 12), and the themes 'race', 'riot' and 'inner city' had become inextricably linked.

The kind of reasoning which either tacitly or explicitly ties the very presence of black people with the threat of crime inevitably contributes to the social and cultural isolation of the black population *within* Britain. From ideas about the 'natural' but transient conflict associated with host–immigrant relations has sprung an enduring stereotype soldering images of racial differentiation on to visions of urban crime and civil unrest. Spatially grounded in the inner city, and largely unrelated to white society, this reconceptualization of racial segregation has displaced earlier concerns (about housing conditions, environmental decay and scarce public resources) with fears about the threat black neighbourhoods pose to the wider urban fabric. This is a direct development of ideas popularized by Powell in the late 1960s but, whereas then the vision was sustained only by marginal voices on the far right, today it gains much wider currency.

Segregation, morality and a resurgence of national pride   The second area of national concern to which ideas about race have been linked, and which segregation now symbolizes, reflects social authoritarianism's much broader campaign against the erosion of national values. In much Conservative thought, a nation's moral order rests fundamentally on public compliance with a set of common norms enshrined not only in law, but also in the conventions of daily life. This, it seems, is guaranteed only when traditional values and lifestyles are shared. Accordingly, in the wake of perceived social disintegration, and in an attempt to resurrect national pride, modern Conservatism has confronted a range of factors thought likely to undermine the 'British' way of life. Prominent among these is the challenge that multi-culturalism presents to the New Right vision of nationhood. Concern about this 'problem' won support for the Conservatives when, in a televised speech on 31 July 1978, Mrs Thatcher extended her sympathy to those who 'are really rather afraid that this country might be swamped by people with a different culture' (cited in Barker 1981: 15).

During the present decade, the supposedly reasonable fears of a white British public about the presence and location of black people have been widely aired. Worries arise principally because of 'the full impact of the immigration which has hit the inner cities of England' (Harvey Proctor, HC 1982/3, 34, 379), because of the damage this might wreak on 'the essential identity of this old, historic nation' (John Stokes, HC 1980, 980, 1092), and because 'parts of London and parts of the West Midlands are unrecognisable from the streets and roads of twenty or thirty years ago' (John Carlisle, HC 1982/3, 37, 232).

Fears that the essence of British culture might 'be lost in a welter of new and different races . . . whose customs will remain unchanged' (Stokes, HC 1980, 980, 1095) have led politicians to reject the Hattersley dictum as a justification for immigration control. The argument that control promotes integration is, for Ronald Bell, little short of hypocrisy. 'We all know,' he urged, 'why we want to limit immigration. It is because we do not want to see too rapid or great a change in the population of our country . . . too rapid and too great a movement damages a community and destroys its sense of identity'. This, he goes on, 'cannot be tolerated if people are to continue to feel a sense of history and destiny' (HC 1979, 975, 300–2). Controls are required not to encourage integration but to ensure that 'England, which has survived for 1000 years, with its incomparable history and contribution to civilisation, can remain recognisably and unmistakably English' (Stokes, HC 1983, 37, 224).

The notion that the presence of black people constitutes a challenge to national values and an affront to the British character is an enduring, only thinly disguised, theme of neo-conservative rhetoric. This has led some to redefine racial prejudice as the attitude of those who refuse to adopt the lifestyle of their chosen country; it has prompted others to portray racism as something black people inflict on whites by demanding special treatment (discussed by Barker 1981; Gordon and Klug 1986); and it has allowed extremists to label black Britons as the Trojan horse of reverse colonialism, ripe for exploitation by the far Left (examined by Bulpitt 1986). The visible presence of black people, embodied in the imagery of segregation, has rekindled a popular patriotism and this, in Murray's (1986) view, helps perpetuate a politically advantageous electoral climate in which the Tories appear as 'the sole and necessary defenders of the nation' (p. 3).

In summary, both as a symbol of the demise of law and order and as a challenge to national unity, 'racial segregation' has become the touchstone for concern about a wider threat to Britain's urban future. Whether because they are potentially disruptive, or because they are culturally alien, the 'black' inner cities have been depicted as a threat to the fragile cohesion of the nation. Moral authoritarianism deals with this in a number of ways.

The authoritarian solution: containing the crisis

While the hallmark of neo-liberalism is freedom and individuality, that of neo-conservatism is the exercise of power and authority by a strong central state. Although much is made of the incompatibility of these views, the strategies they promote may be regarded as complementary rather than contradictory. The strands of New Right thinking are agreed, for instance, in their opposition to state intervention where this entails the direct provisioning of goods, resources and services. Beyond this, however, modern conservatism – with its enthusiasm for the state as a guarantor of legal and moral standards – offers liberalism 'a more coherent conception of nationhood and of the capacities of government' than it would otherwise allow (King 1987: 9). This has been important in devising solutions to the Conservative's reconstructed problem of racial segregation.

In policy terms, the response of the 1980s stands in stark contrast to anything that has gone before. For the first time, an assumption that the problematic features of segregation can be solved (either 'naturally' or via state intervention) by the process of residential dispersal (to encourge assimilation or integration) does not obtain. Now that segregation represents more than a problem of services and resources, now that it has gained currency as a symbolic threat to the moral fabric of society, dispersal no longer seems viable as a means of diluting the effects of black settlement (on the contrary, in a context where the 'immigrant' population is growing most by natural increase, dispersal threatens to extend the boundaries of black Britain).

There are, of course, sound reasons for the demise of dispersal and a relaxing of integrationism. These include the failure of such policies to secure racial equality and mounting evidence that residential clustering and cultural distinctiveness are preferred by some minority groups. The shift away from dispersal is not in itself a cause for concern, but the practices which have replaced it are, since none of the three key trends examined below can be described as anti-racist in intent or effect.

Assimilation Theoretically, 'assimilation' might be held as the ideal solution to a range of race-related problems as defined by the moderate right. The possibility of absorbing the problems of segregation *in situ* has wide appeal, advancing the libertarians' faith in a society comprising individuals rather than social groups while pursuing the conservative quest for conformity to a British way of life. In practice, the pursuit of this assimilationist 'ideal' has taken two directions. In the legislative sphere assimilationist goals have helped to justify the extension of 'aracial' individualism beyond the confines of economic management and across the whole range of social policy. In the cultural sphere, assimilationism has infused the call for one-nationhood and is aligned with a vision of societal integration that is portrayed as superior to multi-culturalism. Both these trends require elaboration.

In the development of legislation, assimilationist rhetoric has provided the basis of a concerted challenge from the Right to the legitimacy of race relations legislation. As Peter Griffiths put it, 'since no case has been made out to show that multiracial societies excel in any way, and since they do not solve the problems of race relations, there seems to be little to gain from their artificial creation' (cited in Barker 1981: 42). In March 1980, John Carlisle referred to immigrants from the New Commonwealth as 'a minority already over-protected by a wealth of legislation, biased rules and numerous statutory boards and bodies' (HC 1980, 980, 1075). In July of that year, three backbench MPs called for the abolition of the Commission for Racial Equality and the repeal of the 1976 Race Relations Act (HC 1980, 987, 1714). The Government had been criticized from the Right for betraying working class whites by upholding 'the harsh, so-called anti-discrimination laws' with increasing vigour (Stokes, HC 1982/3, 34, 398), and in the run-up to the 1983 general election the annual Conservative Party conference seriously debated two motions to repeal this legislation.

Similar reservations about the wisdom of intervening to secure racial equality have been voiced in debates concerning special funding initiatives, 'ethnic' monitoring and contract compliance. The aims of the Local Government Grants (Ethnic Groups) Bill, for instance, were defeated during debate on 12 March 1979 by, among other things, the spectre of a socially divisive form of 'reverse discrimination'. Alan Clarke argued that ordinary white citizens would be keenly aware of their deprivation in the face of a Bill alleged to 'make special provision for people simply because they are coloured' (HC 1978/9, 964, 100). Such a Bill was liable, claimed John Stokes, 'to incense our own countrymen who were born and bred here' and who 'feel that they are being discriminated against' (HC 1978/9, 964, 112). This Bill was lost to the general election and when, eight years later, a new Local Government Bill (1987) was put before the House, critics saw it as a challenge rather than a support to the anti-racist policies of local government (especially where these evoked the principle of contract compliance). Overall, opposition to race-specific (especially anti-racist) legislation, epitomized in the response to a Conservative discussion document (*Realism about Race* 1982), seems to be gaining momentum on the Right (see Fitzgerald 1984).

In practice as well as in principle, the Government has proved reluctant to use special legislation, including race relations legislation, to pursue the cause of racial equality. Between 1979 and 1981, the budget of the CRE was cut, the Commission received little Government encouragement, the Conservative Party's Department of Community Affairs (which had been created to work with 'ethnic minorities') was terminated and bureaucratic responsibility for race-related issues became progressively fragmented (see Studlar 1986). Consistent with libertarian demands, an authoritarian quest for assimilation has helped to ensure that state intervention on behalf of racial *groups* is steadily curtailed.

The assimilationist 'ideal' is not, however, appealing to the authoritarians simply as a justification for aligning the tenor of social policy with that of economic mangement. It also offers a means of boosting political popularity by rousing national pride to an extent not thought possible within the framework of a more plural society. As Francis Pym (1985) implies, unity must be the first social policy of any effective government. The campaign slogan of the early 1980s, 'Labour says he's black, Tories say he's British', thus carried a potentially ambiguous message. Attempting to be both black *and* British might, extending Norman Tebbitt's reasoning, simply confound the inner city 'problem' which is 'more difficult to deal with in a multi-cultural, multi-ethnic society than in a mono-cultural society of single racial origin' (HC 1985, 88, 1001). A dual identity is, moreover, implicitly rejected by the structure of the Conservative Party which, from August 1987, aimed to replace Asian and West Indian Associations with a 'One Nation Forum' which aims to absorb black supporters into the mainstream party (*Daily Telegraph*, 26 August 1987). While it would be wrong to deny the importance of a vociferous group of Tory reformists, present trends confirm the early suspicions of Edmonds and Behrens (1981) that the preferences of the less tolerant populists will continue to gain ground.

To an extent, assimilationist rhetoric has succeeded, and the Right has found some scope for attracting the Asian vote by stressing, for instance, the value of Asian entrepreneurship and reverence for family life. Rich (1986c) suggests that this foreshadows a 'divide and rule' strategy, favouring Asians and marginalizing Afro-Caribbeans. Ultimately, though, the ideals of one-nationhood underestimate not only the exclusivity of this concept, but also the extent of racial inequality in Britan and the potency of black resistance to it.

The racially exclusive undertones of the 'new' nationalism are deftly exposed by Parekh (1986), but it is Miles (1987) who most vividly shows how, throughout British history, English nationalism has been dependent on, and constructed through, the notion of racial differentiation. He argues that during the 1960s and early 1970s, 'the intervention of the state to redetermine who had the right to live within the boundaries of the British nation-state was a concession to, and a legitimation of, racism' (p. 37). This process culminated in the 1981 Nationality Act which brought the definition of citizenship into line with the rights of entry and settlement conferred by the immigration laws. This Act played an important role in the re-establishment of national identity, replacing the expansionist connotations of Commonwealth embedded in the 1948 Act with a more parochial form of patriotism rooted in Britain alone. The irony of the 1981 Act is that 'it is designed to define a sense of belonging and nationhood which is itself a manifestation of the sense of racial superiority created along with the Empire' (Dixon 1983: 173). The fact that it theoretically embraces many black Britons is clouded by the problem that within its many clauses the thinly veiled faces of 'supremacy, chauvinism and racism' are preserved (p. 173).

In the sphere of social welfare, the ideals of assimilation break down at the point of practice. Policies may be formulated as if 'race' were not a fundamental social divide but, especially when the unanticipated outcomes of such policies actually sustain racial inequality, the presumption of even-handedness is unlikely to be widely accepted. From the perspective of many black Britons, the pursuit of assimilationist ideals proves incompatible with both the consequences of economic change and the wider strategies of neo-conservatism. In the face of industrial restructuring, 'the disillusionment, resentment and alienation of the black minority, concentrated in specific areas and excluded from white privileges, is likely to grow' (Dearlove and Saunders 1984: 195). In the context of entrenched racial inequality, the Right's new nationalism appears no less racist than did its Imperialist predecessor (Dixon 1983; Miles 1987): it couples 'backward looking patriotism and nostalgia for Empire' with aspirations for a national homogeneity which makes 'black people – however hard they try to "assimilate" – outsiders' (Murray 1986: 16). Far from encouraging assimilation, a quest for national unity and conformity has produced what DeMont (1980) describes as the ascension of 'race politics' in Britain: the polarization of black and white perspectives on many issues of major importance, encouraged not through any inherent homogeneity among black people but through white legislators' indifference to the specific needs and demands of the black populations. This has not gone unnoticed by right wing populists, who increasingly advance the argument that integrationism is a myth, desired by neither blacks nor 'Britons'. In the wake of this supposed realism other strategies to cope with 'racial segregation' have had to be entertained.

Repatriation   For a vociferous minority on the Right, repatriation has always been the 'logical' culmination of immigration legislation – a link cogently exposed by Miles and Phizacklea (1984). By the 1980s, it seemed to some that arguments centring on nationality might have displaced this immigration–repatriation debate (Rich 1986b). Yet during the 1980s political inclinations towards both immigration control and repatriation have gained renewed momentum.

In 1983, the hundredth Conservative Party conference agreed to debate Harvey Proctor's motion to 'increase the financial and material provision for voluntary repatriation and resettlement'. A pre-debate poll discovered that 55 per cent of delegates supported 'voluntary repatriation', 25 per cent favoured a 'whites only society' and 15 per cent wanted 'compulsory repatriation' (Gordon and Klug 1986: 40). It seems that, far from repatriation being removed from the political agenda, the problems of race and segregation are now constructed in such a way as to provide it with a new rationale. We have seen already that because integration now connotes swamping rather than assimilation, immigration legislation (and the Nationality Act which is its culmination) is regarded less a means of controlling numbers and more a way of maintaining British traditions and institutions. From here, it is but a short step to the view that 'racial harmony and avoidance of strife will be achieved only when the indigenous population see a fall rather than a rise in the total New Commonwealth population resident in the United Kingdom' (Harvey Proctor, HC 1980, 980, 1049). At a time when integrationism has failed to absorb civil strife, and when immigration control is as tight as can be, repatriation is regarded by some as more tenable than ever.

The threat this poses is compounded by a new Immigration Bill published in November 1987 – the first substantial addition to the immigration legislation since 1971. This Bill proposes to remove the right of male Commonwealth citizens, settled in Britain before 1973, to be joined by their wives and children. They will now have to prove their capacity to support a family without recourse to public funds or welfare benefits. While the numbers affected are small (the legislation applies primarily to early Bengali settlers with perhaps fewer than 8000 wives and children overseas) its symbolic implications are unmistakable.[12] Black people in Britain are still to receive only limited access to the rights of citizenship.

Petty immigration legislation simply exacerbates the threat of repatriation which, though still at the bounds of political respectability, continues to reinforce the social isolation of black people, irrespective of where they were born. It also has bearing on the range of other strategies routinely invoked to ensure that 'outsiders', even if they cannot be repatriated, can at least be contained. As Solomos et al. (1982: 31) observe, 'with the concept of "humane repatriation" looming ever more centrally in official thinking on race it need not be conspiratorial to talk of a shift in the balance of state responses from ameliortaion to repression'.

Containment Assimilation is thwarted by resistance; repatriation remains an extreme. Political decision-making has therefore been dominated in the 1980s by the challenge to integrationism that flows from the convenience of 'containment' as a means of controlling black people's discontent. Accordingly, patterns of segregation that are sustained by neo-liberal economic policy tend to be reinforced by the increasingly authoritarian underpinnings of social policy and social control. This helps align physical distance with racial separatism in a process 'justified' as respect for cultural diversity. This powerful combination of ideology and practice carries the seeds of a new segregationism in British public life.

An authoritarian concern for law, order and morality has generated support from the Tory Right for certain interventionist strategies (in the sphere of social control rather than public welfare) which contribute to the social isolation of black people living in relatively segregated areas. It might, of course, be argued that traditional race relations policies have always been more about containment and control than about racial justice (see Moore 1975; Mullard 1985). However, attempts to contain black resistance have become the focus of a much broader attempt 'to bring some kind of order into a society which is widely perceived to be falling apart' (Solomos et al. 1982: 29). Race has become the leading edge of a new ideological thrust to clean up Britain, manage urban conflict and sustain 'traditional' ways of life. Conservative rhetoric has created 'a political context in which tolerance and acceptance, rather than intolerance and rejection [of black people] stand in need of explanation' (Reeves 1983: 164). Once-discrete panics (over race, immigration, crime, welfare, fraud and so on) have been absorbed into the imagery of the inner city, wherein blacks are blamed for a variety of urban ills. The 1980s have become a period of 'crisis management' for governments, and the strategy for managing race relations which has emerged 'prioritizes the option of control and containment of forms of black resistance against racial domination' (Solomos et al. 1982: 15).

The authoritarian assent to interventionism in the sphere of social control extends to both criminal and civil law. With regard to the former, Lord Scarman's inquiry following the Bristol 'riot' of 1980 was expected to form a watershed in the policing of black communities. From it sprang a variety of new initiatives, including the statutory requirement of consultation (introduced by the new Police and Criminal Evidence Act), and a research centre (funded by the Home Office and based at Brunel University) charged to develop training in Community and Race Relations for senior police officers. Yet while Scarman's report *was* innovative in recognizing the permanency of black settlement and dispensing with the imagery of the immigrant, in Rich's (1986a: 209) opinion it still situated black people 'considerably outside the cultural bondage that holds "British" communities together'. The effects of subsequent changes in policing are discussed by Bridges and Bunyan (1983) and Fitzgerald (1987), who both note the extent to which 'law and order' quickly became a euphemism for 'clamping down hard on black people in the inner cities' (Fitzgerald 1987: 3). A recent study by the Institute of Race Relations (1987) claims that modern policing now deliberately targets certain areas, estates, clubs and meeting places in inner city neighbourhoods, giving the impression that 'the police do not consider that a black person, like any other citizen, has the right to enjoy the privacy of his or her own home in peace'. Bridges and Bunyan (1983) go as far as to argue that modern urban policing consists mainly of strategies which aim to 'control and contain the political struggles of the black and working class communities' (p. 106).

The 1980s have also seen losses rather than gains in civil rights for many immigrants and black Britons. Despite being condemned by union leaders as 'reminiscent of the apartheid situation in South Africa' (Gordon 1983: 38), search warrants for illegal immigrants have been issued without bearing suspects' names, effectively requiring 'Asians and West Indians in Britain to carry their passports at all times' (Miles and Phizacklea 1984: 107). By 1983, in a debate on nationality fees, Greville Janner was expressing concern at the new necessity 'for people with Asian names to produce a passport if they are to receive their rights from the DHSS' (HC 1983/4, 50, 145), and two years later David Alton complained that immigrants now faced 'the infringement of the right to movement, the infringement of the right to form relationships, the infringement of the right to live together as a family unit and, in particular, the infringement of the right of all women to equal treatment under the law' (HC 1985, 75, 712).

Separatist principles in the exercise of social control help confirm the 'logic' of racial differentiation as expressed in the organization of space. This imagery is reinforced by the widespread euphemizaton of race, through which a shift from integrationism to segregationism on the part of white society, as well as continuing segregation among black households, is portrayed as a benign index of cultural preference and 'ethnic' diversity.Therefore, if economic liberalism, which claims to address the needs of ostensibly equal individuals, fails to tackle the structural dimension of racial disadvantage, and if public policy remains 'aracial' and effectively colour blind at a time when housing inequalities are expressed as racial segregation, this can all be subsumed in the language of cultural autonomy. Because of this, segregationism, subtly but surely, has become a pervasive racial ideology in neo-conservative Britain. Despite assimilationist 'ideals' and a legacy of integrationist legislation, Tory populism has given the theory and practice of racial separatism, as a form of 'white supremacy', greater force than ever before in political and public life.

Today, moreover, far from being in the shadow of neo-liberal economic policy as a driving force of British conservatism, the revival of moral authoritarianism – with its emphasis on nationhood and social order – is increasingly becoming the flagship of the Right (this trend is discussed by Elliot and McCrone (1987) and Edmonds and Behrens (1981)). The 1980s have witnessed a cultural as well as an economic 'revolution' in the mangement of the nation's fortunes and, as liberal economic goals prove difficult to meet, it is increasingly likely to be a cultural struggle that dominates electoral politics. As a consequence, there is little in the policy agenda for the 1990s to challenge the form or meaning of 'racial segregation'; it remains an expression and a symbol of racial inequality.

Conclusion

Previous chapters gave an account of the pattern and character of 'racial segregation' in Britain, and explored the policy instruments and institutional mechanisms that sustain it. This chapter has taken the analysis one step further by considering how it has been politically possible for the present form of segregation (i.e. coupled with racial inequality) to persist. I have been concerned, therefore, with how racial segregation as a policy-relevant problem is defined and responded to at a national level (the complementary role of local politics is examined by Ben-Tovim et al. (1986) and Rich (1987a), and the local construction and reproduction of racial segregation is the topic of chapter 6). My interest has centred on the political negotiations that determine where and why race and segregation do, or do not, appear on the legislative agenda of national governments, whose decisions seem most crucial in structuring relationships between black and white peoples' residential space.

My aim has been to show how, for more than 40 years, British politicians have regarded racial segregation as a problem. In constructing and addressing this problem, however, attention has consistently centred less on the injustice of racial inequality than on the sensibilities of white voters confronted, successively, by the spectre of overcrowding, the indignity of competition for scarce services and resources, and the insecurity associated with public disorder. These definitions have lent legitimacy to the notion that races are real, and have spawned policies more notable for their role in the reproduction of racial ideology than for their success in tackling the social inequalities expressed in residential space.

For three of the four decades examined, politicians broadly agreed that the 'problem' of segregation was related to the number, concentration and location of 'coloured immigrants', and that solutions lay in cultural adjustment and social mobility, coupled with (and indexed by) residential dispersal. In seeking above all to diminish the visibility of racial disadvantage, and to dilute the impact of immigration on (white) inner city electors, legislators soon adopted dispersal as an over-riding political goal.

Initially, as a 'natural' conclusion to a brief phase of immigration the presumed inevitability of dispersal provided a convenient justification for the non-interference demanded by foreign policy. Subsequently, as a focus of interventionism, the desire to engineer dispersal was presented first (in the absence of any convincing economic rationale) to justify immigration control, and then as the basis of an uneasy bipartisan agreement to 'balance' such controls with the relatively weak provisions of the Race Relations Acts. These strategies were not, however, well suited to solving the problems politicians claimed to address, and by the time attention had turned to the role of the housing system, the shift from redevelopment to renewal had removed the one mechanism (comprehensive redevelopment) that might have allowed dispersal policies to succeed. Thus, despite an outward commitment to the contrary, politicians' attempts to deal with segregation had, by 1979, secured neither residential dispersal nor racial equality in housing.

By the late 1970s, the characteristics of neighbourhoods in which black households were statistically over-represented – epitomized in the volatile and newsworthy 'inner city' – provided the British Right with a convenient platform on which to muster support for its programme of social change. As a symptom of urban malaise, inserted into the debate on law and order and epitomizing the presumed inconvenience of multi-culturalism, racial segregation has acquired a symbolic role in articulating the authoritarian demands, and in sustaining the patriotic imagery, of neo-conservative populism. In practice, solutions to this redefined problem of segregation, when set in the context of neo-liberal economic policy, indicate that the (welcome) demise of 'dispersal' has been succeeded not by a quest for racial justice but by the ascent of a 'new' segregationism.

Segregation now seems acceptable as a phase in the adjustment of market forces, even though social polarization in housing is increasingly implicated in the structuring of racial inequality. As a neutral index of cultural differentiation, segregation seems justifiable as a social practice, even though racially mixed areas are among the most disadvantaged in the country and bear the brunt of new (ostensibly demand-led) authoritarian forms of social control. This marks a break with the past, but there are continuities too.

Now, as in the 1950s, the 'problem' of segregation is constructed in a language that sustains (euphemistically or otherwise) the notion that racial categories are real, without probing the racist, nationalist and segregationist forces which constitute them. In the 1980s, as in the 1940s, 'solutions' as well as problems have been designed almost exclusively by white politicians catering to the demands of a predominantly white electorate. Now, as always, the persistence of racial segregation and its enduring link with racial inequality is a surprise to Governments, but can readily be explained in the light of their actions.

The 1980s mark the culmination of a long political struggle with a problem termed 'racial segregation'. Modern legislators are no nearer than their predecessors to establishing what that is and why it persists, without marginalizing or demeaning the black population. More disturbing still, there is no sign that either the form or the meaning of racial segregation are being challenged (or are even challengeable) at a Parliamentary level. Now more than ever the organization of residential space, and the imagery associated with it, symbolizes black people's exclusion from some fundamental rights of citizenship.

Notes

1 Agnew (1987) discusses the notion of political culture in its more conventional sense as the dominant, internalized value-system of a people or nation.

2 Other typologies focus on the achievements of the Left (Hall 1978; Joshi and Carter 1984; Miles and Phizacklea 1984; Mullard 1985), the role of the Right (Rich 1986c) and the effects of party interactions on the shifting balance of legislation (Bulpitt 1986; Solomos et al. 1982).

3 This periodization is obviously not intended to be discrete or definitive. As a heuristic device it will inevitably understate continuities, and by concentrating on political themes it must sacrifice the complexity of individuals' views.

4 Moore (1987) provides an illuminating account of the negotiations that secured India's participation in the New Commonwealth, formed in 1949.

5 'Operation Westward Ho' began in 1947 as an attempt, supervised by the Ministry of Labour, to recruit workers to the UK from the Polish resettlement camps in Britain, from displaced persons in Germany, Austria and Italy, and from the unemployed elsewhere in Europe (see Harris 1987).

6 The only hint at intervention during this period came in the form of a survey of Colonial Governments during 1947 designed to identify discriminatory legislation, particularly that which applied differently to Europeans and non-Europeans.

7 Miles (1982b) and Miles and Dunlop (1987) have shown that the racialization of British politics during the 1960s was primarily an English phenomenon and was central to the construction of a distinctively English nationalism. In Scotland, the revival of nationalist politics hinged not on opposition to racialized minorities but on opposition to the English. This displaced (possibly temporarily) the salience of race in Scottish politics (although it did not preclude the exercise of racism in Scottish life). Similar arguments might be developed with reference to the Welsh experience.

8 In retrospect, Labour's objections were well founded since there is now evidence that, by limiting the labour force during the early 1960s, Britain may have lost ground relative to the rest of Europe in the process of post-war expansion (see Freeman 1979).

9 The possibility of introducing anti-discrimination legislation was raised as early as 1948 when Bernard Finlay urged a Labour Party conference that the law could be an effective means of containing fascist ideas in the same way that it

controlled defamation, blasphemy and so on. In 1949, Lord Faringdon brought a private member's Bill to the House of Lords advocating the removal of discriminatory clauses from leases and suggesting penalties for discrimination in catering establishments, public houses and employment. These moves failed amid much concern about their inability to counter (and their possibility of enhancing) the effects of communist propaganda in the colonial territories, and without serious discussion of their impact on domestic affairs. The shift of thinking that informed the first successful anti-discrimination Bill is documented by Hindell (1965).

10 Kavanagh (1987: chapter 4) discusses the complexities of this label, which tends to subsume a wide variety of political ideologies drawn from both economic theory and moral philosophy.

11 Reeves (1983) identifies two principal strategies behind the deracialization of political discourse. *Sanitary coding* enables politicians to 'communicate privately racist ideas with a discourse publicly defensible as non-racist' (p. 90), while *imaging* allows a speaker to avoid the terminology of race but to insert an unmistakable racial awareness into the public mind by 'intuitively or consciously' selecting images 'which the audience can be relied on to capture in a predictable way' (p. 201).

12 Ironically, this removal of male migrants' rights is Britain's reply to a ruling by the European Court that the existing immigration rules discriminate against women. Rather than extend the rules and increase the rights of women, Government opted to pursue the cause of equality by diminishing the rights of men.

6 'Common Sense' Racism and the Limits to Resistance

The average person in the ordinary little street in village or town just does not know what the colour bar means.

F. W. Skinnard, 6 May 1949

By asserting that racial segregation is problematic, Governments can win credit from the electorate even when policy solutions sustain inequality. But popular exculpation cannot be taken for granted. Politicians must constantly appeal to, or create, a public 'common sense' which supports – or fails effectively to challenge – their preferred legislative programme. This chapter considers how and why the public accepts or rejects, reproduces or challenges, the salience of 'race' in the structuring of space.

There are many kinds of 'common sense' which sustain segregation. There is a common sense that guides political decision making, a common sense that perpetuates the taken-for-granted mechanisms of institutional racism and a common sense that guides daily routine. So far, by focusing on this 'wisdom' in key decision-makers, I have depicted racial segregation as the product of political and economic forces that are largely beyond the influence of individual will. I will now argue that there is also scope for the common sense racism that infuses public life to play a part – perhaps a fundamental one – in sustaining the form, defining the meaning and securing the popular legitimacy of this iniquitous division of residential space.

I recognize, of course, that it is only within a relatively narrow margin that consumer choice shapes residential patterns, especially at the lower end of the housing ladder. This does not, however, mean that people passively accept their lot. Symbolically, and through a range of social practices, the public can choose from, and create, alternatives in the organization of neighbourhood life. Here I shall be concerned with the role of popular racial consciousness in that wider political struggle for space. I shall argue that 'racial segregation' is not simply a product of markets and institutions, nor even a legislative convenience: it is also a way of life – a medium in which power is contested and an arena in which social and political identities are shaped. In the broadest sense, this chapter is concerned with the construction of residential space by that most fundamental unit of liberal democracy, the voting public.

'Common sense' racism

Eyles and Evans (1987) show that there is a complex relationship between popular consciousness and political ideology. This is a contentious issue, and commentators are divided over the extent to which popular racism flows from, or mobilizes, racial antipathy in the legislature. The review that follows identifies some important links between these two areas of opinion (without implying causality).

Opinion polls conducted during the 1950s reveal relatively widespread indifference among white Britons to the presence of black people. Between half and three-quarters of the population in 1951 and 1956 agreed with the principle of unrestricted entry for colonial workers, and while there *is* evidence of prejudice, discrimination and racial violence, the public generally subscribed to the Commonwealth ideal that was so actively fostered by contemporary politicians (see Banton 1983, 1985). Most (three-quarters of the population) saw only benefits in the Imperial–Colonial relationship, and they shared Governments' faith in the robustness (and superiority) of British cultural norms.

Increasing levels of public anxiety are recorded towards the end of the 1950s and these also mirror the concerns of Parliament. In 1958, as politicians contemplated the delicacies of immigration control, Gallup Polls showed that over one-third (37 per cent) of the public thought black people should not be allowed to compete with whites for jobs, over half (54 per cent) thought they should not be given access to council housing and almost two-thirds (65 per cent) wanted black people excluded altogether through strict immigration controls. As time went on, these sentiments became explicitly segregationist. Rose et al. (1969) found that around a third of residents in five sampled boroughs regarded the presence of 'coloureds' as a major local problem: 31 per cent thought them bad for the neighbourhood, 25 per cent worried about intermarriage and 22 per cent feared that whites would be outnumbered.

By the mid-1960s, race-related problems had become a 'fact' of daily life. White Britons shared the sentiments of political leaders and displayed an enduring pessimism concerning the future for race relations. Studlar

(1974) shows that between 1959 and 1972 over 40 per cent of the population consistently believed that feelings between black and white people were deteriorating, and around half believed that the presence of black people would bring serious social problems.

More recent evidence suggests that public opinion is increasingly aligned with the imagery of neo-conservatism. The popular euphemization of race is nowhere near as thoroughgoing as it has been in the world of high politics, but there are two aspects of New Right thinking that seem particularly pervasive in the population at large. First, reflecting political objections to race-targeted public policy, surveys have shown that at least a third of the British population now believe that attempts to secure racial equality 'have gone too far' (Banton 1985: 67). In accordance with this, between a fifth and a quarter of whites are opposed to positive action to ensure that 'black, Asian and other ethnic minorities' do not suffer unfairly in the spheres of education, work and housing (Anwar 1981/2). Secondly, the assimilationist ideals of one-nation conservatism are reflected in the discovery that fully 40 per cent of the public (mainly whites) are resistant to the notion that blacks should preserve their own cultural identity (Brown 1984). The political corollary of this desire for social homogeneity is concern about the prospect of conflict where diversity persists. It is significant, then, that in 1982, 40 per cent of the public associated racial strife with the location of 'ethnically' mixed neighbourhoods, and that over half those replying to the British Social Attitudes survey believe that 'race riots' will be an enduring characteristic of Britain's urban future (Jowell and Airey 1984).

There are, then, strong parallels between public and political conceptions of race-related problems. The differences between those (such as Ashford 1981; Dummett and Dummett 1969) who regard this as the product of 'strong leadership' and those (including Freeman 1979; Studlar 1974) who attribute it more to politicians' 'responsiveness to the public' might partly be resolved by recognizing two qualitatively different (if overlapping and mutually reinforcing) forms of racial antipathy.

'Top-down' influences on public opinion may best be expressed in a form which Husbands (1979) terms 'low level' racism – a sentiment which infuses daily life and is widely but abstractly expressed by a broad cross-section (perhaps a majority) of the population. Whether through contentious legislation, via political discourse and rhetoric, or by its use of the mass media, the world of high politics must bear some responsibility for the general atmosphere of intolerance and hostility revealed by opinion polls.

On the other hand, there are forms of racial antipathy that exhibit marked variations according to demographic, socio-economic and locational criteria. Such variety seems less likely to be accounted for by the pervasiveness of political culture than by the public's direct experience (actual or, more commonly, perceived) of the consequences of living in a multi-racial society. These 'bottom-up' influences contribute to what Husbands (1979) terms 'experiential racism' – a reaction by white Britons to those broad patterns of local socio-economic change that are outside their control and that coincide with (but of course have no necessary causal relationship with) the presence of black people – either at home or at work. Variations in the expression of such sentiment might be expected to coincide with the selective impact of socio-economic change, and with the labour and housing market characteristics of the different areas in which black people live. Experiential racism might also be the form in which 'common sense' segregationism is most clearly articulated.

Exclusionary tendencies in a 'vertical' sense can be discerned in the growing evidence that racial antipathy is often strongest in the lower socio-economic groups (Freeman 1979). According to the experiential thesis, this must partly reflect the insecure position of (actual and aspiring) waged workers at times of economic decline or during periods when economic inequality is most marked. This explains the common observation that when times are hard, working class whites do not express solidarity with their black counterparts, but instead attempt to secure for themselves (usually to the exclusion of blacks) privileged access to jobs, homes and welfare benefits (Joshi and Carter 1984). In the same vein, Miles and Phizacklea (1979, 1981), and Phizacklea and Miles (1980) show how, among the white working class, perceptions of black people have become linked with perceptions of material hardship and local economic decline.

The experiential component of common sense racism may, it seems, partly be a product of struggles within the occupational order. However, Husbands's (1983) survey of working class electors in several large cities suggests that popular racism (both overt and implicit) may be even more closely contingent on anxieties concerning residence. He examined the relationship between racial antipathy and three aspects of daily experience – housing and neighbourhood, education and social services, and jobs and promotion. By far the most marked levels of antipathy were expressed in relation to the first of these. Half the sample claimed that their neighbourhood had been deteriorating as a place to live in and 39 per cent spontaneously attributed this to factors associated with the presence of immigrants and foreigners. The public displayed a widespread tendency to agree with statements like 'house values go down when immigrants move into a neighbourhood', 'in some areas of our towns there are so many immigrants that white people feel out of place' and 'in some cities there are so many immigrants that white people find it difficult to get the housing they want' (Husbands 1983: Appendix). No statements relating to education, services and jobs gained the same intensity of support as these. This does not necessarily imply that the spheres of employment and education are any less important than housing in reproducing racial inequality in material terms. Rather, it suggests that, at a symbolic level, sentiment generated in a variety of public spheres can become focused at a neighbourhood scale, wherein territory and family life are rooted. This hypothesis is borne out in a range of other studies, which together provide a powerful indication of how resistant white Britain is to the prospect of residential integration (see Miles and Phizacklea 1979; Ratcliffe 1981; Robinson 1984/5, 1987).

From the early 1970s, when 25 per cent of the population spontaneously blamed their own racial antipathy on deteriorating living standards and competition for housing (Butler and Stokes 1974), to the 1980s, when one in five people believe black households should avoid living in 'white' neighbourhoods (Brown 1984), popular consciousness has been infused with segregationist inclinations. These might be overtly hostile or benignly paternalistic, and they may be more or less strongly related to political ideology, but they exhibit considerable local variability and seem especially acute in those socially and environmentally stressed urban areas where black people are most likely to live. The consequences are more than apparent to the black population. Almost 70 per cent of the black people interviewed by Anwar (1981) felt that the status of racial minorities in Britain was declining; half believed that race relations as a whole were deteriorating. Whereas only one-fifth of black people included in the 1974 PEP survey thought racial discrimination and disadvantage were making life worse then than five years earlier, by the time of the 1982 PSI survey that figure had risen to over 50 per cent. The disturbing conclusion must therefore be not only that racist and (increasingly) segregationist sentiments are actively sustained by whites, but also that this impinges directly on black people's own sense of well-being.

It would be dangerous, and theoretically unwarranted, to leap uncritically from the world of attitudes to that of behaviour. None of the sentiments identified above – neither high nor low level, ideological nor experiential, racism – can be regarded as predictors of action. They do, however, provide a reservoir of procedural norms that not only tacitly inform routine activity, but are also available to legitimize more purposive, explicitly racist, practices. Widespread racial antipathy does not determine action, but it may invest racially discriminatory or exclusionary behaviour with a degree of normative support. It may therefore increase the social acceptability of direct or indirect racism both to individual perpetrators and to their peers.

The remainder of this chapter is concerned with a range of behaviours informed by common sense racism and by reactions to it. The activities I consider are political in the broadest sense, and my interest is in how far they reproduce and accentuate, or challenge and attenuate, the racialized structure of residential space. I focus particularly on expressions of territoriality: on behaviour that may be read as an instrument of segregation or as a symbol of resistance.

Racism and resistance in the struggle for space

People can, through their capacity for social action, affect the material reality and ideological tenacity of racial segregation. To this end, public behaviour may be regarded simultaneously as social, economic and political in its orientation: such behaviour turns on a struggle for the power required to shape any and all of these facets of daily life. Elsewhere, I have considerd the general implications of this for the reproduction of race (Smith 1986: chapter 7). Here, I shall focus more specifically on those actions that seek to exert a *political* influence, broadly defined. I shall examine, then, a set of behaviours that are practised more or less explicitly in an attempt to alter the nature and effects of policy, either through direct action or through indirect measures which seek to influence (democratically or otherwise) those with immediate access to decision-making power. By exploring a range of activities from voting behaviour to street politics, from harassment and attack to ritual, rebellion and riot, I examine the scope for, and exercise of, common sense segregationism within the current organization of British liberal democracy. Many of these actions are defensive as well as exclusionary in orientation: in this sense both racism and resistance contribute to the reproduction of neighbourhood life.

Racism at the ballot box

We have seen that the major political decisions sustaining segregation were formulated by an all-white legislature which paid little attention to the needs or rights of black people and which has traditionally secured its legitimacy by granting concessions to a white electorate. Here, I want to consider what that electorate demanded, and what sentiments its vote expressed.

Despite concerted bipartisan efforts to keep race at the margins of the political agenda, the British public has, in a variety of surveys, signalled concern about the political management of race-related issues (McKay

1977). In the mid-1960s it became apparent not only that a racist platform could attract white voters, but also that a neutral or anti-racist stance could lose them. By the 1970s, the far Right had surged back into 'respectable' politics, providing a unique opportunity to interrrogate the racist vote for clues about the organization of residential space.

It may be true (as Anwar (1986) and Lawrence (1978/9) have argued) that parties like the National Front and British National Party have never been a viable entity in British politics.[1] Nevertheless, there is a sense in which support for these groups might be interpreted as a microcosm of more widespread patterns of racial antipathy among the electorate. This interpretation does not seem unreasonable, since we know that the Conservative Party lost voters to the Right when it admitted Ugandan Asian refugees in 1972, and 'reclaimed' many of them once its hardline approach to immigrants and immigration was reasserted later in the decade (see Lawrence 1978/9). Voting patterns on the far Right could, therefore, illuminate some characteristics of common sense racism which are more enduring than the party allegiance of their incumbents. If so, the mid-1970s provide a limited but unique opportunity to consider what the racist vote – symbolised in (but not restricted to) electoral sympathy for the extreme Right – means for the organization of urban life.

Right-wing extremism in twentieth-century Britain has taken many forms, ranging from broadly based neo-fascism to the more narrowly focused immigration control societies (these are documented by Nugent (1976)). My concern here is with those ostensibly more 'respectable' organizations that have attempted to win support through the conventional channels of democracy. The most prominent of these is the National Front (NF).

The National Front was formed in 1967 from a merger of the League of Empire Loyalists, the British National Party, parts of the Racial Preservation Society and a number of smaller groups. The party has had a stormy and contentious history, which is fully documented by Billig (1978), Husbands (1983), Taylor (1977/8, 1979, 1982), Walker (1977) and many others. What it *means* to vote for the National Front, however, is not easy to gauge. To some extent, particularly during the height of the party's fortunes, the NF provided a convenient channel for popular protest. Although Taylor (1982) does not see this as the party's primary attraction, he is convinced that during the 1970s the NF provided an outlet for public hostility towards black people and towards New Commonwealth immigration at a time when the established parties were thought to have abandoned the interests of whites. On the other hand, racist voting must also reflect individuals' compliance with at least some part of the far Right manifesto. Some voters must have subscribed to the NF's assertions that whites head a 'natural' hierarchy of races, that 'miscegenation' is part of a conspiracy to destroy this hierarchy and that integrationist sentiments are an attempt to rob white people of their 'natural' supremacy. Other voters may have allied more closely with the views of the 'National Party of the United Kingdom' which held that 'the British People must preserve their distinct racial character', by preventing the immigration of 'non-British stock' and by encouraging the 'humane repatriation' of 'all coloured and other racially incompatible immigrants, their dependents and descendants' (cited by Nugent 1976).

Racist voting may, then, express a variety of emotions but exclusionism and separatism provide a common core. It is tempting to take the analysis further by appealing to Italian fascism, German nazism, or the Le Pen cult in modern France. However, a more promising avenue is exposed by Husbands (1983), who concentrates on domestic trends in racist voting and draws attention to their striking spatial variability. This distinctive geography seems much more likely to be explained with reference to local culture and experience than by appeal to foreign affairs.

Although electoral support for the far Right has generally been small, there are some areas where the NF has attracted a substantial proportion of the vote. (Equally, there are other regions, notably Scotland, where explicitly racist or fascist organizations made scarcely any impact during the 1970s). In seats contested in the general elections of 1970 and 1974, NF support averaged between 3 and 3.5 per cent of votes cast, and in local elections during 1976 this climbed to 8.9 per cent. These averages mask considerable clustering within a few locales. In the general election of February 1974, NF candidates in Hackney South and Leicester East polled 7.4 and 9.4 per cent of the total vote, respectively, and in October that year, the Hackney poll also increased to 9.4 per cent. In local elections in 1976, the NF took 18 per cent of the vote in Leicester and won two seats on the council in Blackburn; in the GLC elections of 1977, the NF exceeded 15 per cent of the vote in four seats, and there were 11 seats altogether where more than 10 per cent of voters supported the NF candidate.

This spatial clustering of the racist vote has an importance of its own, irrespective of the socio-economic and demographic attributes of electors.[2] Husbands (1983) found that in those economically declining urban neighbourhoods where the far Right has secured substantial electoral support, it is primarily spatial (locational and residential) rather than social criteria that distinguish NF sympathizers. It is the realm of home and neighbourhood rather than the world of work that most directly determines susceptibility to NF support. While this vindicates Savage's (1987) claim that working class voting patterns are increasingly determined by issues related to locality rather than occupation, as an expression of common sense segregationism it does require elaboration.

From research documented by Husbands (1983) and Taylor (1979) it is possible to elicit three ways in which the racist vote might be interpreted as racially exclusionary or separatist in intent. First, the NF consistently received most support in constituencies where the black population formed more than 5 per cent of residents. This suggests that racist voting is part of a white backlash against the local presence of a relatively large black minority. According to Husbands (1979), this backlash occurs both in declining industrial areas (where competition for jobs is fierce) and in relatively prosperous locales (where black and white workers attracted to jobs are forced to compete for housing). In such zones NF sympathizers were 20–30 per cent more likely than others to be concerned about neighbourhood deterioration and to blame this on their black neighbours. Other beliefs, especially about the relationship between black youths and certain types of crime, also characterized these sympathizers. In short, racist voting in areas where the black population forms a relatively high proportion of the total seems to be a direct reaction to the (perceived) impact of residential mixing on a locality's lifestyle, organization and resources.

Secondly, Taylor (1979) shows that throughout the 1970s support for the NF was disproportionately high in voting districts which themselves contained few black people, but which lay adjacent to districts in which the black population was statistically over-represented. This suggests that racist voting is at least partly a reaction to the perceived threat of residential integration. Husbands's (1983) data support this hypothesis, showing that fears relating to *potential* territorial encroachment by black households are one of just three key attitudinal discriminators between NF sympathizer and others. This suggests that racist voting refers to fear of outsiders, resistance to change and apprehension in the face of an uncertain future. In these circumstances, a vote for the extreme Right is a symbolic opportunity to 'exercise a generalised form of defensive self-expression' (p. 108) which is both exclusionary in principle and segregationist in intent.

Finally, the symbolism of the racist vote may be rooted in local history and tradition. The electorate in some areas, for instance South Shoreditch and North Bethnal Green in London, have nurtured a tradition of racist voting throughout the twentieth century (Husbands 1982). Racism, it seems, can be an expression of local culture. It is one signifier of the parochialism that is often associated with life in working class Britain. Paradoxically, the exclusionary and segregationist form this takes may reflect the fact that in Britain, unlike the USA, the social distinctions between residential neighbourhoods are not always clear cut. It is, ironically, 'the absence of clear boundaries and of their associated psychological certainties' that mobilizes NF sympathy (Husbands 1983: 146). A facet of residential segregation in Britain that some have found encouraging (its blurred edges) can combine with local sentiment to strengthen the 'racial' boundaries of residential space.

To summarize, the expression of racist sentiment through political allegiance is one way in which the white working class, with its limited ability to manipulate residential space, can pursue segregationist preferences in everyday life. The 1970s provided a unique 'window' through which to view this. The racist vote – which has never before, or since, been quite so readily isolated – can be read as a symbolic attempt by whites to contest territory and racialize the social identity of their neighbourhood. Whether as a protest against residential mixing, as resistance to the prospect of spatial integration or as a cultural expression of attachment to territory, the racist vote indexes a popular segregationism which sustains rather than challenges the divisive legacy of public policy.

If the racist vote provides a glimpse of the territorial nature of racial antipathy, the 'ethnic' vote may be read as an index of the scope for black resistance through the ballot box. Such 'resistance' must be seen not simply as a reaction to right-wing extremism, but rather as a much broader attempt to secure change in a legislative system that has traditionally ignored black people's interests.[3]

The scope for racialized minorities to participate effectively in representative politics may partly be gauged from their success as election candidates. Locally, black people have made some gains, though they remain under-represented as councillors (see Anwar 1986). Nationally the position is much bleaker, since the widespread (though poorly substantiated) belief that black candidates are an electoral liability has impeded their selection as prospective parliamentary candidates (Bochel and Denver 1983; LeLohé 1983).[4] Even in the 1979 election, the five black candidates who stood were placed in unwinnable constituencies, and although 18 black candidates were fielded in 1983, none was elected. When black MPs entered the House of Commons after June 1987 it was for the first time since 1929 – even then, three of the four were elected with reduced majorities for Labour.[5]

While it is tempting to assume that black candidates are the choice of black voters, and therefore enhance the representation of black people's interest in Parliament, analysts greet this with qualified support. For party preference rather than candidates' identities guides the apportionment votes, and success for black politicians has depended less on attracting black voters than on securing safe seats (Crewe 1979). Thus, although the election of black MPs cannot fail to increase Parliament's sensitivity to race-related issues, their role must be compromised while political success depends on white voters.

Fundamentally, the key to black people's ability to exercise their political rights lies in the strength and efficacy of the black vote itself. This has been limited on two counts, both of which are a consequence of the numerically small voting constituency. The first constraint flows from trends in registration and turnout; the second is imposed by a system of representative democracy which devalues the vote of minority groups.

Black voters represent a much smaller proportion of the electorate in Britain than they do in the USA (where the rising number of black office-bearers is often regarded as a major success of the civil rights movement). However, the problems posed by low numbers have traditionally been exacerbated by under-registration and by low turnouts at general elections. This has been accounted for by black people's limited interest in British politics, by their disproportionate lack of faith in the potential for individuals to influence Government and by their fear of harassment from the far Right or the immigration authorities once their names appear on the electoral roll – this is apparent from the GLC Political Attitudes Survey (1984), cited in Fitzgerald (1987) (see also Anwar 1987; Layton-Henry and Studlar 1985; Ratcliffe 1981).

Patterns of registration and turnout are nevertheless, changing. In 1964, les than half the country's 'Commonwealth immigrants' were registered to vote (Deakin 1965). By 1983, the figure had risen to 78 per cent and was approaching that of the white population, which then stood at 81 per cent (Anwar 1987). Although this represents a consistent increase among Asians (from 73 per cent in 1974 to 79 per cent in 1983), it indicates a fall in the registration of Afro-Caribbeans (from a peak of 81 per cent in 1979 to 76 per cent in 1983 (according to Anwar 1984, 1986, 1987)).[6] In both groups, however, the potential impact of the black vote is still seriously impaired in the inner cities, where black people are only half as likely to register as whites, who are themselves heavily under-registered (Todd and Butcher 1982). This is particularly serious given that it is in the inner city constituencies that the greatest proportion of black voters live.

Turnout is almost as important as registration in determining voting strength and throughout the 1970s turnout steadily increased among black voters while remaining more or less static among whites (Studlar 1986). Afro-Caribbeans' turnout has always been more depressed and less consistent than that of the Asians, however, so that by 1983, 81 per cent of Asians as compared with 60 per cent of Afro-Caribbeans and whites voted in the general election. One suggestion for the discrepancies between

Asian and Afro-Caribbean voting patterns is the more marked over-representation of the latter in the lower socio-economic groups, whose likelihood of voting is always relatively low (Welch and Studlar 1985). Ratcliffe (1981), however, interprets the Afro-Caribbean strategy as a deliberate and symbolic rejection of the ballot box in the face of governmental indifference to racial disadvantage.

Loss of voting power through under-registration or low turnout is particularly critical for minority groups, whose impact within two-party, 'first-past-the-post' politics is already inherently limited (Crewe 1983). Despite this, and despite the cultural and ideological fragmentation of the black population, Afro-Caribbean and Asian electors have a potential advantage in advancing the shared interests of the black populations (limited though these may be) by evincing overwhelming support for the same political party. Even allowing for some loss of the Asian vote to the Centre or the Right, by 1987 a Harris poll carried out for the Hansib newspaper group discovered sustained support for Labour among 72 per cent of the black electorate (*Independent*, 3 June 1987). This means that black people account for an increasing proportion of the Labour vote at a time when overall support for the party appears to be waning.[8] This has led to speculation about the bargaining power that might accrue to black voters, despite their small numbers, by virtue of their control over the 'ethnic marginals' (constituencies in which a deterioration in black people's support for Labour could lose the seat in an election).

The number of ethnic marginals was estimated at somewhere between 14 and 37 in the 1983 election and, in view of their importance, Anwar (1986, 1987) has argued that the very fact of segregation is beginning to give black voters unprecedented bargaining power within the conventional channels of British democracy. However, the work of Fitzgerald (1983), Layton-Henry (1983) and Studlar (1983) is not so optimistic.

In 1983, despite the fact that most black voters in the 'ethnic' marginals retained their allegiance to Labour, a large proportion of these seats were lost. Even black electors who rejected their Labour candidate did not boost the poll of a rival party: these people simply did not vote. There was, then, no notable 'swing' in the black vote from one party to another, and even if there had been, it may not have substantially altered the result (which was primarily determined by the behaviour of white electors). Similarly, in the Conservative marginals, despite black people's over-whelming support for Labour, their collective voting power did not win a single seat. Even in constituencies such as Brent, Southall and Ladywood, where black people constitute more than 40 per cent of the population, the black vote may not be decisive (at least while the alternative to voting Labour is not to vote at all). In the average Labour constituency, where the population is between 9 and 22 per cent black, prospective MPs still have most to gain from the support of local whites.

The insensitivity of modern British democracy to the votes of minority groups is not, it seems, very greatly offset either by black people's political concentration within the Labour Party or by their spatial concentration within the 'ethnic' marginals. The disheartening fact of this political geography is that in the very areas where black people are most likely to live, the major parties retain the option of canvassing the anti-'immigrant' vote; as Banton (1984) realistically observes, racists probably continue to outnumber black people both in the electorate at large and among Labour partisans. In the light of this, Fitzgerald (1987) argues that Labour's anti-racism may ultimately prove to be more rhetoric than reality, and is therefore likely to 'exploit black communities' while benefiting 'only a charmed circle of black people through a process of political nepotism' (p. 34). Parliamentary politics appear to offer few opportunities for non-whites, at least in the medium term.

The impact of the black electorate on *local* politics in some areas is indisputable: it underlies the adoption of anti-racist programmes by Labour-led local authorities and it has encouraged the Labour party to transgress a longstanding bipartisan complacency over race-related issues. Nationally, however, neither the actual nor the potential impact of black voters is very large. It seems that although residential segregation may provide a basis for enhancing the power of the black electorate locally, it simply provides a basis for marginalizing the black vote nationally. Ironically, the first of these features can only encourage self-segregation as a strategy for assembling local political influence (at a time when the power base of local politics is increasingly usurped by the political centre), while the second encourages a form of political segregation which is reflected in the continuing struggle to establish a role for black sections within the Labour Party.[9]

Attack and defence

Voting behaviour represents (among other things) only a veiled assertion of territorial prerogative, and this is based on mobilizing the conventional channels of liberal democracy. However, racially exclusionist sentiments also infuse the exercise of 'street politics', which routinely include racist harrassment, attack or terrorism. Such violence has only received political and journalistic recognition during the past decade, but racial terrorism has been common in Britain throughout the present century. Its full extent can now be appreciated from a range of case materials collated by the Commission for Racial Equality (1981, 1987), the Federation of Black

Housing Organisations (1986), the Greater London Council (1984), the Runnymede Trust (Klug 1982), Searchlight (1982) and many other organizations. Other researchers (including Brown 1984; Fryer 1984; Gordon 1983) provide detailed analyses of the now-familiar catalogue of insults, assaults, graffiti, damage and arson that regularly threaten black people. Causing psychological harm, physical injury and death, such attacks are described by a Home Affairs Committee (1986) as the most shameful and dispiriting aspect of race relations in Britain.

Many official documents (e.g. Home Office 1981) contend that harassment and attack are the product of spontaneous direct racism perpetrated by individuals or unorganized collectivities. Other reviewers (e.g. Layton-Henry 1986) attach much more weight to the coordinated activities of right-wing extremists. For my purposes, personal racism and political extremism can be seen as part of a continuum of separatist behaviours exercised (among other things) to preserve both national exclusivity and neighbourhood segregation.

Since the systematic monitoring of racial attack is a recent and very patchy undertaking, any attempt to interpret trends or patterns must be treated with caution. It is obvious, though, that even allowing for an increase in the reporting and recording of incidents, the 1980s have witnessed an escalation of racial violence, both in England and Wales (Gordon 1986a) and in Scotland (MacEwen 1986). The Home Office claims that victimization rates for this kind of offence stood at 51.2 (per 100 000) for Afro-Caribbeans and 69.7 for Asians at the beginning of the decade, and Brown (1984) suggests that this is an underestimate.

Attempts to interpret the significance of racial violence must take into account both the widespread and indiscriminate pattern of attacks and a marked localization of more intense persecutions. I shall consider these separately.

The pervasive and routine nature of racial violence is documented by Gordon (1986a), who shows that there are very few areas with black residents where attacks have not been reported. Moreover, whereas white victims of violence are most at risk in the areas (the inner parts of the major conurbations) and in the age groups (youthful) where crime rates generally peak, black people are at risk wherever they live and across all age bands (Brown 1984). This dispersed pattern of racial harassment can be accounted for by a combination of two factors: the indiscriminate direct racism associated with extremist politics or with the sentiments they inspire; and widespread institutional complacency.

The rejection of representative democracy in favour of street politics among activists on the far Right is documented by Taylor (1982). He shows how, by the 1980s, the National Front had lifted sanctions against its members' more disreputable activities. At about this time, too, the literature of the 'fascist' fringe became extremely violent, forecasting a slide into thuggery which dominated the agenda of a panel of enquiry into racial harassment set up by the GLC Police Committee in 1984. This investigation identified the organized far Right as an important source of attacks on both individuals and organizations. These attacks are directed more or less randomly against black people wherever and whenever the opportunity arises. Given the broader objectives of the groups involved, such indiscriminate violence may be interpreted as a broadly exclusionist gesture, aiming ultimately to rid Britain of black people and to establish an all-white society.

One reason why this broad spectrum of opportunities to commit racial violence is exploited is the failure of the major institutions to produce an effective deterrent. Housing departments have attracted a great deal of criticism for their inflexibility (particularly in rehousing victims or evicting the perpetrators of racial violence). Even Schedule 2 of the 1985 Housing Act, which provides for the eviction of tenants who are 'guilty of conduct which is a nuisance or annoyance to neighbours', has not always persuaded local councils of their authority to act. Many housing departments have, however, proved amenable to change, and a recent survey by the Commission for Racial Equality (1987) found that over half (56 per cent) have some explicit policy for dealing with racial harassment. Nevertheless, eviction policies are difficult to enact, and only a handful of cases have been pursued. In practice the most feasible strategy has been to transfer the victims within a shrinking public sector stock, usually moving them into poorer quality properties in already segregated areas.

The police also have an important role in containing racial attacks and they are, if anything, more open to the charge of complacency than are the housing departments. (According to the CRE's (1987) survey these two services only liaise formally on the issue of racial violence in 44 per cent of local authorities.) The police have been accused of trivializing harassment, of penalizing victims (often challenging their right to residence in the UK), of failing to respond to calls for help and of preferring to opt for civil action rather than a criminal prosecution (see CRE 1987). Despite demands for reform, in November 1986 the Association of Chief Police Officers restated its opposition to adopting new measures and argued that present guidelines were working effectively. The police claim that their scope to act is limited by a lack of evidence or motive, and by the fine line between civil and criminal assault. Critics claim that they are preoccupied with a narrow 'criminal justice' model of response which regards every incident as discrete and self-contained, defines the severity of the offence only according to measures of physical injury or damage, and is often obsessed with catching offenders at the expense of serving victims. Whatever the reason, modern policing is reluctant to recognize that racial attack may be a way of life in some locales; it seems unable to respond to the *prospect* of violence which impinges on the well-being of whole communities and restricts the lifestyles of many individuals.

There *are* some signs of improvement: many forces now make an effort to encourage victims to report their experience and special provisions have been made in sensitive areas, for instance East London, to investigate racially motivated incidents. The Metropolitan Police have formally acknowledged that a racial incident occurs not only where officers perceive a racial motive, but where allegations of racial motivation are made by *any* person (see Gregg 1987). Nevertheless, many black people continue to regard the police response as inadequate, placing complacency and inactivity alongside a much broader catalogue of oppression and mistreatment. This explains why the GLC (1984) was moved to include police violence with a range of other attacks in its broader survey of racial harassment.

Against a background of widespread and general vulnerability, exploited by the far Right and facilitated by institutionalized apathy, there are noticeable patterns of intensification and localization of racist violence. Most obviously, clusters of violence occur in areas where the most vulnerable black people – Asians – live. The Home Office (1981) found that 43 per cent of incidents with Asian victims showed evidence of a racist motive; a poll in Newham in 1985 estimated that almost a quarter of the Asian population had been victimized in that year (cited in the *Independent*, 5 November 1986, p. 2); and in Glasgow, a small survey of 50 Asians found that at least half had suffered racist graffiti or attack, while over 90 per cent had been victims of racist abuse (MacEwen 1986). Asians, especially Bangladeshis, are most vulnerable to attack, and racial violence is often targeted towards the areas they occupy.

Secondly, Husbands (1982) has shown that violence tends to become localized in neighbourhoods which have a well-established tradition of extremist politics. Here, racial attack can be interpreted in terms of 'some form of very locally based and socially transmitted vigilantist culture whose origins go back at least to the anti-Semitic agitation that occurred at the turn of the century' (p. 21).

Thirdly, attacks tend to cluster in areas where black people form a small minority of the population, but appear to be challenging the territorial preferences of whites (this trend was noted in the report of the Home Affairs Committee (1986)). The force of sentiment here is evident from Phillips's (1986) research in Lambeth, where housing officials commonly receive 'unsolicited hostile comments from white tenants not wishing to see Bengalis moving in'. The consequences for those who do move are reviewed by the FBHO (1986), who show that many women and children are effectively confined to their homes. This prospect of violence and intimidation is a strong disincentive to black households who might otherwise wish to move away from the poorer properties in which they are over-represented.

Finally, research focusing on council housing identifies a clustering of attacks on old run-down estates suffering from poor housing and environmental conditions and from a lack of community facilities. In these areas, racial violence appears to be part of a broader environment of disadvantage (although we know little, so far, about the incidence of attacks in similarly run-down areas of the private sector).

The spread and localization of racial violence together testify to the exclusionary and segregationist nature of common sense racism. The widespread incidence of attack provides evidence of a general desire, in some segments of the public, to challenge black people's rights to participate in and remain part of British society. These attacks are therefore indiscriminate and wide-ranging; they are fostered by extremist politics; and they are facilitated by lethargy or impotency on the part of key public agencies. Where such violence is particularly localized and intense, it may also be read as an expression of territoriality – as a popular means of asserting social identity, of defending material resources and of preserving social status. Racial attack is, from this perspective, a segregationist as well as an exclusionary practice, effected to keep or force black people out of particular urban neighbourhoods.

The irony of this analysis is that because institutional responses have been so ineffective, black resistance tends itself to be segregationist, occurring largely in the form of individual and collective strategies of 'defensive withdrawal'. At an individual level, most persecuted families choose not to wait for the courts to assist them but prefer to transfer to other, usually more segregated, neighbourhoods (see FBHO 1986). The Bethnal Green and Stepney Trades Council (1978) argue that Asians remain segregated within the poorer parts of the housing stock because harassment and intimidation have created 'no go' areas in better neighbourhoods. The GLC (1984) inquiry also collated a range of evidence to show how black people are effectively forced to refuse better quality accommodation in more desirable areas because they fear attack.

A similar pattern of defensive withdrawal characterizes the communal forms of resistance to racial harassment which have developed in some particularly vulnerable areas. Defence committees were formed in many parts of London following repeated outbreaks of racial violence in the late 1970s. On 29 July 1978, the Standing Conference of Pakistani Organisations, the Indian Workers Association and the Federation of

Bangladeshi Organisations issued a joint statement calling for their members to join self-defence groups to fight racism in the face of the apparent impotency of the police (Gordon 1983). By 1982, there was extensive support for the principle of self-defence groups among black people (especially among Afro-Caribbean males) throughout England and Wales, and in November 1985 a GLC-sponsored conference, 'Time to Act', endorsed the principle of collective resistance. This received further support in March 1987 at the fourth annual conference of the Labour Party Black Section group, and defence committees now exist in a number of major cities, most notably in London and the North-West.

Defensive resistance takes a number of forms, and might include campaigning or pressure group politics as well as protection (the estate-based campaign against racist attacks in Brent, for instance, succeeded in persuading the council to write a 'neighbourly conduct' clause into its tenancy agreements in 1984). Despite adverse publicity, very few of these groups are vigilantist in orientation: for the most part, they are defensive rather than offensive, they aim to deter rather than provoke and they favour withdrawal rather than confrontation. Important though this is, it means that both racial attack and defensive resistance encourage the practice of segregation, and sustain the imagery of segregationism, in the course of daily life.

Ritual and rebellion

Defensive withdrawal may characterize routine reactions to racist behaviour, but there are occasions when 'race' becomes a vehicle of resistance and acts as a catalyst for more confrontational forms of social action. These occasions are not as idiosyncratic as politicians like to think, and they may play an important role in the social structuring of urban space.

Each time there is an outbreak of violence in the major cities, politicians and journalists respond as if it were unusual or unprecedented. Yet civil unrest and popular protest are not new in Britain: race-related disturbances have been common throughout the present century and their chronology and character are now relatively well documented (see Fryer 1984; Jacobs 1986; Unsworth 1982). The most widely quoted incidents of the past two decades include the Chapeltown riots in Leeds in 1972, 1974 and 1975, the Notting Hill Carnival riots of of 1976, 1977 and 1987, violence in London's East End and in Southall in 1978 and 1979, the familiar chronology of rioting in St Paul's Bristol in 1980, in Brixton, Southall, Liverpool 8, Handsworth and numerous others in 1981, and further outbreaks in many of the same districts in 1985 (a log of events in the

1980s is provided by Solomos (1986b)). Yet what the press called 'copycat' riots in 1981, the police called 'routine disturbances', indicating that, with or without mass media sensationalism, racial tension routinely prevails in much of urban Britain.

While every 'riot' has its own unique character – related to local histories and traditions, and to a peculiar combination of 'precipitating' events – collectively, they embody some enduring principles of urban life and culture. Just what these principles are is the subject of considerable theoretical debate (some of which is summarized by Benyon 1987; Keith 1987, Lea 1982; Taylor 1984), but I shall explore one part of this, focusing on those aspects of civil unrest that are broadly political and that impinge on the defence and appropriation of territory. From this perspective, it is helpful to regard 'riot' as just one end of a continuum of collective behaviours, along which various types of contest (symbolic and explicit) for power and resources (including control over space) are positioned.

Cohen (1980, 1982) has probably given the most thorough account of the political role of collective behaviour in his analysis of the Notting Hill Carnival as a 'contested cultural performance'. He depicts Carnival as a 'ritual of rebellion': it has a cathartic element (which may ultimately work to sustain a status quo) and a confrontational element (which makes it a vehicle for articulating protest and expressing resistance). There is a fine line between catharsis and confrontation, so that, even at the best of times, 'Carnival is uneasily poised between compliance and subversion' (Cohen 1982: 35). When the balance is tipped too far, Carnival slips into riot; and while the former may be interpreted as 'a joke with the established order', the latter denotes a much more serious debate. Carnival uses territory to celebrate culture and identity; riot is anchored to place through defensive confrontation.

Cohen's study and a recent, related, piece by Jackson (1988) lay the groundwork for conceptualizing popular protest as a mode of political bargaining that is exercised when conventional channels for negotiation are unavailable or ineffective. From this perspective, civil unrest in the 1980s can be seen as the culmination of a long history of collective bargaining by riot. This theme is taken up by Lea (1982), who relates an increase in public disorder to the growing frustrations of inner city communities whose demands and aspirations have not been channelled effectively into those institutional patterns of political compromise which more usually characterize capitalist democracy. Davies (1986), too, argues that riots are a form of civil resistance necessitated by black people's political marginality. These authors articulate more fully what Home Office research now implies, namely that riots are the political voice of those whose statutory rights of political expression are effectively blocked (see Field 1982). Collective violence might therefore be read as a 'politics of last resort', the increasing prominence of which has, in Unsworth's (1982: 74) opinion, effectively converted 'sections of the inner city population into an unstable extra-parliamentary opposition constituting a reminder of the fragility of representative democracy as a device for channelling dissent in times of deep economic, social and political crisis'.

There is, then, a general agreement in the theoretical literature that civil unrest has a political component, and there is increasing empirical evidence that, despite attempts to play down the 'racial' element of riot, black people have used this as a symbolic vehicle for articulating their concerns. Analyses by Peach (1986b) and Keith (1987) show unequivocally that, of all deprived urban areas, those which have proved most volatile over the past decade are the racially mixed inner cities. Keith's (1987) analysis shows, further, that there is an important distinction between riot and the mindless criminality that may often accompany it. In Brixton in 1981 only 58 per cent of those arrested for looting, as compared with 73 per cent of those arrested for riot, were black. Rioters tended to be older, on average, than looters and lived nearer to the core of the disturbances. It seems, in fact, that there were two kinds of unrest: 'one was a highly localized, full-scale confrontation with the police, involving a broad cross-section of people from a very small area of Brixton; the other, which occurred some distance away from this, was an opportunistic reaction to the collapse of public order' (Keith 1987: 286).

It is the element of 'full-scale confrontation' rather than opportunistic deviance which has articulated the frustrations of the black communities. However, by its very nature riot is not a considered representation of carefully specified demands; it is a spontaneous and symbolic gesture of resistance to the power structure of a society in which black people are often treated as second class citizens. Because it is spontaneous, it is linked with participants' home locale or territory; because it is symbolic, it is directed at the most visible presence of white authority – the police. Policing, therefore, lies at the heart of urban conflict in modern Britain. The police are the most tangible expression of the state in civil society, and if the exercise of social control seems unsympathetic to the cause of racial equality, it is the police who will bear the immediate brunt of collective resistance. Accordingly, Clare (1987), Peach (1986b) and D. Smith (1987) all argue that the policing of black communities lies at the core of modern urban unrest.

Tension between the police and black people, which became increasingly apparent during the 1970s, culminated in 1979 when the National Front attracted massive police protection for its election rallies in areas with relatively large black communities. The most explosive confrontation that year occurred in Southall, where a properly organized peaceful protest against the National Front attracted excessive police presence (mustered in an attempt to erect a 'neutral' barrier between NF supporters and black demonstrators). Only an unofficial enquiry now testifies to the extent of the violence which followed, and this criticizes the police for alienating black protesters, undermining their confidence and violating 'any sense they might otherwise have preserved that they are part of the society within which they live' (Dummett 1979: 11). If anything, the riots of the 1980s seem to have been even more directly precipitated by conflict between the police and black people. Usually, such outbreaks of unrest have been linked with insensitive police tactics, such as the raid on a black club in St Paul's in 1980, the notorious 'Swamp 81' operation against street crime in Brixton in 1981, and the shooting of Cherry Groce and death of Cynthia Jarrett, which lay at the centre of unrest in Brixton and Tottenham in 1985.

Popular protest in the 1980s may, at root, be an attempt to express fundamental grievances relating to civil rights and national belonging. In practice, however, these grievances are articulated through conflict with the police as the visible presence of state authority. Through riot, broad issues relating to the meaning of citizenship and acces to democracy are writ small, and protest is organized around more general local struggles for employment, shelter and equality before the law. Gilroy (1987) thus depicts riot as a demand for local control that is manifest when, 'unable to control the social relations in which they find themselves, people have shrunk the world to the size of their communities and begun to act politically on that basis' (p. 28). Riot, he argues, has forged a strong association between identity and territory; segregation, he implies, enhances the potency of 'race' as a vehicle for resistance.

I have already shown (in chapter 5) how race-related civil unrest contributes to the racialization of residential space, and therefore to the construction of racial segregation as a major urban problem. Here it seems that, in everyday life as well, ritualized protest reinforces the alignment of racial identity with the organization of space. In the short term, this offers marginalized minorities an effective (or noticeable) way of handling or expressing their sense of powerlessness. It may even win concessions that are denied by the conventional channels of representative democracy. Ultimately, however, such concessions may be more symbolic than real (Solomos 1986b) and because they are secured through practices which legitimize the imagery of racial segregation, in the longer term violent protest may only exacerbate the political marginalization of those living in the inner city neighbourhoods. For while riot uses territory as a cultural resource, it also asserts the relevance of territory as a focus of social control or containment. In this sense, the organization of civil unrest in the 1980s reinforces the territorial basis of 'racial' separatism both at the level of common sense perceptions and behaviours, and in the eyes of government.

Conclusion

Popular politics, broadly defined, helps to explain how and why racial segregation – as a practice and a symbol – is reproduced through the 'common sense' of daily life. The popular wisdom which sustains segregation may be inspired by political culture, but it is continuously re-negotiated as deprived communities struggle to make sense of their urban experience. Although ordinary people can rarely influence the forces which produce residential space, they all participate in a range of social activities which invest that space with meaning. There *is*, therefore, scope to bargain for some kind of control over the organization of local life, and this barganing is frequently organized around the principle of race (as a basis for exclusionism, separatism or resistance). This contest for power and resources is partly located in the realm of ideas, images and attitudes, where racial consciousness is shaped; but a 'common sense' racial awareness goes on to inform, and legitimize, public conduct and social behaviour.

Examining a range of public behaviours with a broadly political theme, I have identified three practices that seem particularly influential in sustaining the 'racial' dimension of residential segregation. First, I examined the orientation of voting behaviour, isolating the racist vote and drawing out its exclusionary, and probably segregationist, implications. It seems that the 'ethnic' vote is powerless to challenge this, unless by *using* segregation to amass political power (a strategy which has so far had limited success, and then only at a local level).

Secondly, I indicated how the orientation of street politics has both exclusionary and segregationist underpinnings. On the one hand, racial attack forms part of a general attempt by the far Right to remove black people from British territory. On the other hand, racial violence has been more widely appropriated by an active minority of working class whites who, conscious, of their own marginal status, fear the social and material consequences of residential integration, and use harassment or violence to prevent it. Again, the most effective forms of black resistance are strategies of defence and withdrawal. Ironically, these sustain segregation while (and for the wrong kinds of reasons) perpetuating the view that black people wish to remain segregated in the kinds of neighbourhoods they currently occupy.

Finally, the organization of civil unrest has been examined as a mode of political bargaining adopted by otherwise marginalized communities. Riot is, in part, a quest to secure political influence in those areas (the inner cities) and in those communities (racialized minorities) where representative democracy works least well. This quest is spontaneous, symbolic and aimed at the police as representatives of white authority. In practice, riot both expresses and forges a link between identity and territory, but while this has allowed race to become an effective vehicle for resistance, often securing short-term concessions for the communities involved, it is also a strategy which contributes to the imagery of racial segregation. As such, it sustains the language of racial categorization, assents to separatist practice and preserves the basis of racial inequality.

The world of 'common sense' – of habit, routine and taken-for-granted action – is ultimately where politics and policy are legitimized. Without public assent, the reproduction of racial inequality and the tenacity of 'racial segregation' could not be secured. Yet all the evidence suggests that, currently, ordinary people use the fact of residential differentiation to articulate their racial consciousness, so sustaining segregation both as a social practice and as a cultural symbol. For the public at large, racial segregation is significant not just as a pattern of production or consumption, nor even as a politically constructed problem, but rather as a socially constructed way of life. It is implicated in the differential distribution of resources, but at the same time it *is* a resource. Because of this, those who live it, police it and analyse it each face a rather different moral dilemma. Their views may differ, too, on a programme for reform – a topic addressed in chapter 7.

Notes

1 Electoral support for the National Front almost doubled between 1970 and 1977, but the party has never succeeded in securing more than 1 per cent of the national vote. At the height of its popularity, the party attracted no more than 1 in 30 votes in the seats it contested at a general election, and 1 in 12 votes for candidates in local elections (Taylor 1979).

2 Racist sympathies are generally found to be most marked (or most explicit) among the working classes, although Taylor (1979) shows that such antipathy is by no means absent from substantial sections of the middle class.

3 Black people's interests are not, of course, homogeneous or intrinsically different from other public interests. However, because Britain cannot claim to have eliminated racial inequality or discrimination, there is an extent to which

'being black adds a dimension to black people's political experience which white people will never share' (Fitzgerald 1987: 10).

4 In the early 1900s, each major party had a Parliamentary representative from the Indian subcontinent but for almost half a century between 1929 and 1987, the House of Commons was exclusively occupied by white MPs. Until the present decade, the few black candidates who were put forward tended to be placed in unwinnable seats. The only exception was David Pitt, who nevertheless lost Clapham for Labour in 1970.

5 Three black Labour MPs now represent London constituencies: Bernie Grant for Tottenham, Paul Boateng for Brent South and Diane Abbot for Hackney North/Stoke Newington. Although, in London as a whole, Labour gained an average of 1.2 per cent on its previous share of the vote, these candidates saw their majorities fall by 13.6, 6.9 and 3.6 per cent, respectively. In contrast, Keith Vaz, elected to Leicester East, turned a Conservative majority of nearly 2 per cent into a Labour majority of nearly 4 per cent: he increased his party's share of the vote by 9.2 per cent, which is over four times the average (of 2.2 per cent) for Labour candidates in the East Midlands.

6 Registration of whites peaked in 1974 at 94 per cent, and the figure has gradually declined since then.

7 This support appears to relate mainly to Labour's role as the party of the working classes. A Harris poll in 1983 (cited by Fitzgerald 1987) shows that whereas 31 per cent of Asians and 7 per cent of Afro-Caribbeans support Labour because it represents black people, 64 and 76 per cent, respectively, prefer Labour as the party most likely to advance their class interests.

8 A duplicate ballot conducted by the CRE in 1979 amongst 3225 voters in 24 constituencies found that 90 per cent of Afro-Caribbeans and 86 per cent of Asians, but only 50 per cent of whites, voted Labour (see Anwar 1986: 74–76). This racial polarization of the vote was only slightly less marked in 1983, although by 1987, a Harris poll indicated that Asians' support for Labour had fallen to 67 per cent, while support from the Afro-Caribbean communities remained strong, at 86 per cent.

9 This strategy has achieved little success, and has been opposed by over 90 per cent of delegates at the Labour Party conferences of 1984–7.

7 Critical Interpretations of 'Racial Segregation'

Don't let's be purists and stand outside, for we can't fight the system bare-handed. We don't have the tools, brothers and sisters; we've got to get the tools from the system itself . . .

A. Sivanandan, *Race and Class*, 1983

I have now identified several levels of analysis which an adequate understanding of 'racial segregation' must embrace. These levels include empirical insight into *what form* segregation takes (chapters 1 and 2), a conceptual understanding of *how* segregation is sustained (chapters 3 and 4) and a critical appreciation of *why* segregation is able to persist in a racially inequitable form (chapters 5 and 6). Together, these analytical themes indicate that the 'racial' dimension of residential segregation is a product both of material struggles and ideological conflict. As a residential pattern, therefore, specifically *racial* segregation reflects and structures enduring inequalities in access to employment opportunities, wealth, services and amenities, and to the package of civil and political rights associated with citizenship. As ideology, on the other hand, segregation-ism builds from the objective deprivation of black people to a subjective acceptance that racial differentiation has a logic of its own; it provides a reservoir of common sense justifications for discriminatory policy and separatist practice.

The study of racial segregation is therefore about much more than housing and urban research; it is an issue which penetrates far beyond the analysis of neighbourhood structure, organization or change. Because society is spatially constituted – that is, because distance does constrain or enable access to services, resources and the opportunity structure of a nation – the form of residential differentiation has far-reaching implications for individuals' quality of life. Because society is also expressed through ideas and meaning systems, the theme of segregation is important in the constitution of society – by which I mean not just patterns of socialization and exchange at a neighbourhood level but rather the structuring of social relations (and the legitimization of the structuring of social relations) on a national scale. In short, residential segregation both expresses racial inequality and sustains the salience of race: it is the material embodiment of, and symbolic inspiration for, a racial ideology whose impact on the structure of social relations is increasingly pronounced.

Summarizing what this means in Britian today, my conclusions fall into two parts. I begin by formalizing my preferred interpretation of racial segregation, restating my view that whatever else segregation represents – an economic or cultural resource, a focus of social organization or a locus of self-help – *racial* segregation is fundamentally and inextricably bound into an imbalance of power and resources between Britain's black and white populations.

My theoretical generalizations here are based on and, for the moment, restricted to Britain's experience, with its distinctive attributes as a democratic welfare state and its distinctive role in the histories of imperialism, colonialism and capitalism. Conflict and inequality are, of course, racialized in many other countries: white supremacy and black resistance are found throughout the world. Yet, as I argued at the outset, the constitution and reproduction of racial inequality is a negotiable, contestable, diverse and changeable process. It is bound into particular historical, cultural, political and economic contexts, whose varying effects can only be grasped through comparative research (influential examples include the work of Cell (1982), Cox (1948), Fredrickson (1981) and Van den Berghe (1967, 1970), and the collections edited by Clarke et al. (1984) and Jackson (1987)). My own observations are therefore just one piece in a much more complex (though equally disturbing) mosaic.

Having outlined an interpretation of racial segregation in Britain, I move on to consider some principles of political organization and policy orientation that might work towards reform. Here, my comments are 'critical' in the sense outlined by Offe (1984), who argues that if social science is to conceptualize problems adequately, analysts must not be bound by an interest in policy-relevant solutions. In Offe's opinion, solutions circumscribed by an existing policy agenda will simply reproduce the status quo that generated the problem. The role of the analyst is not, therefore, to inform policy directly, but rather to raise questions, expose options and direct research towards the forces for democratic change. Following this model of critical social science I show that racial inequality is a product of political neglect and has been tackled via an unnecessarily narrow range of policies. There *are* more just alternatives and Britain, unlike many other societies divided by 'race', has a political infrastructure which could promote reform. This opportunity issues a crucial challenge to the integrity of representative democracy.

The highest stage of white supremacy?

Empirically, the segregation of racialized minorities may (but will not necessarily) become less intense in future years (as the black population increases in size and gains access to larger, more diverse chunks of urban space). As a measure of economic, social and political inequality, however – i.e. as a factor sustaining the material basis of racial differentiation – the evidence presented in chapters 1–6 suggests that residential segregation in Britain is becoming more, not less, potent as the twentieth century draws to a close (a point amplified in Smith 1989). This is because, symbolically and in practice, the existence of segregation testifies to a systematic undermining of the rights of black people – rights which, in Britain, are related to participation in the economy, to the receipt of essential state-subsidized services and to the political and civil liberties associated with freedom of expression and equality before the law. These themes are considered separately, although it is their simultaneity on which a proper theorization of racial segregation must rest.

Economic rights: employment and ownership

At the heart of most research on the broad theme of residential segregation is concern for its importance in relation to the accumulation of material wealth and the expression of economic power. Accordingly, residential differentiation has often been discussed as an outcome of the relationship between capital and labour which is expressed in the production and utilization of urban space.

It is important to acknowledge that, at root, the quality, cost, desirability and availability of housing is a function of the production of the built environment. This, in turn, is determined by the politics and economics of capital accumulation which, in Britain, have meant that housing is often in short supply (especially at the cheap end of the market), uneven in quality and spatially differentiated to reflect booms and slumps in the building industry. This itself ensures that the distribution of housing will reflect patterns of wealth and status in society as a whole. Because of this, the work of Harvey (1982, 1985a, b) and of Rogers and Uto (1987), which begins with a theory of the production of urban space, is an indispensable starting point for any adequate theorization of racial segregation.

The quality, condition and desirability of dwellings also reflects the *use* of space and propety, and it is at this point of consumption that residential differentiation becomes most directly implicated in the process of racial categorization. This was illustrated in chapter 2, which shows that the fact of residential segregation both expresses and determines the relative inability of black people to exercise their right to full participation in the British labour and property markets.

Initially, patterns of segregation (established during the 1950s and 1960s) simply reflected the distribution of labour demand (for a 'replacement' workforce) and the location of cheap housing. Segregation became an expression of racial inequality because processes which regulate the acquisition, allocation, modification and exchange of property establish systematic variations in the costs and benefits of consuming residential space. At first, the form of segregation testified to the poor wages of migrant workers and to their over-concentration in vulnerable or marginal industries (as well as to systematic, often overt, discrimination in the labour market).

Housing systems do not, however, simply provide an arena for the display of wealth achieved (or deprivation experienced) by virtue of a position in the division of labour. They are also a medium able systematically to confer or restrict access to the wide range of economic rights (to employment and to the accumulation of wealth through property ownership) which, in principle, accrue to able-bodied members of free-market democracies. Chapter 2 therefore went on to show how, in a spatially restructuring economy, early patterns of segregation came to exert a direct bearing on black people's employment opportunities and property rights. With recent shifts in the organization of capital, residential segregation has become more, not less, important in controlling black people's access to economic rewards. Both regionally and within cities, simply because of where they live, black people are now less likely than whites to retain or secure employment, or to have the opportunity to use housing to store and accumulate wealth.

Chapter 3 showed that these difficulties are compounded by the high degree of locational inertia built into the housing system by inter- and intra-regional differences in house price inflation. I argued that black owner occupiers – who are disproportionately clustered within the most depressed segments of the housing market – find it increasingly difficult to move to take advantage of the more buoyant sectors of the economy or to realize the capital stored in their homes (especially Asians who, as owners, are over-represented in the depressed markets of the North). Black council tenants, too, live in the least saleable portions of the public rented stock, and have little prospect of transferring to gain access to areas where labour markets are secure and the local economy is strong (since these are also the areas where black people have been under-represented as council house tenants, but where public sector sales have proceeded most rapidly (see Dunn et al. 1987)). This means that as the 'commodification' of housing and increased subsidies for low-cost home ownership extend the opportunity to invest in property across the class structure, existing forms of segregation decrease black people's relative ability to accumulate wealth in this manner (even though, in absolute terms, many black home owners have made substantial capital gains by participating in the housing market).

To summarize, while 'racial' segregation initially expressed the geography of demand for cheap migrant labour during a period of labour shortage, it persists in a form which effectively regulates the workforce at a time of labour surplus. The organization of residential space may therefore be regarded as a component of that 'structural racism' which Cross (1986) argues is concentrating black people socially and economically into areas of greatest economic decline at a variety of spatial scales. To this end, however, segregation is not simply about wealth and resources. It is also about imagery and ideology. In order to sustain the material inequalities conferred by residential segregation, racial ideology must increasingly take a form less concerned to justify labour extraction than to legitimize 'a process of separation, containment and control' (Cross 1986: 87). Such an ideology was 'unpacked' in chapter 5, which identifies segregationism as a potent source of legitimacy for racially divisive public policy.

This conceptualization of racial segregation as an ideological justification for, as well as a material expression of, differential access to economic rights has a bearing on the main area of theoretical debate in the study of residential segregation more generally – that concerning its role in reproducing the class structure of society. While analysts are divided on the question of whether segregation *could* mobilize collective action to advance shared material interests (the debate is summarized by D. Harris (1984)), most agree that in practice it often does not. The process of racial differentiation is rarely discussed in this literature, yet because of its ideological connotations it adds a dimension to residential segregation which might help explain why territory has so far failed to act as a catalyst for effective collective action whether predicated on class interests (as discussed by Preteceille 1986) or on a shared mode of consumption (as examined by Saunders 1986).

'Race' is a principle of social stratification which cuts across occupational and tenure categories. 'Racial segregation' is therefore the territorial embodiment of a structure that, at the level of meaning and common sense experience, weakens rather than strengthens cleavages within the division of labour or the organization of consumption. At an ideological level, therefore, segregationism impinges on a struggle for the mind of labour in ways that seem functional for capital; it is part of a project which aims to 'forge a consciousness favourable to the perpetuation of the capitalist order' by seeking out ways 'to draw social distinctions along lines other than between capital and labour' (Harvey 1985b: 116). This implies that just as the dominant ideological underpinning (racism) of the racialization of migrant labour might be seen as undermining the ability of labour to gain control over production, so the ideological underpinning (segregationism) of the racialization of residential space can be seen as undermining the territorial basis of class solidarity (and, indeed, of any other form of social solidarity grounded in the collective experience of material deprivation – except, perhaps, that organized around the principle of race itself) in the sphere of consumption.

From this economic perspective, both the material facts and the ideological construction of racial segregation can be said to play a part in facilitating the accumulation function of the state. However, neither segregation nor segregationism is only or necessarily functional for capital. In Britain, this simple model is complicated above all by the development of social policy.

Welfare and well-being

T. H. Marshall (1950, 1975, 1981) has argued that universal access to satate-subsidized welfare is the morally just way to offset the inequalities generated as economies grow. This vision of welfare as a fundamental right of citizenship was shared (to varying extents) by Butler, Beveridge and Bevan, and provided the foundation upon which Britain's welfare state was constructed. Although housing has never been a fully socialized service in the same way as education or health, it is nevertheless true that for more than 20 years (and throughout the main period of immigration from the West Indies, South Asia and East Africa) housing (as shelter) was regarded by successive Governments (albeit with varying commitment) as one of the more prominent social benefits of British citizenship (some implications of this are explored in Clapham et al. forthcoming).

Because of the provisions of the 1948 Nationality Act, most black people (immigrant or otherwise) have not only been required to contribute to the welfare state, but have also, theoretically, been as eligible as white indigenes to gain access to public housing (and to any other social service) as their needs dictate. With the advent of a welfare state to cushion the hard edge of industrial capitalism and to compensate in kind for inequalities in wealth, the eocnomic impetus for racism and segregation-ism should have been weakened, if not removed. If racial segregation persists within a welfare state it might therefore be due as much to the differential distribution of welfare rights as to the organization of economic opportunities.

Confirming this suspicion, modern commentators increasingly argue that racism (and sexism) lurk deep in the heart of Britain's welfare ideal (see Williams 1987). The Left as much as the Right have traditionally sought to protect rather than extend the social rights of citizenship (Cohen 1985), and successive rounds of immigration legislation (a form of exclusionism that is biased against black people) are overlaid with laws dispensing benefit eligibility according to immigration status (a form of internal control drawing the principles of racial separatism to the heart of domestic affairs).

Ever since the Commonwealth Immigration Act was passed in 1962, immigrants have faced restrictions if they seem likely to make recourse to public funds (both Cohen (1985) and Gordon (1986b) draw attention to this). In 1985, 'public funds' were explicitly defined to include supple-mentary benefit, housing benefit, family income supplement and housing under the Housing (Homeless Persons) Act of 1977. Even the process of family reunion now rests on independence from state subsidy. Reviewing the consequences of this, Gordon (1986b) argues that the law has created 'not only a group of second-class claimants but a group of second class citizens whose right to family life and security of residence here is undermined . . . a class of people, mainly black, who do not have the normal welfare rights of other permanent residents in Britain' (p. 31). The significance of this is not, in Cohen's (1985) view, so much that some black people are excluded from state benefits because of their origin or residency status (although this *is* a cause for concern). It is rather that the onus is put on all black people to prove their entitlement in ways that are not required of the majority of whites. Johnson (1987b) therefore argues that, despite the theoretical eligibility of black people for welfare benefits and despite their disproportionate contribution to the welfare state (through labour and taxation), their ability to secure state-subsidized services and resources is deteriorating relative to that of their white counterparts.

All these processes find expression in the housing system. Chapter 3 explains how a failure to coordinate housing provision with immigration policy in the post-war years helped to exclude black migrants from their right to rent at subsidized rates. The timing of the shift from redevelopment to renewal closed off another avenue into subsidized renting, and those black people who subsequently qualified for council accommodation were limited to the older properties or flatted estates of the inner cities. By the time housing provision for general needs had ceased, with council stock being sold to sitting tenants at remarkable discounts, black people were decidedly disadvantaged in the kind of capital 'asset' they could obtain. All this has not only sustained the material basis of segregation, but has enhanced its role as a medium for racial inequality.

As a welfare benefit, subsidized shelter has been systematically (if ostensibly unintentionally) denied to the black community; because this finds expression in the form of residential segregation, it also has implications for access to a range of other welfare services and resources – including education and health care – that are spatially organized to favour some (usually more affluent) areas of cities rather than others. Thus, racially differentiated access to welfare rights is both expressed in the form of segregation and transmitted through segregation into other areas of the welfare state. In this sense the dispensation of state-subsidized welfare has compounded rather than counter-acted those racially divisive effects of the economy encapsulated in residential space.

It must also be acknowledged that social and economic policy are intimately related. It would be naive to interpret the welfare state as a manifestation of the altruistic face (or even of the grudging conscience) of advanced capitalism. Social policy developed, in part at least, because it was needed to win public consent for the concept of wage labour and for the risks associated with it (see Offe 1984). It is, from this perspective, a means by which the state seeks to legitimize its economic strategy. I have already argued (in the previous section) that racial segregation has a direct role in justifying as well as assisting the process of capital accumulation. Here, I suggest that this ideological role extends to the promotion and justification of state legitimation – a process concerned not only to secure the conditions for capital to circulate, but also to make these conditions acceptable to the electorate, ensuring that those already in power retain political control.

Social policy has always helped to secure popular support for economic strategy by appearing to 'mop up' any disadvantageous effects of slow growth or decline. From this perspective a welfare state was required in post-war Britain both to secure the reproduction of labour power and to abate the unrest that springs from material deprivation (George and Wilding 1976). In one sense, therefore, social policy is designed to play a broadly integrative role in a class-divided society, helping to regulate conflict and minimize civil unrest. However, to succeed, this process has both impinged on and relied upon the process of racial differentiation. As a consequence, my interpretation of racial segregation as a medium for the dispensation of welfare rights takes on a significance far beyond that relating to the relative effectiveness of state-subsidized services. Indeed, at an ideological level it offers some clues as to why the dispensation of such services is *necessarily* discriminatory.

Jessop (1982) points out that although there are various means of securing legitimacy for state activity, most may be described as either one- or two-nation strategies. The latter aims for only limited legitimacy – the kind conferred by strategically significant sectors of the population. In managing racial inequality and the associated problem of segregation, the evidence of chapters 3 and 4 is that, in Britain, legislators have preferred a two-nation approach. To this end, 'race' (while by no means the only relevant criterion) has proved to be one of the politically safest principles on which to distinguish these two 'nations'. By limiting the concessions allowed to a black minority, policies can symbolically enhance the status or standing of even the relatively deprived among a white majority. Therefore, the theme of greater access to welfare for white Britons and less for black 'immigrants' dominated political debate – nationally and locally – for more than three decades. Legislators regarded privileged access as axiomatic, and the principle became embedded in the rules and procedures of local institutions. Even (especially) supposedly 'aracial' housing policy may be regarded as a vehicle through which the state, 'by differentially empowering or dis-empowering the relevant social groups, biases the extent and the specific "utility" of social policy for these groups' (Offe 1984: 106).

Obvious, if formally disguised, evidence of discrimination in the allocation of scarce resources can, by conferring a sense of privileged access on those who receive state benefits, defuse the potential dissatisfaction of the white majority, albeit at the expense of the well-being (and electoral support) of a racialized minority. Thus, as a material expression of inequalities generated by the exercise of state benevolence, the 'racial' dimension of residential segregation diverts the attention of politicians and the public away from the economic roots of social inequality. As an ideological device, symbolically distinguishing those more entitled from those less entitled to realize their welfare rights, segregationism interacts with popular conceptions of citizenship and nationhood. It helps foster a sense of national identity and exclusivity in a 'privileged' majority, so increasing the salience of race and diminishing the relevance of class as a fundamental social divide.

If differential access to the citizenship rights embedded in social policy has been so influential in sustaining racial inequality, it might be argued that the present Government's attempt to dismantle the welfare state could advance the cause of racial justice. There are at least four reasons why such reasoning is flawed. First, it can be argued that Marshall's vision of welfare as a universal right has never properly been realized (see Hindess 1987). If the 'strategy of equality' has never been implemented, then social policy could not be expected to undermine the economic logic of racial differentiation. Secondly, it is obvious from the earlier discussion that there often *is* an economic logic guiding racial ideology and an economic basis for racial inequality. This will not be directly affected (though it might be more acutely exposed) by withdrawing state intervention in the sphere of social policy. Thirdly, history cannot be erased simply through legislative change, even if this does remove some of the clumsiness that has been associated with state intervention. The 'commodification' of housing is taking place against a backdrop of systematic inequalities in what was the public sector; these inequalities are being exacerbated rather than ameliorated by the shift in public subsidy to owner occupation. Finally, it has to be recognized that the salience of race could ultimately be determined not in the dispensation of economic or welfare rights but rather in the domain of political and civil rights, to which I shall now turn.

Politics and citizenship

Citizenship in the formal sense refers to the availability of political as well as social and legal rights. For Marshall this meant mass enfranchisement, the right to participate in political parties and pressure group politics, and more general opportunities for social participation in the conduct of public life. In a *de jure* sense, all British citizens share these privileges. In practice, the evidence of chapters 5 and 6 is that there has been little scope for effective participation by black people in the decisions which most directly affect them. This systematic political exclusion helps explain why racial inequalities can remain so entrenched in the social and spatial organization of public life in Britain.

Chapter 5 shows how, as a policy-relevant problem, racial segregation has been constructed by white politicians catering to a predominantly white electorate. It has become a symbol of the difficulties besetting multi-racial societies, and has spawned solutions with little effect on the intensity of segregation or the entrenchment of inequality. Instead, the imagery of racial segregation has provided a rationale and a focus for a range of practices that undermine black Britons' basic civil rights.

On a national scale, the problem mix labelled 'racial segregation' raised public concern about the size and concentration of the black population and mobilized support for a range of policies to diminish the visibility of racial disadvantage. This helped to legitimize the notion of repatriation and placed faith in spatial dispersal but, most importantly, it gave impetus to a series of Immigration Acts which progressively stripped away the rights of entry and settlement conferred on Commonwealth citizens in 1948. The 1981 Nationality Act, which brought eligibility for citizenship into line with eligibility for settlement, marks the culmination of this process, confirming that, in essence, British nationality is a racially exclusive concept. Black people overseas have largely lost their rights to citizenship and had them replaced by a label which carries no right to entry or settlement and is not transmissible between generations.

Racial segregation has informed a racially exclusive nationalism; but it has also acted as focus for the repressive actions that are required from time to time (especially during crises of legitimacy) to assert the authority of the state. Gilroy (1987) argues that the vision of black people as a 'malignant wedge' in the inner city not only helps construct a social group whose identity is incompatible with the label 'British', but also draws the sting of the law and order campaign which has been so central to the popular revival of moral authoritarianism. This has been possible because, as a politically constructed problem, racial segregation makes vivid reference to the supposed volatility of the 'black' inner city, legitimizing new strategies of containment which (whether inadvertently or explicitly) work to sustain racial separatism without challenging white supremacy.

From a political perspective, however, segregation is not simply a medium for the reproduction of racial inequality: it is also a potential power base. It could, in theory, offer the black electorate a symbolic platform from which to claim both short-term concessions and longer-term change in the organization of economic rights and public subsidy. Chapter 6 examined the possibilities for this, but concluded that, because of the way in which British democracy is presently organized, the gains have so far been few. That most fundamental political unit – the voting public – has been more articulate in sustaining segregation than in pursuing anti-racism or even encouraging integration. Despite the visibility of riot and rebellion, black resistance has so far been more notable for eliciting political rhetoric than for securing social reform.

Residential differentiation, then, is bound into the politics as well as the economics and sociology of race. By interrogating racial segregation, we are forced to acknowledge that the black population in Britain cannot simply be conceptualized as a racialized fraction of the working class, nor even as an underclass, marginalized by the welfare state as well as the economy. Black people are also politically marginal and politically marginalized; they are electoral fragments effectively prevented from using their basic democratic rights to alter the structures which apportion the privileges (though not the obligations) of citizenship according to racist criteria. In this sense, it appears that in Britain, as in the USA and, indeed, South Africa, racial segregation is most fundamentally an expression of 'the monopoly by the dominant group over the political institutions of the state' (Cell 1982: 14).

To summarize, the evidence of previous chapters suggests that 'racial segregation' in Britain may be theorized as a material and symbolic expression, and determinant, of racially differentiated access to some basic rights of citizenship. As such, it is a medium through which the salience of race is sustained. In material terms, segregation is implicated in the unequal distribution of economic opportunities, welfare resources and political potential between Britain's black and white populations. Ideologically, segregationism has camouflaged these inequalities and may therefore be seen not only as functional to capital, but also as an aid to the legitimizing, repressive and delegitimizing roles of the state. It is, nevertheless, political exclusionism which lies at the root of racial segregation; it is through politics that the axes of social inequality are racialized; and it is in the struggle for political power that racial ideologies are sustained. With this in mind, and from a conviction that what I have outlined *can* be changed, the final section offers a comment on the prospects for reform.

Reform, revolution or more of the same?

Political strategies

Political exclusionism, whether by design or neglect, is ultimately what sustains the character of racial segregation in Britain. It follows, if this is true, that a prerequisite for effective reform is a change in the balance and orientation of decision-making power. The status quo might be challenged through a variety of strategies, but is unlikely to give way unless several combine.

Although it is increasingly obvious that the conventional channels of representative democracy have failed the black electorate, particularly at the level of national government (see Ashford 1981; Bulpitt 1986), there are two ways of extending the democratic process to challenge this. First, even while black people remain under-represented in elected office, it might be possible to extend the consultative process to provide them better access to key decision makers.

A precedent for this can be found in the work of the House of Commons Select Committee on Race Relations and Immigration, which between 1968/9 and 1977/8 consulted widely with community relations bodies and representatives of Asian and Afro-Caribbean organizations. Banton (1985: 80) describes this committee as 'a major vehicle for the making of government policy in its special field'. The fact remains that it failed to secure the one concession in most demand: a new central gency for race relations. It also failed (through lack of funds) to commission sufficient research to sustain its programme of inquiry.

In 1979, the Select Committee system was reformed. Existing bodies were disbanded and replaced by 14 all-party investigative committees charged 'to examine the expenditure, administration and policy of the principal government departments and associated bodies' (standing order, June 1979, para. 1). The new committees are more powerful than their predecessors, which is an optimistic sign, although there is also concern over their low priority in the eyes of the present Government. It is unfortunate, too, that during the 1980s, race relations and immigration has been 'relegated' to the status of a sub-committee (and not necessarily a permanent one) of the Home Affairs Committee.

The achievements and limitations of the new sub-committee are considered by Nixon (1986). Its greatest success was an investigation into 'Race Relations and the "Sus" Law' (April and August 1980), which led to the abolition of a piece of legislation (Section 4 of the 1824 Vagrancy Act) which was widely known to have been applied in a racially discriminatory manner. Equally important, but less obviously influential, was its report on 'Racial Disadvantage' (July 1981), which, despite the impact of the urban riots of that year, failed to establish a formal body in the Home Office to coordinate the race-related work of other departments. Moreover, the sub-committee made little progress in its reports on 'Proposed New Immigration Rules (February 1980), and 'Numbers and Legal Status of Future British Overseas Citizens without other Citizenship' (March 1981). According to Nixon (1986), these topics proved too controversial for an all-party group to handle: the committee split along partisan lines and this inhibited the formulation of coherent recommendations.

The new committee system undoubtedly has a bearing on Government policy making, not only through investigation and reports but also by its impact on the cultural climate of Parliamentary affairs. If nothing else, the existence of a sub-committee on race relations and immigration retains these themes on the political agenda. Although, when reviewing the entire committee system, Marsh (1987) concludes that consultation with extra-parliamentary interest groups has so far been patchy and unsystematic, he does acknowledge that the committees *could* work to extend the scope of representative democracy. This might enhance the political voice of Britain's black communities, particularly if a system of co-opted representation was developed. By opening up this route, Governments could build on the demonstrable preference of black groups for cooperation with, and integration into, the present system of liberal democracy (a preference discussed by Jacobs (1986)).

A second path to reform within the ambit of representative democracy might seek to enhance the electoral influence of black voters. This could most readily be achieved in one of the following ways. First, the mainstream parties could develop a greater commitment to the demands of their black supporters. This is beginning to occur in the Labour Party now that black people form an increasing proportion of its electorate. The crucial test, though, will come if the Party regains power, since as a government its record of support for minority groups is only slightly less blemished than that of the Conservatives.

Alternatively (or additionally) the effectiveness of the black vote could be enhanced by electoral reform. Proportional representation increases the scope for minority groups to participate in mainstream politics and, if accompanied by a system of multi-member constituencies, it might also encourage more local parties to place black candidates in safe seats. Moreover, the introduction of proportional representation in Britain would probably be based on the principle of single transferable vote (rather than the party list system), which Crewe (1983) argues to offer the best opportunities for black electors. Unfortunately for those who find hope in this kind of change, the election of June 1987 suggests that it is unlikely to gain support, despite increasing interest on the Labour Left.

For the most part, scope for reform within the traditional confines of representative democracy is currently (though not inherently) limited by a lack of commitment to the principle that greater racial equality is a contribution to the common good. Structurally, there is a point beyond which no further concessions to black people's interests can be made while the most powerful political positions are held almost exclusively by whites. There is, however, an alternative route to reform – through extra-parliamentary pressure groups and interest group politics.

This alternative is gaining support as a reaction to the marginalization of anti-racism in mainstream politics and as a reflection of the apparently increasing potency of informal social action. Giddens (1987) argues that the orientation of local social movements around a single theme can often usefully concentrate the forces for change. Although the very existence of such movements testifies to social tension and the potential for conflict, it may also illuminate 'previously undiagnosed characteristics of, and possibilities within, a given institutional order'. The scope and diversity of groups campaigning for racial justice is apparent from reviews provided by Ben-Tovim et al. (1986) and Jacobs (1986). Broadly, a distinction may be made between those whose membership is mixed and those mobilized exclusively around the concept of their black identity.

Alliances of black and white activists sprang into life during the 1970s (to resist the increasing popularity of the National Front) but were often short-lived, were frequently perceived to be extremist and were, in the eyes of many, eclipsed by the work of local community relations councils. Such groups did succeed in bringing the problem of racism and the concept of anti-racism to the forefront of political interest, but the apportionment of power within them has given cause for concern. Haynes (1983: 22) articulates the problem from the perspective of the black participants: 'If whites were there, they were there because they were in the leadership role. If they could not have that role then they undermined the organization of the movement.'

There must, then, be a role for a distinctively black politics in the struggle to secure a less unequal distribution of political power. There has always been a range of *de facto* blacks-only interest groups, which include workers associations, black women's organizations and movements centred on the principles of self-help or religious mobilization. Although these do not add up to a systematic political campaign, Gilroy (1987) argues that pressure group politics articulated through 'race' have growing potential.

Unfortunately, this has often proved difficult to realize. Locally, state bureaucracies have proved able and willing to undermine the activities of black interest groups by controlling access to information, expertise and material resources (Ben-Tovim et al. 1986). Nationally, despite an appearance of sympathy for collectively articulated demands, few fundamental changes followed the civil unrest of the early 1980s (Solomos 1986b). Banton (1985) offers an explanation for this, arguing that, in contrast to the process of, say, industrial bargaining, there are no legal standing and no formal mandate for black leaders to negotiate the kinds of contractual agreement (concerning rights and resources) on which so much of civil life hinges. In states like Britain, where corporate bargaining often bypasses representative democracy, informal political allegiances carry relatively little weight.

It is still possible to argue that the shared historical experience of colonialism and discrimination could (and perhaps should) provide an effective basis for collective action by black people. Rex (1986b) argues that the prospects for overcoming what he calls 'the heritage of slavery' depend crucially on the capacity of black people in Britain to act collectively. This in turn rests on the development of a 'black consciousness' which 'asserts the dignity of black people and their claim to equal treatment' (Rex 1986b: 133–4). Although the cultural diversity of the black populations means that such cooperation must be limited (perhaps to issues like self-defence, the principles of anti-racism and the laws against discrimination) it may already be a potent force for change. This is Gilroy's (1987) view when, reworking a well-worn literature on urban social movements, he argues that the articulation of collective demands through the idea of race depends as much on identification with locale as with a position in the division of labour (although among the unemployed, these obviously overlap). Effectively, the very intensity of segregation, together with awareness of the inequality it symbolizes, may be a spur to collective action. The existence and imagery of 'racial segregation' may be not only an instrument of racism but also a catalyst for resistance to it.

There are, to summarize, at least five political strategies which might be used to secure black people a greater, and fairer, say in political decision making, particularly at a national scale. (These strategies are not mutually exclusive: their coordination may be crucial.) Representative democracy might be extended by reorganizing the Select Committees, by reforming the power structure of individual political parties or by changing the system of electoral representation. None of these options is currently under debate, but it is the last which holds most promise. Alternatively, representative democracy might be bypassed (or supplemented) by pressure group politics. Mixed groups have achieved some successes in this respect, but the alternative – a distinctly black politics – may ultimately be most appealing for symbolic as well as strategic reasons. This strategy may seem unlikely given the wide range of populations it would have to unite, but it is a movement that could derive substantial impetus from the material inequalities experienced through the practice of segregation.

Ultimately, Sivanandan (1983) is realistic in his call for alliances – between the anti-racist struggle and the struggles of women, gays and lesbians; and between black people and the working class more generally. He argues that 'the whole purpose of knowing who we are is not to interpret the world, but to change it'. Thus, he claims, black people 'don't need cultural identity for its own sake, but to make use of the positive aspects of our culture to forge correct alliances and fight correct battles' (p. 11). It is with a view to the practicalities of forging alliances and operating a power-sharing coalition that my final comments are made. For when the battle for effective enfranchisement is won, a question will still remain and a struggle will still be waged. These will centre on the normative principles that are required to guide the apportionment of economic and welfare rights in a market democracy.

Public policy

I have argued that, by one route or another, the key to reform lies in securing an adequate representation of black people's interests in the process of political decision making. No amount of resolve by a white political elite can displace the need for a more equitable system of power-sharing. Yet even when such a system is achieved, it cannot be assumed that policy will change without resistance, or that conflict will disappear. The hallmark of democracy is debate about the appropriate means to reach contestable ends, and even the most sincere advocates of anti-racism or racial justice are divided over the aims of their projects and the way to achieve them.

Surprisingly, reformists in the race relations industry rarely consider what 'success' (however remote it may seem) should look like. There is too often a tendency to aspire to some abstract state of 'racial equality' without specifying how this might be recognized, and without acknow-ledging that equality is just one of several normative criteria by which public policy is guided and against which its effectiveness may be gauged. My concluding remarks suggest why these considerations are important.

Following Offe (1984), and viewing the task of social science as critique rather than prescription, this section does not advocate or evaluate specific policy instruments (such as racial monitoring, equality targets and so on). My intention is rather to outline the options that are theoretically available to politicians, showing that the debate of the past decade has been unnecessarily limited. The choice between the models I describe cannot, however, be made simply on technical or empirical grounds. Each has its own set of political presuppositions, and each, when implemented, advances a particular set of political interests.

Table 6 identifies four broad models for the political promotion of material and social well-being. It indicates that attempts to secure specifically *racial* justice might be regarded both as an effort to meet the collective needs of the black populations, and as an attempt to secure black people's rights as individuals. In general, the balance between needs-based and rights-based policies, as well as the detail of their scope and content, has varied over the years, reflecting changes in the economy and in political ideology. The four models (which are 'ideal types' rather than discrete policy prescriptions) give some idea of the wide range of options, of the aims and objectives associated with them, and of their relative strengths and weaknesses.

Currently, the policy framework within which race-related legislation falls (by this I mean legislation with an implicit as well as an explicit bearing on racial inequality) is closest to model 1. This framework can, to some extent, accommodate both the reformist and the populist factions of Britain's New Right. It is a rights-based model which stresses the primacy of economic, notably property, rights as a route to securing self-determination and contentment within a market economy. This approach prefers to pursue equality of opportunity for individuals in the market

Table 6 Models of intervention to achieve racial justice

	Model 1	Model 2	Model 3	Model 4
Point of intervention	Individual	Individual	Group	Group
Principle of intervention	*Rights* Securing economic efficiency, preserving property rights	*Rights* Securing universal rights of citizenship: political, civil and social	*Needs* Meeting general economic needs	*Needs* Meeting special needs A Technical B 'Structural'
Means of intervention	Market deregulation plus minimum state subsidy for those medically or legally out of the workforce	State provisioning in cash or kind	Vertical (income) redistribution	Horizontal redistribution A To cope with age, illness and handicap B To compensate for disadvantage and discrimination
Criteria for judging success	Economic prosperity, equal opportunity in the market place, fully protected property rights	Egalitarianism: an extension of effective rights to welfare, justice, political participation and employment	Equality of outcome in material circumstances	A Attainment of minimum standards B Attainment of quotas of representation through equity[a] or privilege[b]

[a] The guarantee that like cases are treated alike.
[b] Forms of positive discrimination (see text).

place rather than to subsidize equality of (economic and material) outcome between social groups. It recognizes that a degree of inequality is necessary to reward effort and stimulate initiative, but argues that market mechanisms contain sufficient integral checks and balances to undermine this if it becomes systematic or excessive. Generally, therefore, the market is seen as a more efficient and effective means of distributing goods and services than is the state.

Concessions are, however, made for those unable, through ill health, mental incapacity, old age or frailty, to compete in the economy. Their needs are regarded as 'special' (rather than general or 'normal'), in the technical sense that they are said to require special kinds of building adaptations and special forms of care. In effect, to win popular legitimacy, the rights-based approach in model 1 is forced to draw selectively on the collective needs-based approach summarized by model 4. But only a narrow range of 'special' needs (and, therefore, only a limited set of deserving groups) is recognized: those listed under column A, which is concerned with the kinds of social disadvantage that can be portrayed as technical rather than structural or political in origin.

'Structural' needs (column B) are not drawn into model 1, less because they are irrelevant than because they are expected to dissolve 'naturally' in a competitive market. Segmentation decreases market efficiency, so that if racial discrimination were shown to be, and perceived to be, uneconomic it would (assuming that the aim of participating in a market is to maximize profits and minimize costs) gradually peter out. The more perfect the competition (i.e. the smaller the extent of state intervention) the more obviously inefficient would racial discrimination become, and the more vigorously would it be purged by those in control of the forces of production. This kind of reasoning has prompted governments to argue that 'non-commercial' equal opportunities policies (including contract compliance) are not only unnecessary but might actually inhibit economic growth (see Jenkins and Solomos (1987) for an assessment of this).

Fortunately in view of the tenacity of model 1, there appear to be grounds for exploiting this economic argument. Dex (1986) concludes a comprehensive review of the British literature by observing that it *does* cost employers to discriminate, and by arguing that a government-led stand against racism could significantly enhance industrial efficiency, productivity and profitability. According to this evidence, the elimination of racial discrimination could help to further some broad aims of neo-liberal economics. (At the same time, of course, it is possible that white employees would perceive this as a threat to their own security, and that a surge of popular racism might both disrupt the economy and fragment the working class.)

What is most disturbing about the debate over whether and how model 1 confronts racial inequality is not that the neo-liberal argument may be fallacious, but that it is stripped of moral content (and indeed, that it takes economic efficiency as the measure of morality). Model 1, it is said, will work for racial justice because discrimination works against the efficiency of the market. The implication, of course, is that should racial discrimination *increase* market efficiency (which a Marxian perspective would imply), then its persistence would not give cause for concern (which is what some observers suggest has occurred).

Although model 1 accepts (and encourages) 'moderate' inequalities in income, wealth and social well-being, it is ideologically unable to accommodate the possibility that either economic opportunities or material outcomes are systematically structured to advance the interests of some groups while impeding those of others. The model rests its case on the essential autonomy of individuals, the efficiency of the market and the sanctity of property rights. Yet the evidence I have reviewed suggests that this model (which has now been in place for almost a decade) is not race-neutral, but simply colour-blind. It cannot offer the average black Briton the same range of opportunities and securities that it offers his or her average white counterpart.

Nevertheless, model 1, supplemented by a concession to particular categories of special need, has secured wide-ranging political, popular and intellectual appeal. Much of its popularity rests on its links with a political concern for Britain's performance in a world economy, on its respect for the integrity and autonomy of individuals, and on its support for the principle that individuals should retain and accumulate the rewards of personal effort. These qualities are packaged in a way that portrays model 1 as superior to the concerns of the traditional Left, which has tended to be preoccupied with collectively articulated demands and with group rather than individual needs.

Some aspirations of the 'old' Left are summarized in model 3, which argues for a general redistribution of wealth (in cash or kind) as compensation for the income inequalities generated by a market economy. In its pure form this model does not easily address inequalities that are not determined by income (these related sources of stratification have tended to be seen as superficial, short-lived diversions). However, the development of black consciousness and the success of feminism have prompted the Left to extend its traditional concern with the 'vertical' redistribution of wealth between classes (model 3) to a model (4B) which recognizes the salience of structured inequalities occurring within, or cutting across, class strata.

Although the present Government recognizes only a limited range of the 'horizontal' inequalities encompassed by model 4, in principle there is nothing to prevent this policy-relevant area of social disadvantage being defined more broadly. In the past decade, therefore, left-wing local governments have devoted a great deal of energy to this end. They have sought to tackle specifically racial disadvantage, and in doing so have regarded black people as having certain 'special' needs which are not met either by the market or by those instruments of social policy that aim for a vertical redistribution of wealth. This special treatment is commonly justified by two sets of arguments. The first hinges on the relevance, in some circumstances, of defining the needs of black households in technical terms; the second adds a structural dimension to the notion of special need in an attempt to embrace a history of racism and discrimination. The reasoning behind these arguments deserves spelling out.

It is obvious to most analysts that immigration history, as well as its legacy in the socio-economic profile of the black population in Britain, generates particular needs for housing, social services and educational provision. In the sphere of housing, for instance, neither the public nor the private sector contains sufficient dwellings that are large enough (in relation to cost and location) to cater adequately for the extended families comprising some Asian households. As a consequence there has been both overcrowding and the splitting of families, both of which have contributed to the overall disadvantage experienced by Asians. Clearly, then, there are ways in which black people may be at a disadvantage from the operation of mainstream policies simply by virtue of their demography and settlement history, and while 'technical' needs related to recency of immigration are recognized to a limited extent through the provisions of Section 11 funding,[1] there are compelling reasons to extend model 4A to take black people's 'special' needs more fully into account.

A second set of arguments supporting an extension of model 4 addresses the distinctive problems posed to black people by a history of direct and indirect racial discrimination. The 'special' needs this kind of experience generates are, it is argued, specific to the black population, and can be countered only through explicitly 'race-aware' strategies. Such needs are not therefore 'technical': they are not generated by any 'objective' requirement for special housing, care or medical support; they originate rather from the construction of race as a criterion for the differential distribution of scarce resources, and in this sense they are structural needs. However, whereas technical disadvantage refers to problems which can be discretely defined according to ostensibly 'objective' criteria, and therefore addressed in an apparently apolitical, pragmatic manner (by securing some minimum standard of provision for those in need), the criteria for intervening to combat structural disadvantage, and the aims of intervention, are much more contentious. Opinion is divided as to whether equity (the guarantee that like cases will be treated alike) or privilege (the possibility that like cases will not be treated alike) is the more appropriate basis from which racially just (i.e. anti-racist) policies should build.

Affirmative action and positive discrimination both allow special (preferential) treatment to be given to individuals not according to need, merit or restitution of personal rights, but rather according to group criteria (such as 'race') which are logically irrelevant to the action concerned. This is a way of making resources and opportunities available to people in particular (disadvantaged) categories irrespective of their individual need. This is not unprecedented in British policy (area-based urban policy and the use of 'intelligence' to discriminate between individuals in the education system are both forms of positive discrimination) but it has never been an integral part of race relations legislation.[2]

Common justifications for positive discrimination are: (a) that it is a just instrument by which society can offer group compensation for past discriminatory practice; (b) that, because of extensive, demonstrable, bias in the exercise of discretion, affirmative action is the only hope of providing black people with equal opportunities in the long run; and (c) that policies promoting group interests might be justified by appeal to a higher aim such as social integration or the maintenance of public order. According to Edwards (1987), positive discrimination does not occur when individuals are assisted because the boundaries of their group correspond with (or are constructed by) a particular form of deprivation. Such assistance is simply a response to need, or the restoration of a right.

With this in mind, persuasive though the above reasoning may be, my own feeling is that as a long-term solution for Britain positive discrimination may not be the most fruitful way forward. This is because a model which dispenses with 'equity' – however persuasive the reasoning – assigns group membership greater importance than individual rights. Group membership may be a way of bargaining for resources or winning political concessions in the short term, but ultimately the anti-racist cause must hinge on dispensing altogether with the idea of race as a principle by which to apportion (and deny) wealth, status and well-being.

The alternative to positive discrimination identified by model 4B, and the basis of race relations legislation in Britain, is the principle of equal opportunity. Although it is enshrined in the 1976 Race Relations Act, this means of addressing black people's needs has not been vigorously implemented, and it is only in the past five years or so that local authorities and the CRE have begun to show any real commitment to it. At its most developed, this principle guides local governments' anti-racist programmes which, despite their appellation, and though they take many forms, share a commitment to exposing discriminatory legislation and to confronting personal and institutional racism.

Symbolically, as well as in material terms, the anti-racist movement represents an important advance over the apathy that characterized local government throughout the 1960s. This attempt to broaden the special needs model of state intervention to encompass racial disadvantage must, therefore, be welcomed. Anti-racism is too easily ridiculed by the Right and sensationalized by the mass media. In truth, the demands of the movement have rarely been outlandish, and the policies involved are seldom unprecedented in other areas of legislation. Moreover, some form of race-aware policy – based on either equity or privilege – may be one (and perhaps, under some political arrangements, the only) effective means of alleviating racial inequality.

Nevertheless, the anti-racist movement also epitomizes the essential paradox and ultimate limitation of adopting a special, 'racial', needs approach in tackling racial inequality. In practice, this perspective:

appears to endorse the idea that racial groups are real in the sense of being fixed and exclusive. Race is presented as preceding racism and having the same status as 'national origins'. Race is differentiated from the question of colour (phenotype) but what it is remains unspecified. It is presented as an unproblematic common-sense category. Its existence can be taken for granted and the political problems which attend it are reduced to the issue of prejudice. (Gilroy 1987: 143–4)

All policies implemented within the ambit of model 4 must, however appropriate in the short term, ultimately sustain the social reality of race. This kind of approach falls broadly into Banton's (1985) vision of promoting racial harmony as a public good, and therefore represents a step towards a multi-racial rather than literally anti-racist society (the importance of this distinction is demonstrated by Morgan (1985)). Because of this, it is important to recognize that the special needs approach advocated in model 4 is not the only, nor necessarily the most suitable, alternative to the 'market-rights' model (1) outlined above. Model 2 presents a second possibility, which is as concerned as model 1 with individuals' rights but much less convinced that the market will secure them. The models may be contrasted as follows.

Advocates of the market model have successfully infused the collectivist principles of traditional Toryism with libertarian notions of freedom and individuality. In this model, the principle of freedom has been opposed to the end of equality, even though critics argue that the liberty this offers is limited, referring mainly to the average 'healthy, employed, educated, white adult male' (King 1987: 10). Model 2 also links collectivist principles – those of social democracy – with concern for individuals' integrity, but these concerns stem from a more inclusive moral philosophy based on the rights of citizenship.

The approaches typified in models 1 and 2 differ fundamentally, therefore, over the priority they assign to the rights individuals need to secure self-determination and social participation. Model 1 places faith in access to economic and property rights (equal opportunity in the market place), while model 2 regards the protection of a wider range of citizenship rights – political, civil and social – as an essential prerequisite of social justice (a concept which subsumes, but does not displace, racial justice). The difference between the models is, then, a moral one, involving a debate over who should benefit from market productivity.

Model 2 is based on recent attempts within political science and social policy to revitalize some principles of the citizenship theory that underpinned the post-war welfare state (see Deakin 1987; D. Harris 1987; King 1987; Turner 1986). Reworking the ideas of Marshall, Tawney and Titmuss, this model presents an important challenge to the assumptions of model 1 by arguing that a comprehensive concern for social justice can be advanced without sacrificing either the integrity of the individual or the efficiency of the economy. Model 2 differs from model 1 not over the importance of economic efficiency and personal autonomy, but by recognizing that markets can, and do, fail – both technically (as a distributive mechanism) and morally (as a force for social cohesion). Accordingly, economic success is a priority only as a means to an end. D. Harris (1987), for instance, assents to the legitimacy and potential prosperity of a market democracy, but in a context which balances the right to accumulate wealth against the right to receive welfare and the obligation to minimize hardship. It is this balance which offers the widest range of individuals an opportunity to sieze life chances, practise a chosen lifestyle and exercise their civil rights.

Given the differing primacy of property rights and more general citizenship rights in the two models, they must also differ in their views about the legitimacy of state provisioning: one seeks to minimize and tightly circumscribe public spending to finance tax concessions; the other seeks to re-introduce the principle of universally available (though selectively used) social policy. There is an economic and philosophical argument to justify the strategy embodied in model 2.

King (1987) provides the most comprehensive economic argument for the viability of state intervention of the kind required by this model. His work confirms that the citizenship model is sensitive to economic constraints and prizes highly the right to work. To this end he advocates a modified Keynesianism with a strengthened labour policy, using the work of Therborn (1986) to support his view that this gives better guarantees of economic buoyancy than does monetarism. Most importantly, the model provides the basis on which to establish a National Economic Employment Corporation along the line suggested by Nuti (1985/6) and Rustin (1985). This would extend the right to employment, re-introducing important elements of Keynesian macro-economic planning but retaining some reverence for market forces in an international context. Given black people's particular vulnerability to cycles of unemployment and to the spatial selectivity of industrial restructuring, this kind of safeguard will go a long way to restoring their opportunities to participate fully in the economy.

Deakin (1987) and D. Harris (1987) make a complementary argument for adopting model 2 grounded in moral philosophy. Such a model, they argue, is about integration and mutual support and so offers a very different notion of social belonging from that embraced by one-nation conservatism. It is, according to Deakin, concerned with the creation of a society that secures loyalty through guarantees of mutual aid and 'fellowship', rather than through the strictures of competitive capitalism which offer slim hopes of rich reward. The key to success in this respect, and a strength of the 'new' citizenship theorists over their predecessors, is an extension of public participation in the affairs of the state. This marks a move away from the paternalistic and corporate socialism of previous decades towards a more open, participatory social democracy. It includes, fundamentally, a commitment to conferring the mass public with a capacity to make real choices, even though the consequences 'may not always be to the liking of those who believe they know best' (Deakin 1987: 187).

This, of course, flies in the face of political trends in the last decade: it rests on decentralization rather than centralization of fiscal and political power; on respect for, rather than suspicion of, the exercise of local initiative; and on a willingness to formalize social obligations, rather than an insistence that voluntary effort or individual altruism are sufficient in a climate of uncompassionate individualism. Nevertheless, the promise of transition to a more participatory social democracy may well be the most compelling reason for preferring model 2, particularly given the suspicion with which both the liberal and authoritarian elements of traditional conservatism have regarded mass enfranchisement.

Despite the promise this new model holds, it should not be seized uncritically in a society divided by 'race'. Even putting aside the practical and political difficulties of implementing the model, there are reasons why the social democratic ideal may not always provide the best attack on racial inequality. Ben-Tovim et al. (1986) are wary of 'universalizing' policy frameworks, arguing that they fail to distinguish black people's experience of discrimination from white people's experience of inequality. Such frameworks tend to conflate racism with the kinds of prejudice experienced, for instance, by white Australians in Britain, and they can lend legitimacy to both a patronizing integrationism and a 'colour-blind' assimilationism. Moreover, the very notion of citizenship must be suspect in a society which has worked systematically to exclude black people from wearing that badge. So far, few advocates of model 2 have considered how the extension of rights among a national core might systematically curtail the rights of those at the periphery, and only Turner (1986: 47) cautions that 'we need to discuss citizenship always within the context of national conflicts and colonial development'.

The dangers of model 2 are as real as the benefits, and it will not automatically guard against the colour-blind idealism that has so effectively legitimized racial inequality over the past 40 years. However, some reworking of traditional citizenship theory does seem to offer the best hope of effecting a transition between the 'race-aware' policies required if black people are to exercise their full range of citizenship rights, and the 'race-neutral' policy framework that must be the ultimate goal of a truly anti-racist society.

In promoting this transition, there can be no question of denying the persistence of *cultural* variety, in all its forms. As D. Harris (1987: 149) specifies it, the goal of the citizenship model is 'to provide everyone with the wherewithal to enjoy and participate in the benefits of pluralism'. The 'enemy' is not heterogeneity itself but merely 'those differences which are connected with the process of exclusion and domination'.The model therefore celebrates culture, but systematically undermines the salience of race and the legitimacy of racial ideology. It supports anti-racism not in isolation, but as a prerequisite for developing the more general values of citizenship. This openly acknowledges the need for 'positive intervention designed explicitly to promote the interests of those who face insuperable disadvantages in current circumstances' (Deakin 1987: 184). The model is ready to accommodate a Bill of Rights that secures the well-being of minority groups as well as of the individuals comprising them (the precedents for which are discussed by Rich (1987b)).

Of the four approaches summarized in table 6, only model 2 seems adequate to respond to the weight of evidence accumulated in previous chapters. Throughout the book, I have argued that the fundamental aim of a just society must be to ensure that specifically racial differentiation has no material or ideological rationale. The ultimate end is that of effective (rather than euphemistic) deracialization – that is, to remove the salience of appearance or national origin as a principle for the differential distribution of rewards and life chances (again, I would emphasize that this says nothing about the legitimacy or otherwise of cultural practices which are not organized around the projects of exploitation or usurpation).

This demands policies able both to undermine the material basis of racial inequality and to erode the symbolic significance of racial ideology. Model 2 offers hope on both these counts. First, it tackles the differential distribution of economic, welfare, political and civil rights which I have suggested are all fundamental to the reproduction of racial inequality. Since the model is organized to advance the universal rights of individuals rather than (but not at the expense of) the collective rights of black people as a group, it both pre-empts the racialization of inequality and links a quest for racial justice with the broader project of alleviating social and economic disadvantage overall. Secondly, because its primary emphasis lies with the integrity of the individual, the cultural and ideological underpinnings of racial categorization are also undermined. In this sense, the model not only confronts the structural origins of racial inequality but also challenges a cultural blindspot in white society which has always denied black people their individuality. Such reasoning is not yet complete and may be controversial, but it does have a bearing on whether the future holds reform, revolution or more of the same.

Notes

1 It is significant that it was the Left who tried to extend this service to meet the changing requirements and character of the black population in Britain (whether immigrant or not).
2 A form of 'soft' positive discrimination is built into the 1976 Race Relations Act. It allows special educational, training and welfare facilities to be provided for minority groups (Section 35) and makes provision for pre-employment or promotion training for the minority labour force where such people are obviously but inexplicably under-represented as employees (Sections 37 and 38).

L. I. H. E.
THE BECK LIBRARY
WOOLTON RD., LIVERPOOL, L16 8ND

Chronology of Main Political and Policy Events[a]

		Events relating to	
Date	Government/ prime minister	Immigration, nationality and race relations	Housing/urban policy
1945	*Labour* Attlee		
1948		British Nationality Act	
1949			Housing Act
1951	*Conservative* Churchill		
1954			Housing Repairs and Rents Act
1955	Eden		
1957	Macmillan		
1958		Notting Hill 'riots'	
1961		South Africa leaves Commonwealth; Britain applies to join the EEC	
1962		Commonwealth Immigration Act	
1963		Britain refused entry to EEC	
1963	Home		
1964			Housing Act

Date	Government/ prime minister	Events relating to	
		Immigration, nationality and race relations	*Housing/urban policy*
1964	*Labour* Wilson		
1965		Race Relations Act	
1966			Local Government Act
1968		Race Relations Act; Immigration Act; Kenyan Asian 'crisis'	
1969			Housing Act; Local Government Grants (Social Needs) Act
1970	*Conservative* Heath		
1971		Immigration Act	Housing Act
1972		Ugandan Asian 'crisis'; Britain enters EEC	Housing Finance Act
1974	*Labour* Wilson		Housing Act
1976	Callaghan	Race Relations Act	
1977			Housing (Homeless Persons) Act
1978			Inner Urban Areas Act
1979	*Conservative* Thatcher		
1980		Urban unrest (Bristol)	Housing Act
1981		British Nationality Act; urban unrest (wide-spread)	
1985		Urban unrest	Housing Act
1987		Immigration Bill	
1988		Immigration Act	'Action for Cities'; Housing Act

[a] Only events referred to in the text are included.

References

Aldrich, H. E., Cater, J. C., Jones, T. P. and McEvoy, D. 1981: Business development and self-segregation: Asian enterprise in three British cities. In C. Peach, V. Robinson and S. Smith (eds), *Ethnic Segregation in Cities*, London: Croom Helm, 170–92.

Agnew, J. 1987: *Place and Politics. The Geographical Mediation of State and Society*. London: Allen and Unwin.

Anwar, M. 1981: *Race Relations in 1981*. London: Commission for Racial Equality.

Anwar, M. 1981/2: Public reactions to the Scarman report. *New Community*, 9, 371–3.

Anwar, M. 1984: *Ethnic Minorities and the 1983 General Election*. London: Commission for Racial Equality.

Anwar, M. 1986: *Race and Politics*. London: Tavistock.

Anwar, M. 1987: The participation of Asians in the British political system. Paper presented to the conference on South Asian Communities Overseas, Oxford.

Ashford, D. E. 1981: *Policy and Politics in Britain. The Limits of Consensus*. Oxford: Basil Blackwell.

Association of London Authorities 1988: *Black People, Ethnic Minorities and the Poll Tax*. London: ALA.

Association of Metropolitan Authorities 1985: *Housing and Race. Policy and Practice in Local Authorities*. London: AMA.

Ball, M. 1983: *Housing Policy and Economic Power: the Political Economy of Owner Occupation*. London: Methuen.

Ball, M. 1986: The built environment and the urban question. *Environment and Planning D: Society and Space*, 4, 447–64.

Ballard, R. 1983: Race and the census: what an ethnic question would show. *New Society*, 12 May, 212–14.

Banton, M. 1972: *Racial Minorities*. London: Fontana.

Banton, M. 1977: *The Idea of Race*. London: Tavistock.

Banton, M. 1983: The influence of colonial status upon black–white relations in England, 1948–58. *Sociology*, 17, 546–59.

Banton, M. 1984: Transatlantic perspectives on public policy concerning racial disadvantage. *New Community*, 11, 280–7.

Banton, M. 1985: *Promoting Racial Harmony*. Cambridge: Cambridge University Press.

Barber, A. 1981: Labour force information from the National Dwelling and Housing Survey. *Research Paper 17*, London: Department of Employment.

Barker, A. 1978: *The African Link: British Attitudes to the Negro in the Era of the Atlantic Slave Trade, 1550–1807*. London: Franck Cass.

Barker, M. 1981: *The New Racism. Conservatives and the Ideology of the Tribe*. London: Junction Books.

Barry, N. P. 1987: *The New Right*. London: Croom Helm.

Bassett, K. and Short, J. R. 1980: *Housing and Residential Structure*. London: Routledge and Kegan Paul.

Ben-Tovim, G. and Gabriel, J. 1982: The politics of race in Britain 1962–79. 1. Review of the major trends and of recent debates. In C. Husband (ed.) *'Race' in Britain. Continuity and Change*, London: Hutchinson, 145–72.

Ben-Tovim, G., Gabriel, J., Law, I. and Stredder, K. 1986: *The Local Politics of Race*. Basingstoke: Macmillan.

Bentham, G. 1986: Socio-tenurial polarization in the United Kingdom, 1953–83: the income evidence. *Urban Studies*, 23, 157–62.

Benyon, T. 1987: Interpretations of civil disorder. In J. Benyon and J. Solomos (eds), *The Roots of Urban Unrest*. Oxford: Pergamon Press, 23–41.

Bethnal Green and Stepney Trades Council 1978: *Blood on the Streets*. London: BGSTC.

Biddiss, M. B. (ed.) 1979: *Images of Race*. Leicester: Leicester University Press.

Billig, M. 1978: *Fascists: A Social Psychological View of the National Front*. London: Academic Press.

Bochel, J. and Denver, D. 1983: Candidate selection in the Labour Party: what the selectors seek. *British Journal of Political Science*, 13, 45–60.

Boga, N., Deane, T., Grubb, S., Middleton, R., Robertson, S. and Tay, L. 1986: Anti-racism for the private rented sector. Report for London Against Racism in Housing. London: Anti-Racist Housing Working Group. (Unpublished report.)

Bonnerjea, L. and Lawton, J. 1987: *Homelessness in Brent*. London: Policy Studies Institute.

Booth, P. and Crook, T. (eds) 1986: *Low Cost Home Ownership*. Aldershot: Gower.

Bosanquet, N. 1983: *After the New Right*. London: Heinemann.

Bovaird, A., Harloe, M. and Whitehead, C. M. E. 1985: Private rented housing: its current role. *Journal of Social Policy*, 14, 1–23.

Brennan, J. and McGeever, P. 1987: *Employment Prospects of Graduates from Ethnic Minorities*. London: Commission for Racial Equality.

Bridges, L. and Bunyan, T. 1983: Britain's new urban policing strategy – the Police and Criminal Evidence Act in context. *Journal of Law and Society*, 10, 85–107.

Bristow, M. 1976: Britain's response to the Ugandan Asians Crisis: government myths versus political and resettlement realities. *New Community*, 5, 265–79.

Bristow, M. 1978/9: Ugandan Asians: racial disadvantage and housing markets in Manchester and Birmingham. *New Community*, 7, 203–16.

British Nationality Act 1981: *Public General Acts – Elizabeth II*, chapter 61. London: HMSO.

Brown, C. 1984: *Black and White Britain*. London: Heinemann.

Bulpitt, J. 1986: Continuity, autonomy and peripheralisation: the anatomy of the centre's race statecraft in England. In Z. Layton-Henry and P. B. Rich (eds), *Race, Government and Politics in Britain*, Basingstoke: Macmillan, 17–44.

Butler, D. and Stokes, D., 1974: *Political Change in Britain*, 2nd edn. London: Macmillan.

CACR, 1961: National Union of Conservative and Unionist Associations, Conservative Annual Conference Report. London: Conservative Central Office.

Carter, B., Harris, C. and Joshi, S. 1987: The 1951–55 Conservative government and the racialisation of black immigration. *Immigrants and Minorities*, 6, 335–47.

Castles, S. with Booth, H. and Wallace, T. 1984: *Here for Good. Western Europe's New Ethnic Minorities*. London: Pluto Press.

Castles, S. and Kosack, G. 1985: *Immigrant Workers and Class Structure in Western Europe*, 2nd edn. Oxford: Oxford University Press.

Cater, J. 1981: The impact of Asian estate agents on patterns of ethnic residence: a case study in Bradford. In P. Jackson and S. J. Smith (eds), *Social Interaction and Ethnic Segregation*. London: Academic Press, 163–83.

Cater, J. C. and Jones, T. P. 1979: Ethnic residential space: the case of Asians in Bradford. *Tijdschrift voor Economische en Sociale Geografie*, 70, 86–97.

Cater, J. C.and Jones, T. P. 1987a: Community, ethnicity and class among South Asians in Britain. Paper presented to the Conference on South Asian Communities Overseas. Oxford.

Cater, J. and Jones, T. 1987b: Asian ethnicity, home-ownership and social reproduction. In P. Jackson (ed.), *Race and Racism*, London: George Allen and Unwin, 191–211.

Cater, J., Jones, T. and McEvoy, D. 1977: Ethnic segregation in British cities. *Annals, Association of American Geographers*, 67, 305–6.

Cell, J. W. 1982: *The Highest Stage of White Supremacy*. Cambridge: Cambridge University Press.

Centre for Contemporary Cultural Studies 1982: *The Empire Strikes Back*. London: Hutchinson.

Central Housing Advisory Committee 1969: *Report on Council Housing: Purposes, Procedures and Priorities* (the Cullingworth Committee). London: HMSO.

Central Statistical Office 1987: *Regional Trends 22*. London: HMSO.

Clapham, D., Kemp, P. and Smith, S. J. Forthcoming: *Social Policy and Housing*. Basingstoke, Macmillan.

Clapham, D. and Kintrea, K. 1986: Rationing, choice and constraint: the allocation of public housing in Glasgow. *Journal of Social Policy*, 15, 51–67.

Clapham, D. and Maclennan, D. 1983: Residualisation of public housing: a non-issue. *Housing Review*, 32, 9–10.

Clapham, D. and Smith, S. J. 1988: Urban social policy. In J. English (ed.), *Social Services in Scotland*, Edinburgh: Scottish Academic Press, 216–33.

Clare, J. 1987: The ratchet advances another turn. In J. Benyon and J. Solomos (eds), *The Roots of Urban Unrest*, Oxford: Pergamon Press, 61–5.

Clark, D. 1977: Immigrant responses to the British housing market: a case study in the West Midlands conurbation. *Working Paper 7*, Bristol: Research Unit on Ethnic Relations.

Clarke, C., Ley, D. and Peach, C. (eds) 1984: *Geography and Ethnic Pluralism*. London: Allen and Unwin.

Clarke, W. A. V. 1982: Judicial intervention as policy: impacts on population distribution and redistribution in urban areas in the United States. *Population Research and Policy Review*, 1, 79–100.

Cohen, A. 1980: Drama and politics in the development of a London carnival. *Man*, NS 15, 65–87.

Cohen, A. 1982: A polyethnic London carnival as a contested cultural performance. *Ethnic and Racial Studies*, 5, 23–41.

Cohen, S. 1985: Anti-semitism, immigration controls and the welfare state. *Critical Social Policy*, 5, 73–92.

Commission for Racial Equality 1980: *Reports of Two Formal Investigations* (M. G. Midda and D. S. Services Ltd; Allen's Accommodation Bureau). London: CRE.

Commission for Racial Equality (Race and Housing Forum) 1981: *Racial Harassment on Local Authority Housing Estates*. London: CRE.

Commission for Racial Equality 1983: *Collingwood Housing Association Ltd. Report of a Formal Investigation*. London: CRE.

Commission for Racial Equality 1984a: *Race and Council Housing in Hackney*. London: CRE.

Commission for Racial Equality 1984b: *Race and Housing in Liverpool: a Research Report*. London: CRE.

Commission for Racial Equality 1985a: *Walsall Metropolitan Borough Council: Policies of Housing Allocation*. London: CRE.

Commission for Racial Equality 1985b: *Race and Mortgage Lending*. London: CRE.

Commission for Racial Equality 1987: *Living in Terror. A Report on Racial Violence and Harassment in Housing*. London: CRE.

Commonwealth Immigration Act 1962: *Public General Acts – Elizabeth II*, chapter 21. London: HMSO.

Community Relations Commission 1977: *Housing Choice and Ethnic Concentration*. London: CRC.

Cox, O. C. 1948. *Caste, Class and Race*. New York: Doubleday.

Crewe, I. 1979: The black, brown and green votes. *New Society*, 12 April, 1976–8.

Crewe, I. 1983: Representation and the ethnic minorities in Britain. In N. Glazer and K. Young (eds), *Ethnic Pluralism and Public Policy*, London: Heinemann, 258–84.

Crook, A. D. H. 1986: Privatisation of housing and the impact of the Conservative Government's initiatives on low-cost homeownership and private renting between 1979 and 1984 in England and Wales: 1. The privatisation policies. *Environment and Planning A*, 18, 639–59.

Cross, M. 1982a: The manufacture of marginality. In E. Cashmore and B. Troyna (eds), *Black Youth in Crisis*, London: George Allen and Unwin, 35–52.

Cross, M. 1982b: Racial equality and social policy: omission or commission? In C. Jones and J. Stevenson (eds), *The Year Book of Social Policy in Britain 1980–81*, London: Routledge and Kegan Paul, 73–88.

Cross, M. 1983: Racialised poverty and reservation ideology: blacks and the urban labour market. Paper presented to the fourth Urban Change and Conflict Conference, Clacton-on-Sea.

Cross, M. 1985: Black workers, recession and economic restructuring in the West Midlands. Paper presented to the conference on Racial Minorities, Economic Restructuring and Urban Decline, Warwick.

Cross, M. 1986: Migration and exclusion: Caribbean echoes and British realities. In C. Brock (ed.), *The Caribbean in Europe*, London: Frank Cass.

Cross, M. and Johnson, M. 1989: *Race and the Urban System*. Cambridge: Cambridge University Press, in the press.

Crossman, R. H. S. 1975: *The Diaries of a Cabinet Minister, Vol. 1*. London: Hamish Hamilton and Jonathan Cape.

Crowe, E. W. 1980: Cross-voting in the British House of Commons 1945–74. *Journal of Politics*, May, 487–510.

Daghlian, J. and Dalton, M. 1988: *The Housing Needs, Experience and Expectations of Glasgow's Minority Ethnic Populations: The Role of the Housing Associations*. Glasgow: Scottish Ethnic Minorities Research Unit.

Daniel, W. W. 1968: *Racial Discrimination in England*. Harmondsworth: Penguin.

Davies, T. 1986: The forms of collective racial violence. *Political Studies*, 34, 40–60.

Davison, R. B. 1966: *Black British*. London: Oxford University Press for Institute of Race Relations.

Deakin, N. (ed.) 1965: *Colour and the British Electorate*. London: Pall Mall Press.

Deakin, N. 1968: The politics of the Commonwealth Immigrants Bill. *Political Quarterly*, 39, 25–45.

Deakin, N. 1987: *The Politics of Welfare*. London: Methuen.

Deakin, N. and Bourne, J. 1970: Powell, the minorities, and the 1970 election. *Political Quarterly*, 41, 399–415.

Dean, D. W. 1987: Coping with colonial immigration, the cold war and colonial policy: the Labour government and black communities in Great Britain 1945–51. *Immigrants and Minorities*, 6, 305–34.

Dearlove, J. and Saunders, P. 1984: *Introduction to British Politics*. Cambridge: Polity Press.

DeMont, A. J. 1980: Racial politics in Britain and America: divergence and decline. Unpublished paper, Nuffield College, Oxford.

Denney, D. 1985: Race and crisis management. In N. Manning (ed.), *Social Problems and Welfare Ideology*, Aldershot: Gower, 55–75.

Department of the Environment 1980: *Review of the Traditional Urban Programme: Consultative Document*. London: Department of the Environment.

Department of the Environment 1981: *Ministerial Guidelines on the Partnerships, and Programme Authorities*. London: Department of the Environment.

Department of the Environment 1983: *Local Authorities and Racial Disadvantage*. London: Department of the Environment.

Department of the Environment 1984: *The Urban Programme: Tackling Racial Disadvantage*. London: Department of the Environment.

Department of the Environment 1985: *Urban Programme: Minutes of Evidence. Monday 25 November 1985*. House of Commons Committee of Public Accounts. London: HMSO.

Department of the Environment 1986: *Assessment of the Employment Effects of Economic Development Projects Funded under the Urban Programme*. London: HMSO.

Department of the Environment 1987a: *Housing Policy: The Government's Proposals* (Cmnd 214). London: HMSO.

Department of the Environment 1987b: *Tenants' Choice. The Government's Proposals for Legislation*. London: Department of the Environment.

Department of the Environment 1987c: *Housing Action Trusts. A Consultation Document*. London: Department of the Environment.

Department of the Environment 1987d: *Finance for Housing Associations: the Government's Proposals*. London: Department of the Environment.

Desai, R. 1963: *Indian Immigrants in Britain*. London: Oxford University Press for Institute of Race Relations.

Dex, S. 1986: The costs of discriminating: a review of the literature. *Home Office Research Bulletin 22*. London: HMSO.

Dickens, P., Duncan, S., Goodwin, M. and Gray, F. 1985: *Housing, States and Localities*. London: Methuen.

Dixon, D. 1983: Thatcher's people: the British Nationality Act 1981. *Journal of Law and Society*, 10, 161–80.

Doherty, J. 1973: Race, class and residential segregation in Britian. *Antipode*, 5, 45–51.

Doling, J. and Davies, M. 1983: Ethnic minorities and the protection of the rent acts. *New Community*, 3, 487–95.

Dummett, M. 1979: *Southall 23 April 1979; The Report of the Unofficial Committee of Inquiry* (The Dummett Report). London: HMSO.

Dummett, M. and Dummett, A. 1969: The role of government in Britain's racial crisis. In L. Donnelly (ed.), *Justice First*. London: Sheed and Ward, 25–78.

Duncan, O. D. and Duncan, B. 1955: A methodological analysis of segregation indexes. *American Sociological Review*, 20, 210–17.

Dunleavy, P. and O'Leary, B. 1987: *Theories of the State. The Politics of Liberal Democracy*. Basingstoke: Macmillan.

Dunn, R., Forrest, R. and Murie, A. 1987: The geography of council house sales in England 1979–85. *Urban Studies*, 24, 47–60.

Dye, T. R. 1976: *Policy Analysis*. Montgomery, Alabama: University of Alabama Press.

Edmonds, J. and Behrens, R. 1981: Kippers, kittens and kipper boxes: conservative populists and race relations. *Political Quarterly*, 52, 342–8.

Edwards, J. 1987: *Positive Discrimination, Social Justice and Social Policy*. London: Tavistock.

Edwards, J. and Batley, R. 1978: *The Politics of Positive Discrimination: an Evaluation of the Urban Programme 1967–77*. London: Tavistock.

Elliott, B. and McCrone, D. 1987: Class, culture and morality: a sociological analysis of neo-conservatism. *Sociological Review*, 35, 485–515.

English, J. 1982: Must council housing become welfare housing? *Housing Review*, 31, 154–6 and 212–13.

English, J., Madigan, R. and Norman, P. 1976: *Slum Clearance: the Social and Economic Context in England and Wales*. London: Croom Helm.

Ermisch, J. 1984: *Housing Finance: Who Gains?* London: Policy Studies Institute.

Eyles, J. and Evans, M. 1987: Popular consciousness, moral ideology, and locality. *Environment and Planning D: Society and Space*, 5, 39–71.

Falk, R. F., Cortese, F. and Cohen, J. 1978: Utilizing standardized indices of residential segregation: comment on Winship. *Social Forces*, 57, 713–16.

Farley, J. E. 1984: P^* segregation indices: what can they tell us about housing segregation in 1980? *Urban Studies*, 21, 331–6.

Federation of Black Housing Organisations 1986: Racial terrorism. *FBHO Newsletter*, 1, 5.

Fenton, M. 1977: *Asian Households in Owner Occupation*. Working Papers on Ethnic Relations 2, SSRC Research Unit on Ethnic Relations.

Fenton, S. 1984: Costs of discrimination in the owner-occupied sector. In R. Ward (ed.), *Race and Residence in Britain: Approaches to Differential Treatment in Housing*, Birmingham: ESRC Research Unit on Ethnic Relations, 107–12.

Fevre, R. 1984: *Cheap Labour and Racial Discrimination*. Aldershot: Gower.

Field, S. 1982: Urban disorders in Britain and America: a review of research. In S. Field and P. Southgate (eds), *Public Disorder*, London: HMSO, 1–40.

Field, S. 1986: The changing nature of racial disadvantage. *Research Bulletin*, 21, 39–42, London: Home Office Research and Planning Unit.

Field, S., Mair, G., Rees, T. and Stevens, P. 1981: *Ethnic Minorities in Britain*. London: Home Office.

Fitzgerald, M. 1983: Ethnic minorities and the 1983 general election. *Runnymede Trust Briefing Paper*, May.

Fitzgerald, M. 1984: *Political Parties and Black People*. London: Runnymede Trust.

Fitzgerald, M. 1987: *Black People and Party Politics in Britain*. London: Runnymede Trust.

Fitzgerald, M. and Layton-Henry, Z. 1986: Opposition parties and race policies, 1979–83. In P. Rich and Z. Layton-Henry (eds), *Race, Government and Politics in Britain*, Basingstoke: Mcmillan, 100–24.

Flett, H. 1979: Dispersal policies in council housing: arguments and evidence. *New Community*, 7, 184–94.

Flett, H. 1984: Asians in council housing: an analysis. In R. Ward (ed.), *Race and Residence in Britain: Approaches to Differential Treatment in Housing*, Monographs on Ethnic Relations 2, ESRC, 52–80.

Flett, H., Henderson, J. and Brown, B. 1979: The practice of racial dispersal in Birmingham, 1969–1975. *Journal of Social Policy*, 8, 289–309.

Foot, P. 1965: *Immigration and Race in British Politics*. Harmondsworth: Penguin.

Foot, P. 1969: *The Rise of Enoch Powell*. Harmondsworth: Penguin.

Forrest, R. and Murie, A. 1983: Residualization and council housing: aspects of the changing social relations of housing tenure. *Journal of Social Policy*, 12, 453–68.

Fredrickson, G. M. 1981: *White Supremacy*. New York and Oxford: Oxford University Press.

Freeman, G. P. 1979: *Immigrant Labour and Racial Conflict in Industrial Societies*. Princeton, NJ: Princeton University Press.

Frenkel, S. and Western, J. 1988: Pretext or prophylaxis? the malarial mosquito and racial segregation in a British tropical colony. *Annals, Association of American Geographers*, 78, 211–28.

Fryer, P. 1984: *Staying Power. The History of Black People in Britain*. London: Pluto Press.

George, V. and Wilding, P. 1976: *Ideology and Social Welfare*. London: Routledge and Kegan Paul.

Gibson, M. S. and Langstaff, M. J. 1982: *An Introduction to Urban Renewal*. London: Hutchinson.

Gilroy, P. 1987: *There Ain't no Black in the Union Jack*. London: Hutchinson.

Giddens, A. 1981: *A Contemporary Critique of Historical Materialism, Vol. 1*. London: Macmillan.

Giddens, S. 1987: *Social Theory and Modern Sociology*. Cambridge: Polity Press.

Gordon, P. 1983: *White Law*. London: Pluto Press.

Gordon, P. 1986a: *Racial Violence and Harassment*. London: Runnymede Trust.

Gordon, P. 1986b: Racism and social security. *Critical Social Policy*, 6, 23–40.

Gordon, P. and Klug, F. 1986: *New Right Racism*. London: Searchlight Publications.

Gouldner, A. W. 1976: *The Dialectic of Ideology and Technology*. London: Macmillan.

Greater London Council 1984: *Racial Harassment in London*, report of a panel of inquiry set up by the GLC Police Committee. London: GLC.

Gregg, A. 1987: Tenants tackle racial harassment. *Roof*, September/October, 14–15.

Grubb, S. 1987: Race and housing: a note on the role of the Commission for Racial Equality in the operation/application of the Race Relations Act 1976. In S. J. Smith and J. Mercer (eds), *New Perspectives on Race and Housing in Britain*, Glasgow: Centre for Housing Research, 107–23.

Haddon, R. 1970: A minority in a welfare state: location of West Indians in the London housing market. *The New Atlantis*, 2, 80–123.

Hall, P., Thomas, R., Gracey, H. and Drewett, R. 1973: *The Containment of Urban England. Vol. 2: the Planning System: Objectives, Operations, Impacts*. London: Allen and Unwin.

Hall, S. 1978: Racism and reaction. In *Five Views of Multi-racial Britain*, London: Commission for Racial Equality, 23–35.

Hambleton, R. 1981: Implementing inner city policy: reflections from experience. *Policy and Politics*, 9, 51–71.

Hamnett, C. and Randolph, B. 1986: The role of labour and housing markets in the production of geographical variations in social stratification. In K. Hoggart and E. Kofman (eds), *Politics, Geography and Social Stratification*, London: Croom Helm, 213–46.

Harris, C. 1987: British capitalism, migration and relative surplus-population: a synopsis. *Migration*, 1, 47–96.

Harris, D. 1987: *Justifying State Welfare: The New Right versus the Old Welfare*. Oxford: Basil Blackwell.

Harris, R. 1984: Residential segregation and class formation in the capitalist city: a review and directions for research. *Progress in Human Geography*, 8, 26–49.

Harvey, D. 1975: Class structure in a capitalist society and the theory of residential differentiation. In R. Peel, M. Chisholm and P. Haggett (eds), *Processes in Physical and Human Geography*, London: Heinemann.

Harvey, D. 1982: *The Limits to Capital*. Oxford: Basil Blackwell.

Harvey, D. 1985a: *The Urbanization of Capital*. Oxford: Basil Blackwell.

Harvey, D. 1985b: *Consciousness and the Urban Experience*. Oxford: Basil Blackwell.

Haynes, A. 1983: *The State of Black Britain*. London: Root.

Henderson, J. and Karn, V. 1984: Race, class and the allocation of public housing in Britain. *Urban Studies*, 21, 115–28.

Henderson, J. and Karn, V. 1987: *Race, Class and State Housing: Inequality in the Allocation of Public Housing in Britain*. Aldershot: Gower.

Higgins, J., Deakin, N., Edwards, J. and Wicks, M. 1983: *Government and Urban Poverty*. Oxford: Basil Blackwell.

Hindell, K. 1965: The genesis of the Race Relations Bill. *Political Quarterly*, 36, 390–405.

Hindess, B. 1987: *Freedom, Equality and the Market. Arguments on Social Policy*. London: Tavistock.

Hiro, D. 1971: *Black British, White British*. London: Eyre and Spottiswoode.

Hogwood, B. W. 1987: *From Crisis to Complacency? Shaping Public Policy in Britain*. Oxford: Oxford University Press.

Home Affairs Committee 1981: Racial Disadvantage, fifth report from the Home Affairs Committee, session 1980/1. London: HMSO.

Home Affairs Committee 1986: Racial Attacks and Harassment, third report from the Home Affairs Committee, session 1985/6. London: HMSO.

Home Office 1981: *Racial Attacks*. London: HMSO.

House of Commons 1965: Immigration from the Commonwealth, House of Commons Papers, session 1964/5, Cmnd 2739. London: HMSO.

House of Commons 1982: Government reply to the fifth report from the Home Affairs Committee 1981/2, Racial Disadvantage. London: HMSO.

House of Commons Employment Committee 1987: Discrimination in Employment, first report, session 1986/7. London: HMSO.

Housing Act 1969: *Public General Acts – Elizabeth II*, chapter 154. London: HMSO.

Housing Act 1980: *Public General Acts – Elizabeth II*, chapter 51. London: HMSO.

Housing Monitoring Team 1982: *Building Societies and the Local Housing Market.* Research Memorandum 90, Centre for Urban and Regional Studies, University of Birmingham.

Husbands, C.T. 1979: The 'threat' hypothesis and racist voting in England and the United States. In R. Miles and A. Phizacklea (eds), *Racism and Political Action in Britain*, London: Routledge and Kegan Paul, 147–83.

Husbands, C. 1982: East End racism 1900–1980. *The London Juornal*, 8, 3–26.

Husbands, C. 1983: *Racial Exclusionism and the City: the Urban Support of the National Front.* London: George Allen and Unwin.

Husbands, C. 1987: The politics of housing and race: perspectives from Great Britain, the United States and France. In S. J. Smith and J. Mercer (eds), *New Perspectives on Race and Housing in Britain, Studies in Housing 2*, Glasgow: Centre for Housing Research.

Immigration Act 1968: *Public General Acts – Elizabeth II*, chapter 9. London: HMSO.

Immigration Act 1971: *Public General Acts – Elizabeth II*, chapter 77.

Institute of Race Relations 1987: *Policing against Black People.* London: IRR.

Jackson, P. (ed.) 1987: *Race and Racism: Essays in Social Geography.* London: George Allen and Unwin.

Jackson, P. 1988: Street life: the politics of carnival. *Environment and Planning D: Society and Space*, 6, 213–27.

Jacobs, B. D. 1986: *Black Politics and Urban Crisis in Britain.* Cambridge: Cambridge University Press.

Jacobs, S. 1985: Race, empire and the welfare state: council housing and racism. *Critical Social Policy*, 5, 6–28.

James, D. R. and Taeuber, K. E. 1985: Measures of segregation. In N. B. Tuma (ed.), *Sociological Methodology 1985*, San Francisco: Jossey-Bass, 10–12.

Jessop, B. 1982: *The Capitalist State.* London: Martin Robertson.

Jenkins, R. and Solomos, J. (eds) 1987: *Racism and Equal Opportunities Policies in the 1980s.* Cambridge: Cambridge University Press.

Johnson, M. R. D. 1987a: Housing as a process of racial discrimination. In S. J. Smith and J. Mercer (eds), *New Perspectives on Race and Housing in Britain, Studies in Housing 2.* Glasgow: Centre for Housing Research, 159–81.

Johnson, M. R. D. 1987b: Ethnic minorities and racism in welfare provision. In P. Jackson (ed.), *Race and Racism*, London: George Allen and Unwin, 238–53.

Johnson, M. and Cross, M. 1984: Surveying service users in multi-racial areas. *Research Paper, 2.* Warwick: Centre for Research on Ethnic Relations.

Johnston, R. J. 1980: *City and Society. An Outline for Urban Geography.* Harmondsworth: Penguin.

Jones, K. 1967: Immigrants and the social services. *National Institute Economic Review*, 41, 28–40.

Jones, P. N. 1976: Colored minorities in Birmingham, England. *Annals, Association of American Geographers*, 66, 89–103.

Jones, P. N. 1977: Comment in reply. *Annals, Association of American Geographers*, 67, 306.

Jones, P. N. 1978: The distribution and diffusion of the coloured population in England and Wales, 1961–71. *Transactions, Institute of British Geographers*, NS 3, 315–32.

Jones, P. N. 1980: Ethnic segregation, urban planning, and the question of choice: the Birmingham case. Paper presented to the *Symposium on Ethnic Segregation in Cities*, St. Antony's College, Oxford.

Jones, T. P. 1983: Residential segregation and ethnic autonomy. *New Community*, 11, 10–22.

Jones, T. P. and McEvoy, D. 1978: Race and space in cloud cuckoo land, *Area*, 10, 162–6.

Joshi, S. and Carter, B. 1984: The role of labour in the creation of a racist Britain. *Race and Class*, 23, 53–70.

Jowell, R. and Airey, C. 1984: *British Social Attitudes: the 1984 Report*. Aldershot: Gower.

Kantrowitz, N. 1981: Ethnic segregation: social reality and academic myth. In C. Peach, V. Robinson and S. Smith (eds), *Ethnic Segregation in Cities*, London: Croom Helm, 43–57.

Karn, V. 1977: The impact of housing finance on low income owner occupiers. Working Paper 55, Centre for Urban and Regional Studies, University of Birmingham.

Karn, V. 1981: Race and council housing allocations. Paper presented to the Policy Seminar on Race Relations, Nuffield College, Oxford.

Karn, V. 1982: Race and housing in Britain: the role of the major institutions. Paper presented to the Anglo-American Seminar on Ethnic Minorities and Public Policy, Middle Aston House, Oxfordshire.

Karn, V., Kemeny, J. and Williams, P. 1985: *Home Ownership in the Inner City. Salvation or Despair*. Aldershot: Gower.

Karn, V., Kemeny, J. and Williams, P. 1986a: Low income home ownership in the inner city. In P. Booth and T. Crook (eds), *Low Cost Home Ownership*, Aldershot: Gower, 149–69.

Karn, V., Doling, J. and Stafford, B. 1986b: Growing crisis and contradiction in home ownership. In P. Malpass (ed.), *The Housing Crisis*, London: Croom Helm, 125–50.

Kavanagh, D. 1987: *Thatcherism and British Politics. The End of Consensus?* Oxford: Oxford University Press.

Keith, M. 1987: 'Something happened': the problems of explaining the 1980 and 1981 riots in British cities. In P. Jackson (ed.), *Race and Racism. Essays in Social Geography*, London: George Allen and Unwin, 275–303.

King, D. S. 1987: *The New Right. Politics, Markets and Citizenship*. Basingstoke: Macmillan.

Klug, F. 1982: *Racist Attacks*. London: Runnymede Trust.

Lawless, P. 1986: *The Evolution of Spatial Policy*. London: Pion.

Lawless, P. and Brown, F. 1986: *Urban Growth and Change in Britain: an Introduction*. London: Harper and Row.

Lawrence, D. 1978–9: Prejudice, politics and race, *New Community*, 7, 44–55.

Lawrence, E. 1982: Just plain common sense: the 'roots' of racism. In Centre for Contemporary Cultural Studies, *The Empire Strikes Back*, London: Hutchinson, 47–94.

Layton-Henry, Z. 1984: *The Politics of Race in Britain*. London: George Allen and Unwin.

Layton-Henry, Z. 1986: Race and the Thatcher Government. In Z. Layton-Henry and P. B. Rich (eds), *Race, Government and Politics in Britain*, Basingstoke: Macmillan, 73–99.

Layton-Henry, Z. and Rich, P. B. (eds) 1986: *Race, Government and Politics in Britain*, Basingstoke: Macmillan.

Layton-Henry, Z. and Studlar, D. T. 1985: The electoral participation of Black and Asian Britons: integration or alienation? *Parliamentary Affairs*, 38, 307–18.

Lea, J. 1982: Urban violence and political marginalisation: the riots in Britain; summer 1981. *Critical Social Policy*, 1, 59–69.

Lear, A. 1987: Black access to housing association stock. Unpublished Housing Diploma Dissertation, Glasgow University.

Lee, T. R. 1977: *Race and Residence. The Concentration and Dispersal of Immigrants in London*. Oxford: Clarendon Press.

Lelohé, M. J. 1983: Voter discrimination against Asian and black candidates in the 1983 general election. *New Community*, 11, 101–8.

Lieberson, S. 1981: An asymmetrical approach to segregation. In C. Peach, V. Robinson and S. J. Smith (eds), *Ethnic Segregation in Cities*, London: Croom Helm, 61–82.

Lieberson, S. and Carter, D. K. 1982: Temporal changes and urban differences in residential segregation: a reconsideration. *American Journal of Sociology*, 88, 296–310.

Lomas, G. 1975: *The Inner City*. London: London Council of Social Services.

Lorimer, D. A. 1979: *Colour, Class and the Victorians: English Attitudes to the Negro in the Mid-Nineteenth Century*. Leicester: Leicester University Press.

McEvoy, D. 1987: The effects of population distribution on South Asian retail business in Britain. Paper presented to the conference on South Asian Communities Overseas, Oxford.

MacEwen, M. 1986: *Racial Harassment, Council Housing and the Law*, Research Paper 11. Glasgow: Scottish Ethnic Minorities Research Unit.

MacEwen, M. 1987: *Housing Allocations, Race and Law*, Research Paper 14. Edinburgh College of Art and Heriot Watt University Department of Town and Country Planning.

McKay, D. H. 1977: *Housing and Race in Industrial Society. Civil Rights and Urban Policy in Britain and the United States*. London: Croom Helm.

McKay, D. H. and Cox, A. W. 1979: *The Politics of Urban Change*. London: Croom Helm.

MacKenzie, J. M. 1984: *Propaganda and Empire*. Manchester: Manchester University Press.

Maclennan, D. and Ermisch, J. 1986: Housing policy and inner city change. In

V. Hausner (ed.), *Social and Economic Change in the Inner Cities*, Oxford: Oxford University Press.

Maclennan, D. and O'Sullivan, A. 1985: *The Structural Development of Housing Policy in the UK*. Discussion Paper 2. Centre for Housing Research, University of Glasgow.

Malpass, P. 1983: Residualisation and the restructuring of housing tenure. *Housing Review*, 32, 44–5.

Malpass, P. 1986: From complacency to crisis. In P. Malpass (ed.), *The Housing Crisis*, London: Croom Helm, 1–23.

Malpass, P. and Murie, A. 1987: *Housing Policy and Practice*, 2nd edn. Basingstoke: Macmillan.

Marsh, I. 1987: *Policy Making in a Three Party System: Committees, Coalitions and Parliament*. London: Methuen.

Marshall, T. H. 1950: *Citizenship and Social Class*. Cambridge: Cambridge University Press.

Marshall, T. H. 1975: *Social Policy in the Twentieth Century*, 4th edn. London: Hutchinson.

Marshall, T. H. 1981: *The Right to Welfare and Other Essays*. London: Heinemann.

Marrington, D. 1987: From primary right to secondary privilege: an essay in British immigration law. *New Community*, 14, 76–82.

Massey, D. 1984: *Spatial Divisions of Labour*. London: Macmillan.

Massey, D. and Meegan, R. 1982: *The Anatomy of Job Loss: The How, Why and Where of Employment Decline*. London: Methuen.

Merrett, S. 1982: *Owner Occupation in Britain*. London: Routledge and Kegan Paul.

Miles, R. 1982a: *Racism and Migrant Labour*. London: Routledge and Kegan Paul.

Miles, R. 1982b: Racism and nationalism in Britain. In C. Husband (ed.), *'Race' in Britain. Continuity and Change*, London: Hutchinson, 279–300.

Miles, R. 1984: The riots of 1958: the ideological construction of 'Race Relations' as a political issue in Britain. *Immigrants and Minorities*, 3, 252–75.

Miles, R. 1987: Recent Marxist theories of nationalism and the issue of racism. *British Journal of Sociology*, 38, 24–41.

Miles, R. and Dunlop, A. 1987: Racism in Britain: the Scottish dimension. In P. Jackson (ed.), *Race and Racism*, London: George Allen and Unwin, 119–41.

Miles, R. and Phizacklea, A. 1979: Some introductory observations on race and politics in Britain. In R. Miles and A. Phizacklea (eds), *Racism and Political Action in Britain*, London: Routledge and Kegan Paul, 1–27.

Miles, R. and Phizacklea, A. 1981: Racism and capitalist decline. In M. Harloe (ed.), *New Perspectives in Urban Change and Conflict*, London: Hutchinson, 80–100.

Miles, R. and Phizacklea, A. 1984: *White Man's Country*. London: Pluto Press.

Miliband, R. 1982: *Capitalist Democracy in Britain*. Oxford: Oxford University Press.

Miller, N. and Brewer, M. B. 1984: *Groups in Contact. The Psychology of Desegregation*. Orlando, Florida: Academic Press.

Milner Holland 1965: Report of the Committee on Housing in Greater London, Cmnd 2605. London: HMSO.

Minogue, K. and Biddiss, M. (eds) 1987: *Thatcherism: Personality and Politics*. Basingstoke: Macmillan.

Modood, T. 1988: Who's defining who? *New Society*, 4 March, 4–5.

Moore, R. 1975: *Racism and Black Resistance in Britain*. London: Pluto Press.

Moore, R. J. 1987: *Making the New Commonwealth*. Oxford: Clarendon Press.

Morgan, B. S. 1980: The measurement of residential segregation, *Occasional Paper* 11, Geography Department, King's College, London.

Morgan, B. S. 1982: An alternative approach to the development of a distance-based measure of racial segregation, *American Journal of Sociology*, 88, 1237–49.

Morgan, B. S. and Norbury, J. 1981: Some further observations on the index of residential differentiation. *Demography*, 18, 251–6.

Morgan, G. 1985: The analysis of race: conceptual problems and policy implications. *New Community*, 12, 285–94.

Mullard, C. 1985: *Race, Power and Resistance*. London: Routledge and Kegan Paul.

Murie, A. 1986: The right to buy as low cost home ownership: impact and issues arising. In P. Booth and T. Crook (eds), *Low Cost Home Ownership*, Aldershot: Gower, 102–17.

Murray, N. 1986: Anti-racists and other demons: the press and ideology in Thatcher's Britain. *Race and Class*, 27, 1–19.

National Federation of Housing Associations 1982: *Race and Housing: A Guide for Housing Associations*. London: NFHA.

National Federation of Housing Associations 1983: *Race and Housing: Still a Cause for Concern*. London: NFHA.

Newnham, A. 1986: *Employment, Unemployment and Black People*. London: Runnymede Trust.

Niner, P. 1984: Housing associations and ethnic minorities. *New Community*, 11, 238–48.

Niner, P. 1985: *Housing Association Allocations. Achieving Racial Equality*. London: Runneymede Trust (in collaboration with V. Karn).

Niner, P. 1987: Housing associations and ethnic minorities. In S. J. Smith and J. Mercer (eds), *New Perspectives on Race and Housing in Britain, Studies in Housing 2*, Glasgow: Centre for Housing Research.

Nixon, J. 1986: The House of Commons Home Affairs sub-committee and government policy on race relations. In Z. Layton-Henry and P. B. Rich (eds), *Race, Government and Politics in Britain*, Basingstoke: Macmillan, 125–58.

Nugent, N. 1976: The anti-immigration groups. *New Community*, 5, 302–10.

Nuti, D. M. 1985/6: Economic planning in market economies: scope, instruments, institutions. *The Socialist Register*, 373–84.

Newton, K. 1976, *Second City Politics: Democratic Processes and Decision Making in Birmingham*. Oxford: Oxford University Press.

Oc, T. Ethnic minorities, scarce housing resources and urban renewal in Britain. In W. van Vliet, H. Choldin, W. Michelson and D. Popenoe (eds), *Housing and Neighbourhoods*, New York: Greenwood, 91–104.

Offe, C. 1984: *Contradictions of the Welfare State* (edited by John Keane), London: Hutchinson.

OPCS and Registrar General of Scotland 1983: *Census 1981: Country of Birth, Great Britain.* London: HMSO.

OPCS Population Statistics Division 1986: Estimating the size of the ethnic minority populations in the 1980s. *Population Trends*, 44, 23–7.

Parekh, B. 1986: The 'New Right' and the politics of nationhood. In G. Cohen et al. (eds), *The New Right, Image and Reality*, London: Runnymede Trust, 33–44.

Paris, C. and Blackaby, B. 1979: *Not Much Improvement: Urban Renewal Policy in Birmingham.* London: Heinemann.

Paris, C. and Lambert, J. 1979: Housing problems and the state: the case of Birmingham, England. In D. T. Herbert and R. J. Johnston (eds), *Geography and the Urban Environment, Vol. 2*, Chichester: Wiley, 227–58.

Peach, C. 1965: West Indian migration to Britain: the economic factors. *Race*, 7, 31–47.

Peach, C. 1966a: Under-enumeration of West Indians in the 1961 census. *Sociological Review*, 14, 73–80.

Peach, C. 1966b: Factors affecting the distribution of West Indians in Great Britain. *Transactions, Institute of British Geographers*, 38, 151–63.

Peach, C. 1968: *West Indian Migration to Britain: a Social Geography.* London: Oxford University Press for Institute of Race Relations.

Peach, C. 1978/9: British unemployment cycles and West Indian immigration. *New Community*, 7, 40–3.

Peach, C. 1979a: Race and space: a comment. *Area*, 11, 82–4.

Peach, C. 1979b: More on race and space. *Area*, 11, 221–2.

Peach, C. 1981: Conflicting interpretations of segregation. In P. Jackson and S. J. Smith (eds), *Social Interaction and Ethnic Segregation*, London: Academic Press, 19–33.

Peach, C. 1982: The growth and distribution of the black population in Britain, 1945–1980. In D. A. Coleman (ed.), *Demography of Immigrants and Minority groups in the United Kingdom*, London: Academic Press, 23–42.

Peach, C. 1984: The force of West Indian island identity in Britain. In C. Clarke, D. Ley and C. Peach (eds) *Geography and Ethnic Pluralism*, London: Allen and Unwin, 23–42.

Peach, C. 1986a: Patterns of Afro-Caribbean migration and settlement in Great Britain: 1945–1981. In C. Brock (ed.), *The Caribbean in Europe*, London: Frank Cass, 62–84.

Peach, C. 1986b: A geographical perspective on the 1986 urban riots in England. *Ethnic and Racial Studies*, 9, 396–411.

Peach, C. 1987: Immigration and segregation in Western Europe since 1945. In G. Glebe and J. O'Loughlin (eds), *Foreign Minorities in Continental European cities*, Stuttgart: Franz Steiner, 30–51.

Peach, C. and Shah, S. 1980: The contribution of council house allocation to West Indian desegregation in London, 1961–71. *Urban Studies*, 17, 333–42.

Peach, C. and Winchester, S. 1974: Birthplace, ethnicity and the enumeration of West Indians, Indians and Pakistanis. *New Community*, 3, 386–94.

Peach, C., Winchester, S. and Woods, R. 1975: The distribution of coloured immigrants in Britain. *Urban Affairs Annual Review*, 9, 395–419.

Phillips, D. 1981: The social and spatial segregation of Asians in Leicester. In P. Jackson and S. J. Smith (eds), *Social Interation and Ethnic Segregation*, London: Academic Press, 35–58.

Phillips, D. 1986: *What Price Equality?* GLC Housing Research and Policy Report 9. London: GLC.

Phillips, D. 1987a: The institutionalization of racism in housing: towards an explanation. In S. J. Smith and J. Mercer (eds), *New Perspectives on Race and Housing in Britain*, Glasgow: Centre for Housing Research, 124–58.

Phillips, D. 1987b: The rhetoric of anti-racism in public housing allocation. In P. Jackson (ed.), *Race and Racism*. London: George Allen and Unwin, 212–37.

Phillips, K. 1977: The nature of Powellism. In R. King and N. Nugent (eds), *The British Right*, Westmead: Saxon House, 99–129.

Phizacklea, A. and Miles, R. 1980: *Labour and Racism*. London: Routledge and Kegan Paul.

Platt, S. 1987: Future laws and housing. *New Society*, 82, 4.

Powell, J. E. 1969: *Freedom and Reality*. London: Batsford.

Powell, J. E. 1972: *Still to Decide*. Kingswood, Surrey: Paperfronts, Elliot Right Way Books.

Prager, J. 1982: American racial ideology as collective representation. *Ethnic and Racial Studies*, 5, 99–119.

Prager, J. 1987: American political culture and the shifting meaning of race. *Ethnic and Racial Studies*, 10, 63–81.

Preteceille, E. 1986: Collective consumption, urban segregation, and social classes. *Environment and Planning D: Society and Space*, 4, 145–54.

Pym, F. 1985: *The Politics of Consent*. London: Sphere.

Race Relations Act 1965: *Public General Acts – Elizabeth II*, chapter 73. London: HMSO.

Race Relations Act 1968: *Public General Acts – Elizabeth II*, chapter 71. London: HMSO.

Race Relations Act 1976: *Public General Acts – Elizabeth II*, chapter 74. London: HMSO.

Ram, S. and Phillips, D. 1985: Indians in Bradford. Socio-economic profile and housing characteristics, 1971–84, Working Paper 433. Leeds University, School of Geography.

Ramdin, R. 1987: *The Making of the Black Working Class in Britain*. Aldershot: Gower.

Ratcliffe, P. 1981: *Racism and Reaction*. London: Routledge and Kegan Paul.

Rees, G. and Lambert, J. 1986: *Cities in Crisis*. London: Edward Arnold.

Rees, P. H. and Birkin, M. 1984: Census-based information systems for ethnic groups: a study of Leeds and Bradford. *Environment and Planning A*, 16, 1551–71.

Reeves, F. 1983: *British Racial Discourse*. Cambridge: Cambridge University Press.

Reiner, A. 1972: Racial segregation: a comment. *Journal of Regional Science*, 12, 137–48.

Rex, J. 1981a: Urban segregation and inner city policy in Great Britain. In C. Peach, V. Robinson and S. Smith (eds), *Ethnic Segregation in Cities*, London: Croom Helm, 25–42.

Rex, J. 1981b: A working paradigm for race relations research. *Ethnic and Racial Studies*, 4, 1–25.

Rex, J. 1986a: *Race and Ethnicity*. Milton Keynes: Open University Press.

Rex, J. 1986b: The heritage of slavery and social disadvantage. In C. Brock (ed.), *The Caribbean in Europe*, London: Frank Cass, 111–34.

Rex, J. and Moore, R. 1967: *Race, Community and Conflict*. London: Oxford University Press for Institute of Race Relations.

Rex, J. and Tomlinson, S. 1979: *Colonial Immigrants in a British City*. London: Routledge and Kegan Paul.

Rich, P. 1984/5: Doctrines of racial segregation in Britain: 1800–1914. *New Community*, 12, 75–88.

Rich, P. 1986a: *Race and Empire in British Politics*. Cambridge: Cambridge University Press.

Rich, P. 1986b: The impact of South African segregationist and Apartheid ideology on British racial thought: 1939–1960. *New Community*, 13, 1–17.

Rich, P. 1986c: Conservative ideology and race in modern British politics. In Z. Layton-Henry and Paul B. Rich (eds), *Race, Government and Politics in Britain*, Basingstoke: Macmillan, 45–72.

Rich, P. 1986d: The politics of 'surplus Colonial labour': black immigration to Britain and governmental responses, 1940–1962. In C. Brock (ed.), *The Caribbean in Europe*, London: Frank Cass, 36–62.

Rich, P. 1987a: The politics of race and segregation in British cities with reference to Birmingham 1945–76. In S. J. Smith and J. Mercer (eds), *New Perspectives on Race and Housing in Britain*, Glasgow: Centre for Housing Research, 72–106.

Rich, P. 1987b: T. H. Green, Lord Scarman and the issue of ethnic minority rights in English liberal thought. *Ethnic and Racial Studies*, 10, 149–68.

Robinson, V. 1980a: Lieberson's P^* index: a case study evaluation. *Area* 12, 307–12.

Robinson, V. 1980b: Correlates of Asian immigration to Britain, 1959–74. *New Community*, 8, 115–23.

Robinson, V. 1980c: Asians and council housing. *Urban Studies*, 17, 323–31.

Robinson, V. 1981: The development of South Asian settlement in Britain and the myth of return. In C. Peach, V. Robinson and S. Smith (eds), *Ethnic Segregation in Cities*, London: Croom Helm, 149–69.

Robinson, V. 1982: The assimilation of South and East African Asian Immigrants in Britain. In D. A. Coleman (ed.), *the Demography of Immigrant and Minority Groups in the United Kingdom*, London: Academic Press, 143–68.

Robinson, V. 1984/5: Racial antipathy in South Wales and its social and demographic correlates. *New Community*, 12, 116–23.

Robinson, V. 1986: *Transients, Settlers and Refugees. Asians in Britain*. Oxford: Clarendon Press.

Robinson, B. 1987: Spatial variability in attitudes towards 'race' in the UK. In P. Jackson (ed.), *Race and Racism. Essays in Social Geography*, London: George Allen and Unwin, 161–88.

Rogers, A. and Uto, R. 1987: Residential segregation retheorised: a view from Southern California. In P. Jackson (ed.), *Race and Racism: Essays in Social Geography*, London: George Allen and Unwin, 50–73.

Rose, E. J. B., Deakin, N., Abrams, M., Jackson, V., Peston, M., Vanags, A. H., Cohen, B., Gaiskell, J. and Ward, P. 1969: *Colour and Citizenship*. London: Oxford University Press.

Saggar, S. 1985/6: The 1983 Labour force survey and Britain's 'Asian' population: a research note. *New Community*, 12, 418–29.

Sarre, R. 1986: Choice and constraint in ethnic minority housing. *Housing Studies*, 1, 71–86.

Saunders, P. 1986: *Social Theory and the Urban Question*, 2nd edn. London: Hutchinson.

Saunders, P. and Harris, C. 1988: Home ownership and capital gains. Paper presented to a conference on Housing Policy and Urban Innovation (Amsterdam, June).

Savage, M. 1987: Understanding political alignments in contemporary Britain: do politics matter? *Political Geography Quarterly*, 6, 53–76.

Schwartz, J. E. 1980: Exploring a new role in policy making: the British House of Commons in the 1970s. *American Political Science Review*, March, 23–37.

Seager, R. and Singh, G. 1984: Race, housing and equality targets. *Housing*, 20, 25–6.

Searchlight 1982: Violence on London's estates and elsewhere. *Searchlight*, 83: 12–13.

Shah, S. 1979: Aspects of the geographic analysis of Asian immigrants in London. Unpublished D.Phil thesis, University of Oxford.

Sharpe, L. J. and Newton, K. 1984: *Does Politics Matter?* Oxford: Clarendon Press.

Short, J. R. 1984: *The Urban Arena*. London: Macmillan.

Short, J. and Bassett, K. A. 1981: Housing policy and the inner city in the 1970s. *Transactions, Institute of British Geographers*, NS6, 293–312.

Sills, A., Tarpey, M. and Golding, P. 1983: Asians in an inner city. *New Community*, 11, 34–41.

Simmons, I. 1981: Contrasts in Asian residential segregation. In P. Jackson and S. J. Smith (eds), *Social Interaction and Ethnic Segregation*, London: Academic Press, 81–100.

Simpson, A. 1981: *Stacking the Decks: A Study of Race, Inequality and Council Housing in Nottingham*, Nottingham Community Relations Council.

Sims, R. 1981: Spatial separation between Asian religious minorities: an aid to explanation or obfuscation? In P. Jackson and S. J. Smith (eds), *Social Interaction and Ethnic Segregation*, London: Academic Press, 123–35.

Sivanandan, A. 1983: Challenging racism: strategies for the '80s. *Race and Class*, 25, 1–12.

Sivanandan, A. 1986: Britain's Gulags. *Race and Class*, 27, 81–5.

Smith, D. 1976: *The Facts of Racial Disadvantage*. London: PEP.

Smith, D. J. 1977: *Racial Disadvantage in Britain*. Harmondsworth: Penguin.

Smith, D. 1987: Policing and urban unrest. In J. Benyon and J. Solomos (eds), *The Roots of Urban Unrest*, Oxford: Pergamon Press, 69–74.

Smith, D. J. and Whalley, A. 1975: *Racial Minorities and Public Housing*. London: PEP.

Smith, S. J. 1986: *Crime, Space and Society*. Cambridge: Cambridge University Press.

Smith, S. J. 1987: Residential segregation: a geography of English racism? In P. Jackson (ed.), *Race and Racism*, London: George Allen and Unwin, 25–49.

Smith, S. J. 1988: Political interpretations of 'racial segregation'. *Environment and Planning D; Society and Space*, 6, 423–44.

Smith, S. J. 1989: The politics of 'race' and a new segregationism. In J. Moham (ed.), *The Political Geography of Contemporary Britain*, Basingstoke: Macmillan.

Smithies, B. and Fiddick, P. 1969: *Enoch Powell and Immigration*. London: Sphere.

Solomos, J. 1986a: Trends in the political analysis of racism. *Political Studies*, 34, 313–24.

Solomos, J. 1986b: Riots, urban protest and social policy: the interplay of reform and social control. Policy Papers in Ethnic Relations No. 7. Warwick: Centre for Research in Ethnic Relations.

Solomos, J., Findlay, B., Jones, S. and Gilroy, P. 1982: The organic crisis of British capitalism and race: the experience of the seventies. In Centre for Contemporary Cultural Studies, *The Empire Strikes Back*, London: Hutchinson, 9–46.

Southgate, P. 1982: The disturbances of July 1981 in Handsworth, Birmingham. In S. Field and P. Southgate (eds), *Public Disorder*, London: HMSO, 41–72.

Stepan, N. 1982: *The Idea of Race*. Basingstoke: Macmillan.

Stevens, L. et al. 1982: *Race and Building Society Lending in Leeds*. Leeds Community Relations Council.

Stewart, M. 1983: The inner areas planning system. *Policy and Politics*, 11, 203–14.

Stewart, M. 1987a: Ten years of inner cities policy. *Town Planning Review*, 58, 129–45.

Stewart, M. 1987b: Ten years of urban policy. *Local Links*, 10, 6–11.

Stewart, M. and Whitting, G. 1983: Ethnic minorities and the urban programme. Occasional Paper No. 9. Bristol: School for Advanced Urban Studies.

Studlar, D. T. 1974: British public opinion, colour issues and Enoch Powell. *British Journal of Political Science*, 4, 371–81.

Studlar, D. T. 1978: Policy voting in Britain: the coloured immigration issue in the 1964, 1966 and 1970 general elections. *American Political Science Review*, 72, 46–64.

Studlar, D. T. 1983: The ethnic vote 1983: problems of analysis and interpretation. *New Community*, 11, 92–100.

Studlar, D. T. 1986: Non-white policy preferences, racial participation and the political agenda in Britain. In Z. Layton-Henry and P. B. Rich (eds), *Race, Government and Politics in Britain*, Basingstoke: Macmillan, 159–86.

Taeuber, K. and Taeuber A. 1965: *Negroes in Cities: Residential Segregation and Neighbourhood Change*. Chicago: Aldine.

Taylor, S. 1978/9: Race, extremism and violence in contemporary British politics. *New Community*, 7, 56–66.

Taylor, S. 1979: The National Front: anatomy of a political movement. In R. Miles and A. Phizacklea (eds), *Racism and Political Action in Britain*, London: Routledge and Kegan Paul, 124–46.

Taylor, S. 1982: *The National Front in English Politics*. London and Basingstoke: Macmillan.

Taylor, S. 1984: The Scarman report and explanations of riots. In J. Benyon (ed.), *Scarman and After*, Oxford: Pergamon Press, 20–34.

Therborn, G. 1986: *Why Some Peoples are More Unemployed than Others*, London: Verso.

Thomas, A. 1982: Racial discrimination and the Attlee government. *New Community*, 10, 270–8.

Todd, J. and Butcher, B. 1982: *Electoral Registration in 1981*. London: Office of Population Censuses and Surveys.

Turner, B. S. 1986: *Citizenship and Capitalism*. London: George Allen and Unwin.

Unsworth, C. 1982: The riots of 1981: popular violence and the politics of law and order. *Journal of Law and Society*, 9, 63–85.

Unsworth, R. 1985: First and second generation Pakistanis in Slough: social and spatial assimilation. Unpublished PhD thesis, Cambridge University.

Urry, J. 1981: Localities, regions and social class. *International Journal of Urban and Regional Research*, 5, 455–73.

Van den Berghe, P. L. 1967: *Race and Racism*. New York: Wiley.

Van den Berghe, P. L. 1970: *Race and Ethnicity: Essays in Comparative Sociology*. New York: Basic Books.

Walker, M. 1977: *The National Front*. London: Fontana.

Ward, R. 1981: *Race, Housing and Wealth*. Paper presented to the policy seminar on Race Relations, Nuffield College, Oxford.

Ward, R. 1982: Race, housing and wealth. *New Community*, 10, 3–15.

Ward, R. 1987: Race and access to housing. In S. J. Smith and J. Mercer (eds), *New Perspectives on Race and Housing in Britain*, Glasgow: Centre for Housing Research, 182–218.

Ward, R. and Sims, R. 1981: Social status, the market and ethnic segregation. In C. Peach, V. Robinson and S. Smith (eds), *Ethnic Segregation in Cities*, London: Croom Helm, 217–34.

Weaver, G. J. 1980: Political Groups and Young Blacks in Handsworth, Discussion Paper Series C No. 38, Faculty of Commerce and Social Science, University of Birmingham.

Welch, S. and Studlar, D. T. 1985: The impact of race on political behaviour in Britain. *British Journal of Political Science*, 15, 528–39.

Williams, F. 1987: Racism and the discipline of social policy: a critique of welfare theory. *Critical Social Policy*, 1, 4–29.

Williams, J. 1985: Redefining institutional racism. *Ethnic and Racial Studies*, 8, 323–48.

Williams, P. 1977: Building Societies and the Inner City, Working Paper 54, Centre for Urban and Regional Studies, University of Birmingham.

Winship, C. 1977: A reevaluation of indexes of segregation. *Social Forces*, 55, 1058–66.

Winship, C. 1978: The desirability of using the index of dissimilarity or any adjustment of it for measuring segregation: a reply to Falk et al. *Social Forces*, 57, 717–20.

Woods, R. I. 1975: The stochastic analysis of immigrant distributions. Research Paper 11, Oxford University School of Geography.

Woods, R. I. 1976: Aspects of the scale problem in the calculation of segregation indices: London and Birmingham, 1961 and 71. *Tijdschrift voor Economische en Sociale Geografie*, 67, 169–74.

Young, K. 1983: Ethnic pluralism and the policy agenda in Britain. In N. Glazer and K. Young (eds), *Ethnic Pluralism and Public Policy*, London: Heinemann, 287–300.

Young, K. and Connelly, N. 1981: *Policy and Practice in the Multi-racial City*. London: Policy Studies Institute.

Name Index

Subject Index

Africa 111, 116
Afro-Caribbeans 11, 12, 25;
  employment 39–40, 42–3, 62;
  housing 41–2, 53, 55, 56, 57, 59, 75,
  82, 84, 87, 90, 94; and politics 137,
  155–8, 169n.; segregation of 26–36,
  47n., 58, 96, 100
anti-discrimination legislation 18, 49,
  50, 54, 67, 75–6, 102, 106, 113, 115,
  122, 124–5, 135–6, 143, 144–5, 186,
  191; Race Relations Act (1965) 75,
  124–5; Race Relations Act (1968) 75;
  Race Relations Act (1976) 19, 66, 75,
  76, 80, 99, 100, 103n., 136, 196n.
anti-racism 77, 86, 92, 96, 101–2,
  104n., 126, 130, 135, 136, 158, 180,
  183, 184, 185, 186, 191–2, 195
apartheid 1, 16, 58, 141
Asians 11, 12, 25, 137, 161; East
  African 24, 25, 26, 27, 45n., 47n.,
  48n., 56, 77, 152; employment
  39–41, 42–3, 44, 62; housing 41–2,
  53–6, 59, 60, 62, 63, 82, 87–92, 94,
  95, 97, 103n., 104n., 173, 190; and
  politics 137, 155–8, 169n.;
  segregation of 26–36, 47n., 96, 97,
  100
assimilation 114, 117, 135–8, 148

Bangladesh 24, 35
Bangladeshis 25, 26, 34, 39, 82, 83, 84,
  87, 92, 95, 161, 163

Birmingham 32, 33, 34, 37, 43, 47n.,
  62, 71, 72, 78n., 83, 88, 89, 91, 93,
  96, 100
Blackburn 34, 35, 37, 47, 78n., 153
Bradford 34, 35, 62, 78n., 87, 90
Bristol 91, 163
British Nationality Act: (1948) 51, 110,
  137, 175; (1981) 132, 137, 138, 180
building societies 53, 58, 87–9

Caribbean 24, 25, 37, 46n., 47n., 51,
  110, 120, 175
Census: (1961) 45n.; (1966) 46n.;
  (1971) 25–6, 27, 46n.; (1981) 25–6,
  27, 47n.; 'ethnic' question 45n.
citizenship 137; see also British
  Nationality Act
citizenship rights 7, 8, 9, 11, 21, 50, 51,
  103, 105, 110, 111, 114, 131, 139,
  141, 144, 170, 172, 181, 193–6; civil
  140, 141, 166; economic/property 9,
  18, 21, 50, 67, 77, 172–5, 180, 185,
  186–7, 189, 193; political 21, 156,
  179–81; welfare 18, 19, 51, 54, 67,
  77, 93, 95, 96, 175–9, 185
colonialism 2, 3, 109–15, 184
colour bar 16, 20, 114, 115, 124
Commonwealth 108, 109, 110, 111,
  112, 115, 116, 121, 123, 147
Conservative Government 59, 72, 107,
  121, 126, 182, 189–90
Conservative Party 51, 109, 119, 122,

150694